AN ACTOR PREPARES...

TO LIVE IN NEW YORK CITY

AN ACTOR PREPARES...
TO LIVE IN NEW YORK CITY

How to Live Like a Star
Before You Become One

Craig Wroe

Limelight Editions
NEW YORK

First Limelight Edition, May 2003
Copyright © 2003 by Craig Wroe.

All rights reserved, including the right of reproduction in whole or in
part in any form, under international and Pan-American Copyright
Conventions. Published by Proscenium Publishers Inc., 118 East 30th
Street, New York, NY 10016.

Manufactured in the United States of America.

Library of Congress Cataloging-in-Publication Data
Wroe, Craig.
  An actor prepares—to live in New York City / Craig Wroe.—1st
Limelight ed.
      p. cm.
  ISBN 0-87910-986-6 (pbk.)
1. Acting—Vocational guidance—New York (State)—New York. 2. New
York (N.Y.)—Guidebooks. I. Title.
  PN2055.W76 2003
  792'.028'0237471—dc21

                                2003007668

Designed by Mulberry Tree Press, Inc. (www.mulberrytreepress.com)

For
John Ryan
and
Frank Rizzo

ACKNOWLEDGMENTS

I WOULD LIKE TO THANK John Ryan, who years ago casually suggested that I put all of the following into a book both to help my fellow actors, and to keep myself busy between engagements. Thanks too to Frank Rizzo who provided me with constant crucial guidance and inspiration.

I offer my deepest appreciation and thanks to the many friends and colleagues who endured my self-imposed exile while I was working on this book and who offered their invaluable suggestions and contributions. Special thanks to Bill Clarke, Dennis Delaney, Shelley Delaney, Jay Patterson, Bill Kux, Andrea Cirie, Chris Downey, Pamela Nyberg, Eve Eaton, Paul Gamner, Stefano Imbert, Larry Gershberg, Glenn Teller, John Sullivan, Jim Duncan, Charles Karchmer, David Kennedy, Henny Russell, William Gibson, Sharon Washington, Michael Feingold, Reno Roop, Patrick Frederic, Maggie Frederic, Sybil Lines, Todd Phillips, Ellen Ferris, Sarah Stasaitis, Heather Muhleman, Carla Capone, Bob Sacheli, Jim Poles, Matt Loney, Mauricio Alexander, and Dea Lawrence.

Infinite thanks to agents Paul Reisman, Mark Turner and Charmaine Ferenczi at Abrams Artists for their encouragement. Special kudos to my literary agent Maura Teitelbaum, the best agent a writer could ask for.

With my arms spread as wide as I can stretch them, I offer my editor Nina Maynard a resounding, "Thank you this much;" her prowess with a red pen is awe invoking. Mucho appreciation to my publisher Mel Zerman, Jenna Young and everyone at Limelight Editions for their unfettered enthusiasm and collaboration on this

project. Thanks too to artists Annette Berry and Johanna Goodman for the wonderful work they did on the cover.

My heartfelt gratitude goes out to my legit agents Mary Harden,
Nancy Curtis, Michael Kirsten and Diane Riley for their years of
support and friendship. Ditto that sentiment to Tracy Goldblum,
Genine Esposito, Alison Quartin and the entire crew in the Commercial Department at Abrams Artists.

Thanks to the Metropolitan Transit Authority for their $17 un-
limited weekly "Metropass," which made it possible for me to haul
my ass all over the city to research this book.

Thanks also to all of the organizations and businesses and their
representatives who helped make this book as comprehensive as
possible, including Elba Aviles at AFTRA, Marjorie Murray Roop
and Natalie Choi at The Actors' Fund of America, Actors' Equity
Association Business Representative Valerie LaVacco, Dr. Craig
Fishel at the New York Wellness and Chiropractic Center, Gary
Ginsberg at Royal Alliance, actors' accountant Marc Bernstein, Dr.
Barry Kohn and Amanda LaBarbera at Physician Volunteers for
the Arts, Patricia S. Schwadron at The Actor's Work Program,
Ellen Celnik at Common Ground Management (who oversees The
Aurora apartment complex), Merrill Schneiderman at the Na-
tional Institute for the Psychotherapies, Secretary Treasurer of
Actors' Equity Association and Coordinator of VITA site 35006
Conard Fowkes, The Actors' Fund of America, Actors' Equity As-
sociation, Screen Actors Guild and American Federation of Televi-
sion and Radio Actors.

"On any person who desires such queer prizes, New York will bestow the gift of loneliness and the gift of privacy. It is this largess that accounts for the presence within the city's walls of a considerable section of the population; for the residents of Manhattan are to a large extent strangers who have pulled up stakes somewhere and come to town, seeking sanctuary or fulfillment or some greater or lesser grail. The capacity to make such dubious gifts is a mysterious quality of New York. It can destroy an individual, or it can fulfill him, depending a good deal on luck. No one should come to New York to live unless he is willing to be lucky."

—E.B. White
From *Here Is New York*

"If I can make it there, I'll make it anywhere."

—Kander and Ebb

Key of Acronyms Used in Text

AEA	=	Actors' Equity Association (Equity)
AFCU	=	Actors Federal Credit Union
AFM	=	American Federation of Musicians
AFTRA	=	American Federation of Television and Radio Artists
AGMA	=	American Guild of Musical Artists
AGVA	=	American Guild of Variety Artists
AHIRC	=	Artist's Health Insurance Resource Center
AWP	=	Actors Work Program
BC/EFA	=	Broadway Cares/Equity Fights AIDS
CTFD	=	Career Transition for Dancers
DGA	=	Directors Guild of America
HOLA	=	Hispanic Organization of Latin Actors
ISP	=	Internet Service Provider
IATSE	=	International Alliance of Theatrical Stage Employees
SAG	=	Screen Actors Guild
SSDC	=	Society of Stage Directors and Choreographers
TDF	=	Theater Development Fund
VITA	=	Volunteer Income Tax Assistance
VLA	=	Volunteer Lawyers for the Arts
WGA	=	Writers Guild of America

CONTENTS

PART I

Welcome to New York

INTRODUCTION

WELCOME TO NEW YORK—capital of the arts and commerce, fashion and conflict—the greatest city in the world.

For anyone in the performing arts, this is the place to be. No other city has the diversity and quality of live theater, dance and music that we have here in the Big Apple. No other city can boast the numbers of resources, organizations, services, unions, guilds and training institutions that are available to us here. For those actors who are just starting out, there's no better base from which to launch a career. For those who have been working in other parts of the country, New York is the inevitable next rung up the career ladder.

When I told a friend recently that I was writing a guide for actors and others who are moving to New York City to pursue their dreams, he glibly replied, "What more can you tell them except, 'Say your prayers every night and skip lots of meals'?" Much truth is said in jest. We actors have chosen a profession where hard work, kismet, chutzpah and sacrifice are compulsory, and which is especially tough in a town where over 90,000 people call themselves actors, and of those, only 2 percent are employed at any given time.

Besides employment challenges, the city itself can be demanding—it's expensive, dirty, edgy, congested, fast-paced, and curt. For those without drive and a strong constitution, it can chew them up and spit them out, or at the very least, put them on the next bus out of town.

To survive the ups and downs of urban life and the acting profession, it takes equal parts confidence and cunning, stamina and stability, tenacity and even mendacity. And, this practical, in-depth reference can't hurt either (how's that for confidence)!

During the 18 years I've lived in New York, I have become the master of living above my means without paying above my means. Unwilling to sacrifice quality of life to my tight budget, I've devoted a large amount of time, effort and energy to getting superior products, help and services for less. Blessed with a photographic memory, a network of friends and colleagues whom I continually poll for tips on the best and least expensive that New York has to offer, and compulsive organizational skills, I have accumulated mountains of information on everything from how to find an affordable apartment, to inexpensive shopping outlets, quality products and services resources at bargain prices, financial institutions, actors' support organizations, tax preparers, discount providers to actors with union cards, free or cheap entertainment, and low-cost medical and legal providers. After years of living well on an actor's salary, I turn my knowledge and burgeoning files into a source for all in this book.

My design is to provide actors with all the information they'll need to survive and thrive as comfortably and as inexpensively as possible in New York. While this book won't make you a better or more successful actor—you won't learn here how to find an agent, land a Broadway show or become a soap star—it might help make you be a better and more successful resident while you pursue your career.

You're not an actor! Not to worry, anyone on a budget who wants to take full advantage of all the city has to offer can benefit from the information. No matter what your profession, no matter if you're only passing through, inside you'll find a comprehensive and detailed guide to many of the city's inexpensive shopping and services. And, the chapters on New York's free and cheap sites, landmarks, parks, institutions, museums and cultural events are ideal for anyone wanting the best for less.

Now, go out and live like a star before you become one!

PART II

Getting
Settled

FINDING A HOME

THE HORROR STORIES ARE TRUE—apartment hunting in New York is a nightmare for everyone except the very wealthy. Rents are obscenely high, broker and/or "key" fees are exorbitant, and most landlords will not rent without a guarantor on the lease. Also, there are too few apartments, and a lot of those that do exist are uninhabitable hovels in 'iffy' buildings, or smaller than most suburban closets. Welcome to New York.

Forget completely about finding a cheap place to live. It doesn't exist. You swear you know a friend of a friend of a friend who found a rent-stabilized studio in *The New York Times* for only $400 a month? Yeah, and alligators live in the sewers and I swear after a blind date I woke up in a bathtub full of ice to discover that one of my kidneys was missing. It's an urban legend, a lie, or the "friend of a friend of a friend" found his apartment in 1961.

A burgeoning Wall Street and Silicon Alley have altered, irreversibly it seems, the Manhattan real estate market. Stockbrokers and dot-commers who make buckets of money have flooded this tiny island and are willing to pay whatever price a landlord sets, for the convenience of city living. Studios now start at about $1,800 a month, and it's not unheard of for 2-bedrooms to go for $4,500. The junior millionaires have priced us artist types right out of the city. We're now lucky if we can find affordable housing in Newark, Jersey City or the hinterlands of Brooklyn and Queens.

About right now you are thinking, "This guy promised that he was going to show me how to live here cheaply. Now, in chapter one no less, he says that there are no cheap apartments. Why the hell did I buy this book?" Don't shoot me; I'm just the messenger. I don't pretend to know the sure-fire way to find a cheap place to live. What I am able to do is offer some suggestions on how I think you could go about looking for your New York City home. I've drawn on my own experiences as well as those of several friends and colleagues who have had some success tackling this most difficult task. A word of advice: Apartments being as hard to come by as they are, if you find something that is even remotely suitable, take it immediately. If you don't, someone else will. That doesn't mean you should rush into a decision; examine the apartment, the building, the neighborhood and the commute to midtown thoroughly to determine whether you would feel safe and content living there.

PLACES TO START:

The Actors' Fund of America (729 Seventh Avenue at 49th Street—212–221–7300, ext. 257) knows almost everything there is to know about affordable housing in the city and will be happy to assist you in your search. They will answer your questions about the 80/20 lottery (more anon) and give you an updated list of 80/20 buildings to write for applications. They also have a complete list of New York City buildings like Manhattan Plaza, The Aurora and Times Square Apartments where you may write to request a place on their waiting lists. The Fund of America can also help answer inquiries regarding the Section 8 Housing Assistance Program subsidy, including eligibility, apartment availability, and the application process. When you call The Actors' Fund, sign up for their monthly "Affordable Housing" seminars and request a copy of their housing information packet that gives a comprehensive overview of the things you need to know in your search for a New York City home. The Actors' Fund of America receives a high volume of calls regarding housing questions, but leave a message and they will eventually return your call.

The Aurora located at 475 West 57th Street and Tenth Avenue in midtown is a 30-story building that provides affordable supportive housing to special low-income groups, such as seniors, performing arts professionals and people living with HIV/AIDS. Originally intended to be a luxury high-rise, The Aurora was converted into 178 "shared" residential units. This means that each resident has his/her own bedroom unit but shares a living room and kitchen with one or two roommates. Some units share a bathroom with one other person, some have a private bath within the bedroom unit. 27 one-bedroom units serve eligible individuals who have special medical needs.

Eligibility for the building is based on federal guidelines under the Internal Revenue Service Federal Tax Credit Program: A person's annual income from all sources may not exceed $23,500 and should not be less than $13,000. Households of two may apply for a one bedroom if both members are persons with AIDS or are senior citizens with joint incomes not exceeding $27,000 annually or less than $14,000. To apply, contact:

Intake Department/Common Ground Management
475 West 57th Street, 4th Floor
New York, NY 10019
212–262–4502

Bulletin boards can be a real help in the elusive apartment search. Start with the housing bulletin boards at Equity, SAG and AFTRA; many actors willing to sublet list their apartments with the unions when they go out of town for work. Check the boards at your survival job, church or synagogue, as well as social organizations and clubs, bookstores and grocery stores.

You've exhausted all your networking connections and contacts (see below) and still come up empty-handed. The next best way to find an apartment is through the wonderful community-based website **Craigslist** (NewYork.Craigslist.org), which features several low-cost housing options including thousands of apartments for rent, broker and agent listed apartments, rooms for rent, shares, sublets and temporary accommodations. It lists housing swaps as well as sections for home-hunters to itemize what they are looking for. On a recent surf through the site, searching for apartments under $800, I came up with hundreds of listings (granted, most were in the outer boroughs and New Jersey) and almost all were fee-free. (For more on Craigslist, see the chapter on "Shopping").

Even if you have your heart set on residing in Manhattan, unless you are willing to pay an outrageous sum in rent, you should think seriously about **living outside of Manhattan—** in the upper reaches of the island, in one of the boroughs or just across the Hudson River in New Jersey. Finding an apartment in Washington Heights, Inwood, the Bronx, Brooklyn, Queens, Staten Island, Hoboken or Weehawken, will be much less expensive and competitive than Manhattan. To find a place in one of these areas, choose a neighborhood where you might like to live and wander through it. Go up and down the blocks looking for "For Rent" signs. Talk to the people on the street or those sitting on their stoops. Don't be afraid to ask if they know of any vacant apartments. Be nice. Be warm. Smile. Ring the superintendent's buzzer (he or she is the person who oversees the complex and is almost always listed on the buzzer) of any building you particularly like and ask about vacancies. Be nicer, be warmer and smile harder. Give the super and anyone else you meet your contact information, ask them to please call if they hear of anything and offer a reward of $100 or more if they connect you to a place. By doing this, you avoid a steep broker's fee, you are not competing with others and the rents on these apartments are often lower than those that are advertised and shown through agents. Remember though, be nice—and smile. Make them want you to live there.

Known as "the Miracle on 42nd Street," **Manhattan Plaza** is one of the most unique residential complexes anywhere. Built in 1977, Manhattan Plaza was intended to be a luxury condominium building stretching a full city block from Ninth to Tenth Avenues between 42nd and 43rd Streets. As the project neared completion however, the builder filed for bankruptcy protection. Worse, the neighborhood was still considered to be "in transition," meaning no one who could afford a luxury apartment wanted to live in Hell's Kitchen. After an intensive effort on the part of city officials, performing artists and unions, Broadway producers and civic leaders, the U.S. Department of Housing and Urban Development designated Manhattan Plaza eligible to receive a Section 8 Housing Assistance Program subsidy.

The idea behind Manhattan Plaza was to create a community for those who could not otherwise afford to live right in the heart of the theater district. With the federal rent subsidy, performers were offered a chance to live where they "plied their trades," and the elderly and people who had made the area their home for many years were able to stay, helping the neighborhood to retain its character and diversity.

Created as an experiment in housing and performing arts support, almost from the day the first tenant moved in, Manhattan Plaza became the prime catalyst in the redevelopment and preservation of the Westside. It has brought thousands of hard-working, energetic people back into Clinton/Hell's Kitchen and generated a host of commercial establishments, such as theaters, bars, restaurants, cafes, markets, specialty gift shops and bakeries.

Today, roughly 70 percent of Manhattan Plaza's residents earn their living in the performing arts as actors, dancers, directors, writers, singers, technicians, ushers, theater managers or designers. The remaining 30 are the elderly, handicapped and long-term neighborhood residents. Approximately 90 percent of the tenants receive some federal rent subsidy (under the Section 8 program, residents are obligated to pay 30 percent of their annual income to rent with the federal government making up the difference); the remaining 10 percent pay "fair market" rent.

As you can imagine, the desire to live at Manhattan Plaza is great. As you can also imagine, getting in is next to impossible. Because the waiting list is years-long, it is often closed to new applications. I waited (yeah, I'm a resident) four years; a friend of mine who moved in this year waited seven years. Only infrequently does the list open to new applicants; when it does, it is usually announced in the trade paper *Backstage* or *Equity News*. If you see that the list has opened, it will only be open for a few days and may not open again for years, so act immediately. You can also write Manhattan Plaza to ask for notification of the list opening and for the eligibility requirements for residing there:

Manhattan Plaza Business Office
400 West 43rd Street
New York, NY 10036

Having thoroughly spooked you about New York apartments, let me say that I have occasionally heard stories with happy endings. Most of the people I know who have been successful at finding affordable housing have done it by **networking** with their friends and colleagues. Inform everyone you know who lives here that you are looking for an apartment. I mean EVERYONE—friends, relatives, acquaintances, colleagues, friends of friends, friends of friends of friends. Write, call or e-mail and ask them to contact you immediately if they hear of a vacancy. New Yorkers are always hearing about someone who is subletting a place for few months, a colleague who is looking for a roommate, or an apartment that is about to go on the market. I hear about vacant apartments all the time and on average, hook people up with a place a couple of times a year.

BEST BET

Consider becoming a **roommate** to someone who already has a place rather than trying to find your own lease. Ask your friends (the ones you trust and like) if they or someone they know needs a roommate. If no one is looking to share, check the bulletin boards in the members' lounge at Equity (165 West 46th Street, 2nd Floor) and SAG (1515 Broadway) for roommate postings.

While there are **roommate-pairing services,** listed in the Yellow Pages and on the internet (type in "New York Apartment Roommate"), if you try one of these agencies, you will pay a fee. They ask you to fill out forms about the type of apartment and roommate you are seeking, your living habits, and the amount you can spend on rent. Do proceed cautiously as I know no one who has had success with these services. One friend discovered, *after* he moved into his new digs, that his roommate was a drug addict and very violent; the situation got so dire that my friend did a stealth escape one afternoon while his roommate was at work. Another friend put two and two together about his roommate who was bringing beefy guys in leather down to his basement to "watch TV;" one day while the roommate was out, my friend went into the off-limits "TV room" to discover a fully-equipped S & M dungeon. The service I used paired me with a guy who had "two-bedrooms" in Chelsea; one of the two bedrooms, *my* room, was a closet—literally a closet, with a cot placed under *his* hanging clothes. Needless to say I did not take it and cancelled my membership with the service.

Subletting an apartment can be advantageous; it allows you to get semi-settled in the city and have a place to lay your head while you are searching for your permanent home. The bulletin boards at Equity and SAG also have lots of listings for sublets, with new ones posted daily.

One way of beating the hassle and expense of finding your own lease that lots of New Yorkers swear by is **sublet hopping**. This entails putting all your worldly possessions into storage except clothing, some books maybe and a few creature comforts, and living from one sublet to another. By stringing sublets together you may never have to be burdened with finding your own place.

This is much too transient for me, but it works for a lot of people. A guy I met at a party recently told me he has been living this way for 14 years. He claims it has saved him thousands of dollars in broker's fees, furniture, towels, bed linens, decorating costs, kitchen utensils, even telephone and cable installation charges. As he said, "It's helped me remain true to myself and live a purer, simpler life."

I asked him if it didn't make him crazy to always live with other people's stuff. "No. You see, I just visualize that all that stuff is mine. I pretend it's all mine and make up a scenario in my head why I would own that stuff. One time, I sublet an apartment for almost four years from a dancer who was in Europe doing *Cats*. She had this huge collection of Madame Alexander dolls that sat on a shelf over the bed. She told me they were valuable and asked me to never touch them. Well, I created this really great rationalization in my head why I had them. Although, I had a lot of explaining to do to my dates." My kingdom for a lease . . . and my own sofa, and my own tchotchkes!

The **Times Square** residential complex is a small-scale version of Manhattan Plaza. It is also a Section 8 Housing Assistance Program building in the heart of the theater district and has several apartments designated for performing artists. The Times Square differs in size (only 650 units) from Manhattan Plaza and has a much shorter waiting list to get in (about six months). To be eligible, you must be a single adult with a yearly income between $12,500 and $24,840. If you meet these criteria, call and request an application. The apartments are tiny—basically one room half the size of an average bedroom that serves as kitchen, sleeping, living and dining room (fortunately, each room has a decent size bathroom). About all that can fit are a single bed, dresser, small bookshelf, television, table and chair. The pullman kitchen is not great if you love to cook or entertain (not that you could in this small room, unless you had your guests line up in the hallway and come in one at a time): there are two burners, a dormitory size refrigerator and no oven. Despite these drawbacks, the Times Square apartments provide a safe home in the center of midtown, an affordable rent, and a place to hang your hat while you are pursuing your career and hunting for a bigger home. Contact the Times Square office at:

255 West 43rd Street

New York, NY 10036

Phone: 212–768–8989, ext. 2018

The "Apts. For Rent" section of *The Village Voice* is still considered a pretty good way of finding a place. When I came to New York in 1984, I spent several late Tuesday evenings lining up with hordes of others at the Astor Place newsstand, the first place in the city to receive that week's edition. As the papers came off the truck, I would hurriedly grab a copy, throw down some change (it wasn't free back then like it is now) and dash to a nearby coffee shop where I would peruse the apartment ads, circling those that looked interesting or affordable. The objective of all of us in Astor Place at two in the morning was to hightail it to as many landlords as we could early the next day and beat out the multitudes. It took a few weeks, but I did eventually find a place on Amsterdam and 85th. Luckily, it was Thanksgiving weekend and I was the first to reach the landlord. It was also fortuitous that I chose to tell the landlord I was in a different profession; I'd heard most were reluctant to rent to actors, so I created a job for myself (fund-raiser) and gave him the phone number of a friend who I claimed was my employer. My friend vouched for me, the landlord bought it, and the apartment was mine. At the lease signing, he snickered, "At first I thought maybe you were an actor. Well, good thing you're not, 'cause I never rent to actors. Ha, ha."

Times have changed. Besides now being free, the *Voice* also has a website (VillageVoice.com) with a full classifieds section that is posted early Tuesday evenings. You still have to get to the landlord as early as possible the next day and go with a certified check for the amount of the rent, the deposit and the fee when you actually view the apartment. Also, do yourself a favor—have a good "backup" profession to present if you get even an inkling that he or she has an aversion to actors. *The Village Voice* is available from newsstands and distribution boxes around the city.

More and more high price, high-rise apartment complexes are going up all over Manhattan. As the price of real estate here escalates, so do property taxes. Many building owners offer an **80/20 Lottery** to obtain a tax break from the city. This system allows the owners to designate 20 percent of their building's units for low-income recipients giving them a generous rent break, in exchange for a sizable tax reduction. Low-income eligibility is determined by a prescribed earnings ceiling per year. Phone the Actors' Fund of America at 212–221–7300, ext. 257 to hear a message listing buildings currently offering the lottery program. Send a postcard to the addresses given requesting an application. Lottery winners are chosen at random from all the eligible applications submitted. The Actors' Fund can also answer any questions you may have about the program and eligibility. As mentioned earlier, please be patient—your call will be returned; the Fund receives a high volume of queries and tries to answer them all.

If you find yourself at the point of homelessness, the following are a few of the **low cost hotels, hostels and dorms** that can provide life-saving, temporary accommodations while you are looking for a permanent home:

Aladdin Hotel: 317 West 45th Street—212–246–8580

Big Apple Hostel: 119 West 45th Street—212–302–2603

Chelsea Center Hostel: 313 West 29th Street—
    212–643–0214

Chelsea International Hostel: 251 West 20th Street—
    212–647–0010

DeHirsch Residence: 1395 Lexington Avenue at 92nd
    Street—212–415–5650

International Student Center: 38 West 88th Street—
    212–787–7706

Jazz on the Park: 36 West 106th Street—212–932–1600

New York International Hostel: 891 Amsterdam Avenue at 103rd Street—212–932–2300

Sugar Hill International House: 722 Saint Nicholas Avenue—212–926–7030

YMCA Flushing: 138-46 Northern Boulevard, Queens— 718–961–6880

YMCA McBurney: 125 West 14th Street—212–741–9226

YMCA Vanderbilt: 224 East 47th Street—212–756–9600

YMCA West Side: 5 West 63rd Street—212–875–4100

BANKING AND CREDIT CARDS

WITH WALL STREET, the New York Stock Exchange, the NAS-DAQ as well as headquarters or offices of most of the world's leading monetary institutions, New York is truly the financial center of the universe. As a result of mega-mergers and hubris ("We are the Financial Capital of the Universe"), New York's banks have gotten out of control. In midtown and downtown, there are branch offices on practically every corner, vying with Starbucks and The Gap for total domination. Unfortunately, the larger these institutions have become the less user-friendly they are to us poor schmoes who just want plain ol' everyday checking and savings accounts.

For those dealing with small balances, gone are the days of free monthly checking and excellent customer service, and forget about the free toaster you'd get for opening a new account. Although most banks offer free ATM withdrawals, that is where their generosity ends; they more than make up for this benefit with astronomical monthly checking fees, high penalties and impersonal service.

Fortunately, there is a great alternative for actors:

The Actors Federal Credit Union (AFCU), a cooperatively run, nonprofit banking organization, was chartered in 1962 to serve the entertainment community. Any paid-up member of Equity, AFTRA and SAG in good standing, or member of a component organization is eligible to apply for membership. The myriad benefits for members of the AFCU include:

→ 2 convenient office locations:
   165 West 46th Street (Actors Equity Building), 14th Floor—212–869–8926
   322 West 48th (Musicians Local Building), 4th Floor

→ Interest and dividend rates that are competitive with or better than commercial or savings banks

→ Federally insured deposits up to $100,000 by the National Credit Union Association

→ Free checking with overdraft protection for accounts that maintain an average daily balance of $99

→ Two types of overdraft protection—automatic loan from Cash Draw or automatic transfer from regular savings

→ Actorcash (isn't that an oxymoron?) ATM Cards which can be used to access cash from both savings and checking accounts at ATMs worldwide. (I know this is true—I've used my Actorcash ATM Card in Mexico, Hungary, Italy, the Netherlands, France, United Kingdom and Austria and have never had a problem.) Actorcash ATM Cards can be used to make purchases at many stores. Via the CO-OP network, members can make deposits and withdrawals without being surcharged at participating ATMs across the country.

→ Actors Gold and Classic Visa Cards with a 6.9 percent introductory rate and an 11.9 percent fixed rate (well below the typical 17 to 23 percent rates of most commercial banks) with no annual fees and a 25-day grace period. Actors Visa benefits include access to cash at ATM machines worldwide, free travel accident insurance, auto rental insurance, 90-day purchase protection and extended warranties.

→ ActorMiles MasterCard—which allows members to earn credit toward free airline tickets throughout the United States and much of Europe with every purchase

→ Free investment counseling with financial consultants to help you obtain your long- and short-term financial goals. Through mutual funds, fixed and variable annuities, and tax-free and tax-deferred investments, the AFCU will help create a comprehensive investment package that is right for you

→ Touch-tone Teller services—from the convenience of a phone, you may check your balances and cleared checks, transfer funds and make loan payments

→ Free full-service banking via the internet (www.actorsfcu.com) allows members to pay bills, check balances and account histories, apply for loans, transfer balances within accounts and view a complete listing of current rates and services online.

→ Regular savings accounts

→ Individual Retirement Accounts

→ Payroll deduction for direct deposit

→ Deposit by mail

→ Auto loans with an annual auto loan sale

→ Personal loans with rates lower than major New York banks and no prepayment penalty if you repay the loan before it is due

→ Free life insurance, which matches the amount you have on deposit at the time of death, up to $5,000

→ Wire transfers

→ Gift check, money orders and travelers checks

→ US Savings Bond redemption

→ Free notary service

→ Unlimited internet access for only $9.95 per month with the first month free, including four e-mail accounts, 24/7 technical support and up to 20 mb of web space. (See chapter on "Internet Service Providers)

→ The ability to make safe and secure deposits at Manhattan MoneyBranch check cashing offices throughout the city. This service offers members the convenience of multiple locations as well as weekend service and extended hours of access (as early as 7:30 A.M., as late as 8 P.M.). Unlike traditional ATMs, funds deposited at these locations are immediately available for withdrawal. Manhattan MoneyBranch locations:

> 73 Fourth Avenue, between 9th and 10th Streets—212–475–3442
>
> 140 West 55th Street, between Sixth & Seventh Avenues—212–258–2439
>
> 59 West Eighth Street at Sixth Avenue—212–674–0338

→ Over 90 fee-free ATMs located throughout the city, with plans for the installation of several more in the near future. Call or go by either of the Actors Federal Credit Union offices for a complete list of ATM outlets.

I hate to admit it, but for years I resisted my friends' and colleagues' exhortations to join the AFCU. Not that I'm stubborn or anything, but it was hard for me to comprehend that the credit union could be as safe and dependable as a commercial bank. It was only after wretched experiences at three of the New York banking behemoths that I decided to give the AFCU a try. I kick myself for the years I wasted and the money I lost banking with the big boys. It's a no-brainer, with enormous benefits, competitive interest rates and excellent service (not to mention our money stays in the "family" so to speak), there is no better place for actors to bank than the AFCU.

ALTERNATIVE BANKING INSTITUTIONS

If you don't qualify for membership at the credit union, below you'll find a list of some of New York's smaller banking institutions. Although they have a lesser ATM presence than the financial giants (Chase/Citibank/Bank of New York) do, they don't gouge you as terribly through penalties and monthly fees. Call each, ask about locations, rates, fees and interest and do some comparative shopping.

→ **Apple Bank for Savings**—800–722–6888

→ **Carver Federal Savings**—212–876–4747

→ **Doral Bank**—877–313–6725

→ **Emigrant Savings Bank**—212–850–4000

→ **Fleet Bank**—800–841–4000

→ **Greenpoint Bank**—212–681–8470

→ **Sterling National Bank**—212–935–1440

→ **Washington Mutual**—800–788–7000. This bank has recently been advertising "Free Checking that's actually free," with no monthly fees—no matter what your balance, no fee to return cancelled checks, and free standard Online Banking. Definitely worth looking into.

BEATING HIGH CREDIT CARD INTEREST RATES

Do you feel like you are paying too much interest on your credit cards? Does a large chunk of what you pay on your credit card bill go to pay the interest? Do you find it hard to get out of credit card debt because of the accrual of high monthly interest charges? Do you feel helpless when it comes to interest charges? If you answered yes to these questions, I'll bet that you, like most credit card holders, are paying anywhere from 17 to 23 percent interest. It doesn't take Sherlock Holmes to deduce that you should not be paying that much.

"Okay," you say, "but I can't do anything about it." Not true. You can have the rate lowered. That's right, you can have the rate lowered. Here's how. . . .

Call your credit card company and tell them that you feel you are paying too much interest. Say that you have recently been offered a credit card from another bank at a lower rate and you want to cancel your card. The bank representative will almost immediately offer you a rate slightly lower than the one you are paying. The negotiations have begun. Ask for few points more; even suggest the rate you'd like to pay to stay with this bank. There will be some hemming and hawing on their part, some "I have to speak to my supervisor," but they will basically give you what you want. They want to keep your business.

I have done this with every credit card I've ever owned and it has always worked. A year or so ago, I called the bank that oversees my Visa Card account and told them that I was going to be canceling my card. I told them I was offered a card through my union at 6.9 percent the first year and then a fixed rate of 11.9 percent. The woman who was helping me over the phone put me on hold. She came back a few minutes later and told me the bank was going to drop my interest rate to 9.9 percent. With one phone call and about six minutes of my time, I had my credit card interest rate reduced by a substantial five percentage points. Every person that I've suggested this to has been amazed at the results. You will be too.

Note: To avoid high debt and paying interest in the first place, use your credit cards sparingly and pay off as much of your monthly balance as possible.

AVOID PAYING ATM CHARGES

There is a way to avoid paying huge ATM charges (ranging from $1 to $3) every time you use a bank machine not linked to your card to withdraw cash. Stop using those ATM machines. Instead, whenever you do grocery shopping, go to the drugstore or the post office, purchase your items with your ATM/debit card. When the cashier asks you if you want cash back, say yes and request the amount you need (most places have a ceiling of $50). Because you used your card to make a purchase, no added fee or charge is deducted from your account. You can easily save $200 to $300 a year doing this.

GETTING AROUND

GETTING AROUND THE CITY can be costly. To ride the subway and bus system, you have to fork over a hefty $2.00 for each trip, whether it's a long or short trip. That can be very expensive for those of us who have to travel to several places throughout the city in the same day. Fortunately, the **Metropolitan Transit Authority's unlimited MetroCard** provides a potent reprieve from the high cost of transportation. For $21 per week or $70 per month, the MetroCard gives you unlimited use of the subway and bus system, including transfers. This is ideal for actors who need to go back and forth to auditions, survival jobs, classes, etc. Metro-Cards may be purchased at all subway stations as well as newsstands, the Visitor's Center in Times Square (next to the Equity building), and pharmacies and grocery stores bearing a MetroCard sticker in the store window. Note: Bus and subway maps to help you plan your route are available on all buses, at train stations, public libraries, hotel lobbies and visitor centers.

PUBLIC TRANSPORTATION INFORMATION TELEPHONE NUMBERS:

Amtrak—212–630–6400

John F. Kennedy International Airport—718–244-4444

LaGuardia Airport—718–533–3400

Long Island Railroad—718–217–5477

Metro North Commuter Railroad—212–532–4900

Metropolitan Transit Authority Bus and Subway Information—718–330–1234

Newark International Airport—973–961–6000

New Jersey Transit—973–762–5100

Port Authority Bus Terminal—212–564–8484

Port Authority Trans-Hudson Corporation (PATH)— 800–234–7284

Staten Island Ferry—718–727–2508

Native New Yorkers as well as newcomers are occasionally stumped when trying to **find an address on the Avenues in Manhattan.** There seems to be no rhyme or reason to how buildings are numbered. It comes as a surprise that there actually is a handy formula, undoubtedly devised by some algorithm expert with a lot of time on his hands. I won't attempt to explain how it works (as if I knew, I'm an actor for God's sake—I can barely balance my checkbook), but it does. Use the calculator below and you'll arrive within a block or two of where you need to go.

TO LOCATE AVENUE ADDRESSES:

Take the address,
Drop the last digit,
Divide by 2 (unless otherwise noted),
Then add or subtract the number in the second column.
The result will be the nearest numbered cross street.

Note: Do not apply this guide to Broadway below Eighth Street, because many of the cross streets are named rather than numbered; for those addresses, you're on your own!

Avenues A, B, C and D	Add 3
First and Second Avenues	Add 3
Third Avenue	Add 10
Fourth Avenue	Add 8
Fifth Avenue Up 200	Add 13
Fifth Avenue Up to 400	Add 16
Fifth Avenue Up to 600	Add 18

Fifth Avenue Up to 775	Add 20
Fifth Avenue 775 to1286	Subtract 18
Fifth Avenue Up to 1500	Add 45
Fifth Avenue Up to 2000	Add 24
Sixth Avenue/Avenue of the Americas	Subtract 12
Seventh Avenue Below 110th Street	Add 12
Seventh Avenue Above 110th Street	Add 20
Eighth Avenue	Add 10
Ninth Avenue	Add 13
Tenth Avenue	Add 14
Amsterdam Avenue	Add 60
Audubon Avenue	Add 165
Broadway 754 to 858	Subtract 29
Broadway 858 to 958	Subtract 25
Broadway Above 100	Subtract 30
Columbus Avenue	Add 60
Convent Avenue	Add 127
Central Park West	Divide by 10, Add 60
Edgecombe Avenue	Add 134
Fort Washington Avenue	Add 158
Lenox Avenue	Add 110
Lexington Avenue	Add 22
Madison Avenue	Add 26
Manhattan Avenue	Add 100
Park Avenue	Add 35
Pleasant Avenue	Add 101
Riverside Drive (to 165th Street)	Divide by 10, Add 72
St. Nicholas Avenue	Add 110
Wadsworth Avenue	Add 173
West End Avenue	Add 60
York Avenue	Add 4

Finding an address on a numbered street is a lot less compli-cated—follow the charts below and it'll be a breeze. Note: All even addresses are on the south side of the street, odd addresses on the north side.

FOR THE WEST SIDE ABOVE 59th STREET:

ADDRESS:	LOCATED BETWEEN:
1–99	Central Park West and Columbus Avenue
100–199	Columbus and Amsterdam Avenues
200–299	Amsterdam and West End Avenues
300–399	West End Avenue and Riverside Drive

FOR THE WEST SIDE BELOW 59th STREET:

ADDRESS:	LOCATED BETWEEN:
1–99	Fifth and Sixth Avenues
100–199	Sixth and Seventh Avenues
200–299	Seventh and Eighth Avenues
300–399	Eighth and Ninth Avenues
400–499	Ninth and Tenth Avenues
500–599	Tenth and Eleventh Avenues

FOR EAST SIDE ADDRESSES:

ADDRESS:	LOCATED BETWEEN:
1–49	Fifth and Madison Avenues
50–99	Madison and Park Avenues (Park becomes Fourth Avenue below 14th Street)
100–149	Park and Lexington Avenues
150–199	Lexington and Third Avenues
200–299	Third and Second Avenues
300–399	Second and First Avenues
400–499	First and York Avenues (York becomes
Avenue A	below 14th Street)
500–599	Avenue A and Avenue B

TELEPHONE SERVICE

BELIEVE IT OR NOT, but there are many lower-priced alternatives to the phone giants Verizon and AT&T for both home and cellular service:

LOCAL

As I state later in my chapters on "Internet Access" and "Cable Television," **RCN Cable's "Resilink Gold" package** is the best deal out there on cable TV, local and long distance telephone and high-speed internet access. Telephone services include unlimited local and regional toll calling in all of these area codes: 212, 646, 917, 914, 631, 718, 347, 845, 203. Other features include Caller ID Deluxe, 3-Way Calling, Call Waiting ID Deluxe and basic Voice Mail. Also included are low long-distance rates, either 9¢ a minute, or just 7¢ a minute with a $4.95 monthly fee, for calls within the continental United States, with a separate, itemized long distance bill provided. The price tag for all this may sound high, but it's not when you factor in that you are getting cable TV (with expanded HBO and Cinemax channels) and ultra high-speed internet access. If you bought these services through Verizon or Time Warner, you'd pay over $166 a month, and if you bought them separately, you'd pay well over $175 a month. (For a more detailed description, see chapter on "Cable Television".)

LONG DISTANCE

If you opt not to use RCN Cable's "Resilink Gold" as your phone/cable/internet access provider, there are still several ways to cut down on your long-distance bills. The following will help you do just that:

BuyersOnline offers deeply discounted long distance and local long distance in New York State. There is no monthly fee charge; you will be billed $2.50 if your monthly usage falls below $20, which is typical of most long-distance providers. With BuyersOnline you get low international rates, a discounted calling card rate (with no surcharge), and a low-priced domestic 800 number rate for an additional $1 per month. Billing is in 60-second increments; you can pay either online with a credit card or with a check via mailed bill. By joining BuyersOnline, you'll get cash rebates up to 25 percent off the purchase price on every product you buy using their online shopping service. In addition, by simply sharing the savings you enjoy with others, you can earn monthly cash rebates equal to 10 percent of their usage. For more information or to sign up, go to their website at www.buyersonline.com/longdistance.

CallingCard.com offers a standard calling card that can be used from home, work or when traveling with what has to be the lowest long-distance rate around. Even better, rates for most international calls are only slightly higher. Signing up for this plan is incredibly easy: just go to their website at www.callingcard.com, have a credit card handy and open an account. You charge as much as you'd like to your card. You can recharge your card online at any time. Besides CallingCard.com's low rates, there are no access fees, no fees for universal use, no weekly surcharges and no startup fees. Moreover, you can view your call records and account information and manage your account right online. Billing is in full one-minute increments. The company provides 24-hour customer support to help make domestic and international calls trouble-free. Go to their website for more information.

Opex "Value-Plus" long distance provides quality, inexpensive domestic and international phone service. With the

"Value-Plus" plan, there are no monthly fees; billing is in one-minute increments and minimum call length is one minute. Opex also offers low-rate inbound toll-free calls for a service charge of $2 a month. They have several payment options: pay online with a credit card; pay by check with a paper bill mailed monthly; prepay with a credit card (which gives you an additional 8 percent savings off your monthly bill); or use auto-pay, which will automatically deduct your monthly balance due either from your checking account or any major credit card. Other pluses of the Opex plan include up to 100 free state-to-state minutes and 24/7 online customer service. For more information or to sign up, go to their website at www.cognigen.net/opex..

The "Ratesmasher" plan at **ZoneLD.com** is another great money saver. For a very low per-minute rate day or night, you get state-to-state long distance service with an even cheaper rate per minute to five states of your choosing, and low-priced international calls. With the "Ratesmasher" plan, there are no monthly minimums and billing is in 6-second increments. Payment options include either online with a credit/check card or by check via mailed bill. As an incentive to new customers, ZoneLD.com offers 50 free minutes of long distance and discount coupons for online shopping. For more information or to sign up, visit their website at www.zoneld.com or call their customer service at 866–966–3835.

CELLULAR

There are, hundreds of cellular phone plans out there, and it feels like I've researched each and every one. Cell phones are practically indispensable to actors. They provide a fail-safe way for directors, agents, producers and casting people to contact us, especially for last minute appointments. Moreover, our work frequently takes us out of town, and cellular service is the best way to keep in touch with friends, family and business contacts. For quality of service, access, minutes, availability and roaming charges, the following are the superior and most cost-effective cell plans:

I swear by the **Sprint** "Free and Clear plan" for wireless service. For a low rate, you get 4,000 minutes (350 "anytime" and 3,650 night and weekend), all with nationwide long distance that can be used throughout Sprint PCS's national network. The service features free voicemail, numeric paging, caller ID, call waiting and conference calling. In my experience, connections and access are almost always good, billing is straightforward and understandable, and although I've made calls to and from some out-of-the-way places, I've never been charged for roaming. For more information and rates and to activate this service, go to the Sprint website at www.sprintpcs.com or visit one of the many Sprint stores located throughout the city (for locations, check your phone book).

In regard to "anytime" and weekend minutes and price per month, the "Get More" nationwide plan from **VoiceStream Wireless** is an outstanding deal on cellular service. For one low rate, you get 600 "anytime" minutes of airtime, unlimited weekend minutes and with nationwide digital roaming, you pay no roaming charges. Other features include free nationwide long distance (of course), unlimited paging, caller ID, call waiting and call hold, detailed billing and conference calling. You may activate your "Get More" plan through the VoiceStream website (Voicestream.com), by calling 888–787–3267 or by visiting one of VoiceStream's New York City stores (check local listings for locations).

BEST BET

Recently, **Cingular Wireless** introduced its "Rollover Metro" plan, which is comparable to the VoiceStream plan above. For about the same rate, you get 600 "anytime" min-

utes, three-way calling, call forwarding, caller ID, call waiting, nationwide long distance, basic voice mail, and detailed
billing. What makes this plan superior to VoiceStream's, is
that you can roll over unused anytime minutes from month
to month. Cingular usually offers generous rebates on a couple of different phones. For information, rates or to activate
your phone, call Cingular at 866-CINGULAR, visit their
website at www.cingular.com, or stop by one of their city
stores (consult your phone book for the nearest location).

WORKING OUT

WORKING OUT IS ONE of the most important things we can do for our careers—think corsets, tights, nude scenes! Kidding aside, strong, healthy bodies are vital to our craft. We need strength and stamina to sustain a role for two or more hours, eight times a week. By working out we can keep in touch with our bodies so that we can effortlessly create the movement and mannerisms of the characters we are working on. Exercise is also a great way for us to work through our frustrations (we'll have a few), makes us look good, and empowers us with the confidence we'll need in audition rooms everyday.

Membership in most of New York's gyms is prohibitive for an actor's budget. There are mercifully, a few inexpensive alternatives:

Dolphin Fitness Clubs advertise that they "provide an affordable refuge from the overpriced pickup bars often disguised as fitness clubs." I'm not sure that the pickup bar/fitness club analogy applies anymore, but you gotta do what you gotta do to get paying customers, and if they think that's how they are going to sell their clubs, who am I to say they shouldn't? They are however one of the lowest priced health club chains in the city with memberships only $549 for 16 months that allow you access to all of Dolphin facilities citywide. Dolphin Fitness gyms are equipped with state-of-the-art machines, comparable to the machines and free weights you'd find at higher-end clubs. Dolphin also offers numerous classes, including yoga and martial arts. There are 15 Dolphin Fitness Clubs in the New York City area and continued expansion is planned (consult your phone book for the nearest Dolphin Fitness Club location).

The **Fitness Point Health Club** (2514 34th Avenue, Queens— 718–609–0670), a full-service gym in Astoria, offers yearly memberships for just under $200. Yep, you heard right, under $200 ($199 to be exact, and $249 for a two-year membership). Membership includes access to all weights and machines, guest passes, a free session with a trainer and all the aerobic/cardio/yoga/boxing classes that your heart and body can take.

Conveniently located in the heart of the theater district, the moderately priced **Gold's Gym** (250 West 54th Street— 212–307–7760) has 40,000 square feet of free weights and weight and cardio machines on 3 levels. Membership per year is advertised at $998, but don't let that scare you—no one I know who is a member has paid that. Go in, take a tour and then haggle over the rate; depending upon your tenacity, you can bargain your way to a substantial discount of between $200 and $300 off the advertised price. If you are opposed to haggling and are a member of one of the performing unions, Gold's Gym will give you a discount of about $200. Membership includes use of all exercise equipment, sundeck, and unlimited free classes like rebounding, tribal dance, hip-hop, spin, abs of steel, step, body sculpture, Hatha and Jivamukti yoga, cardio Thai boxing, kick boxing and belly dancing. Members are offered, at a cost, onsite medical and chiropractic care and massage therapy.

The **New York City Parks and Recreation Centers** (main number—212–360–8222) feature almost everything you'd find at the upscale gyms, including weight lifting equipment, cardio machines, classes, swimming pools, running tracks, handball/racquetball courts, and climbing walls (the types of things offered at the Centers varies depending upon location). You get all this for an unbelievable $25 per year, $10 per year if you are 55 or older. There are 30 NYC Recreation Centers throughout the city with five in Manhattan. Call the main number for

BEST BARGAIN

outer borough locations; check your White Pages for the nearest location. Manhattan locations include:

→ **The Asser Levy Center**—East 23rd Street between First Avenue and the FDR Drive—212-447-2020

→ **The Carmine Center**—Seventh Avenue South at Clarkson Street—212-242-5228

→ **The Hamilton Fish Center**—127 Pitt Street at Houston Street—212-387-7688

→ **The West 59th Street Center**—Tenth Avenue and 59th Street—212-397-3166

The clean and amiable **Synergy Fitness Clubs** has five Manhattan locations and has the cheapest membership rates I've heard of. Synergy has comparable amenities and classes to the more expensive clubs like New York Sports Club and Equinox and charges only $49 per month (easily half to a third what the super clubs charge), sometimes less when they are offering a special. A friend of mine who is a member told me, "Don't hesitate to bargain with them; after a bit of haggling, my membership is only $360 a year." At each Synergy location there is a good selection of machines, free weights and lots of cardio. Synergy locations:

201 East 23rd Street at Third Avenue—212-679-7300

1438 Third Avenue between 61st and 62nd Streets—
    212-879-6013

4 Park Avenue at East 39th Street—212-545-9590

1781 Second Avenue at East 93rd Street—212-426-0909

700 Columbus Avenue at West 94th Street—
    212-865-5454

The "Ys," as in **YMCA, YWCA and YM-YWHAs** are an inexpensive alternative to the city's pricey boutique gyms. Most "Y" facilities have a good selection of free weights, cardio, Universal, Nautilus (and the like) machines as well as handball/racquetball courts, basketball courts, swimming pools, running tracks, steam rooms, saunas, and myriad classes. The selection does vary at the different locations. Call the "Y" in your area for more information and membership rates.

Vanderbilt YMCA—224 East 47th Street—212–756–9600

West Side YMCA—5 West 63rd Street—212–875–4100

McBurney YMCA—125 West 14th Street—212–741–9210

92nd Street YM-YWHA—1395 Lexington Avenue at 92nd Street—212–415–5729

Manhattan YWCA—610 Lexington Avenue at East 63rd Street—212–755–4500

Chinatown YMCA—100 Hester Street—212–219–8393

Harlem YMCA—180 West 135th Street—212–281–4100

Bronx YMCA—2 Castle Hill Avenue, Bronx—718–792–9736

Greenpoint YMCA—99 Meserole Avenue, Brooklyn—718–389–3700

Flatbush YMCA—1401 Flatbush Avenue, Brooklyn—718–469–8100

Brooklyn Central YMCA—153 Remsen Street, Brooklyn—718–625–3136

North Brooklyn YMCA—570 Jamaica Avenue, Brooklyn—718–277–1600

Bedford-Stuyvesant—1121 Bedford Avenue, Brooklyn—718–789–1497

Prospect Park YMCA—357 9th Street, Brooklyn—
718–768–7100

Long Island City YMCA—3223 Queens Boulevard—
718–392–7932

Flushing YMCA—13846 Northern Boulevard, Queens—
718–961–6880

Brooklyn YWCA—30 Third Avenue, Brooklyn—
718–875–1193

Recently, **24/7 Fitness Club** (47 West 14th Street between Fifth and Sixth Avenues—212–206–1504) was running an ad offering yearly memberships for just $328. Besides access to its fully equipped facilities, this offer also includes classes (i.e., yoga, Afro aerobics, pilates, toning and abs, kick boxing, urban rebounding and boxing), a free personal training session, free body fat analysis and free nutritional information. This club's biggest plus: it never closes. Call or go by for more information.

PERSONAL APPEARANCE

Astor Place Hairstylists (2 Astor Place at Broadway—212–475–9854) used to be *the* place for the terminally hip to get a haircut. In the '80s, this salon was so popular you would have to wait an hour or more on the sidewalk outside until a guy who was perched on a ladder high above the throng would call your number. Over blaring music, barbers named Nick or Tony would ask in Brooklynese, "Whadja wanna do widja haih?" In the chair next to you, someone would be having his (or her) blue Mohawk reshaped, on the other side of you, a guy would be having a map of the subway system buzzed into the back of his head. When done, you would walk out content with your cut and feel slightly cocky that, for the half hour or so that you sat there, you were part of Manhattan's ultra-cool underworld. Best of all, the cut, "local color" and feeling of community cost only a few dollars.

Times have changed and Astor Place Hairstylists has mellowed. The music still blares and the atmosphere is funky and fun, but you see less "out-there" cuts and the crowds out front have diminished. Still, this huge place (three floors, 110 employees) turns out plenty of satisfied customers, and continues to charge very low prices—cuts starts at $11, blow-drys, $12. "Quintessentially New York," says a friend of mine who has his hair cut here every three weeks.

"Barber Shop" (349 West 44th Street, Basement) is a tiny, subterranean, one-chair wonder. Proprietor Nick gives great cuts starting at $9 (and only a dollar or two higher for longer hair) and shaves for $8. Lots of actors go to this place and swear by it. Why pay $60 when you can pay $9?

The **Beauty and Youth Village Spa** (145 Seventh Avenue at Charles Street—212–463–0246), across the street from the RandeeElaine Salon (see below), seems to be in a price war with them; although most services are priced about the same as Randee-Elaine, some things are a dollar or two more or less. Competing for the gay dollar (of course you don't have to be gay to patronize), Beauty and Youth offers discount coupons that can be found in gay periodicals like HX, MetroSourceNY and Next magazines (which may be found at most newsstands, gay bars, restaurants and businesses and on almost every corner in Chelsea). They also have a website—Beautyandyouth.com—with a complete menu of their services with downloadable coupons for treatments and special "Beauty Day" packages.

The **Clairol Product Evaluation Salon** (345 Park Avenue at 51st Street—646–885–4200), which provides services for both men and women, will color, perm, straighten, wash and set hair at no charge. Why, you may wonder? Clairol uses this salon to test its competitors' products in order to improve its own, and constantly needs guinea pigs. No need to worry though, the services here are all done by professional stylists and your desires are treated with utmost care and respect. You may use the Clairol Salon as often as you like either as a walk-in or after you call to make an appointment.

Four **hair salon chains** in the city all do very good work and charge reasonable prices for their services:

> **Dramatics NYC** has eight shops around town that offer a huge menu of salon services at moderate prices. You can do everything from getting a cut to having a deep pore with oxygen complex facial, to eyebrow shaping, to paraffin hand treatment and manicure and underarm waxing. Their press materials promise that "entertainment" is always a feature of their services. I've never patronized this chain, but it's nice to know that there is a salon with a sense of humor. Wash and cuts start at $17.95. Check your phone book for the nearest Dramatics location.

No appointment is necessary at the **filles et garcons** salons. The friends who are regular clients have all raved about the work, and the prices and services are comparable to the other chains. A shampoo and cut for a man is $23, for a woman between $26 and $37. A shampoo and blow-dry is $22 to $25, shampoo/cut/blow-dry is $30 to $35, color is $45 and foil highlights range from $78 and $100. filles and garcons locations are:

760 Third Avenue at 47th Street—212–486–6943

50 West 55th Street between Fifth and Sixth Avenues— 212–586–6585

673 Lexington Avenue at 56th Street—212–688–6655

The chain that is most popular and has the largest presence in New York is **Jean Louis David**. These ultra-hip European-style salons are all over Manhattan and are always bustling and packed with New Yorkers who look a little silly wearing the salon's signature white smocks. The services provided are far from silly; the work is very stylish and satisfying to a loyal and discriminating clientele. Shampoo, massage and cut goes for $22.49; Shampoo, massage, dry set for $28.49; shampoo, massage, cut and dry set for $35.49; shampoo, massage, cut, dry set and either perm, gloss, color or contrast for $88.49. Customers 20 and under get a 20 percent discount. The salons accept "walk-ins" or you may make an appointment. Consult your telephone listings for one of the 11 Manhattan Jean Louis David salons nearest you.

Don't confuse the **Jean Pierre Salons** with the Jean Louis David salons. The Jean Pierre salons are mirror and fluorescent affairs (and the two don't really go together, especially in a beauty salon!), with six full-service venues around the city. The work in them is good and the prices are affordable. A shampoo and cut is $18.30; shampoo, cut and blow-dry is $27.90 to $37.90; blow-dry is $20.20. The salons do color processes starting at $45, highlights with foil starting at $65 and perms starting at $65. Other services provided include body waxing for men and women, facials, full-body Swedish massage, ear piercing and eyelash/eyebrow tinting. You may walk in or make an appointment. Check your phone book for the nearest Jean Pierre Salon location.

A friend of mine has been going to **Limitone Hair Salon** (162 Seventh Avenue South between Perry and Charles Streets—212–675–3865) in the West Village for years and loves it. She is always very pleased with the work they do and can't believe (neither can her friends) that she pays just $20. Wash and cuts for both men and women start at $15 for walk-ins, $20 if you request a particular stylist.

My personal favorite is **Marella's Unisex** (625 Eighth Avenue at 42nd Street—212–868–0127) located inside the south annex of the Port Authority Bus Terminal. Even though Marella's has lots of chairs and barbers, there is almost always a wait of a few minutes, a testimony to this salon's popularity, service and customer satisfaction.

I happened upon Marella's by accident a few years ago as I was coming out of the 42nd Street subway under the Port Authority. Seeing the sign for $11 cuts and needing a trim, I ventured in. I was handed over to Jairo, who asked me what I wanted. "A little cleaned off the sides," I said. He started buzzing me quite close—a lot more hair than I desired was falling all over the brown smock I was wearing. It was too late by the time I protested. Most of my hair was gone. I was very angry and voiced my dismay quite loudly. Jairo, one of the mellowest human beings I have ever met, very gently assured me that this was the best cut for my face (and receding hairline). Although he didn't say it, his whole demeanor oozed, "trust me." As I'd already lost so much hair, I grumpily assented and slouched in the chair, but couldn't watch what he was doing. I decided I definitely would not be coming back, and there was no way I was going to tip the son-of-a-bitch.

When he was done, I looked up poutily, ready to hate what I saw.

I didn't. The cut was very different from how I normally wore my hair, but it wasn't bad. "Okay," I thought, "I'll give him a tip, but I'm still not coming back." Then during the day several friends complimented me on my new haircut. Strangers on the street and in the subway asked me where I had gotten my cut. It continued all week and for the next few weeks. You know the ending of this story—I went back to Jairo and have become a loyal customer.

Cuts at Marella's start at $12 (they've gone up a buck since my first visit) for men, $13 for women; shampoo and blow dry is $8 for men, $16 for women; a shave is $12; color is $23; color and set is $39; perms are $60.

The **Mayfair Beauty Shop** (252 East 73rd Street between Second and Third Avenues—212-535-7038) on the Upper East Side looks like the kind of place where your mother would have had her hair done when you were a kid. The prices here are about what she would have paid as well: a shampoo and cut is an unbelievable $10 and up, blowdrys are $12 and up, color is $12 and up, a manicure and pedicure is $21 and men's cuts are $12. The friend who recommended Mayfair feels she gets a better cut here than at other salons in the neighborhood that charge more than ten times the price. Walk-ins only.

Seek out some of the city's more upscale salons that constantly need **models for student classes**. As a model for these beauticians-in-training, you are charged next to nothing for a haircut and/or coloring. The tradeoff is, you are literally in the hands of students and at their disposal. Although, they are always overseen by a pro, and occasionally the pro will use your cut/color as a demonstration for the students. Note: Most salons will only accept cash for model cuts.

Leading salons that offer model cuts include:

Bumble and Bumble (146 East 56th Street between Lexington and Third Avenues—888-528-6253, ext. 397) does model cuts for $10 to $20 and color for $20. Call to find out when model cuts are offered.

Frederic Fekkai Beaute de Provence salon (15 East 57th Street off Fifth Avenue—212–753–9500) does model cuts or coloring for $30 on Wednesdays beginning at 6:30 P.M. Call in advance for an appointment.

John Sahag Salon (425 Madison Avenue at East 49th Street—212–750–7772) offers model cuts or single process color at $25, and highlights for $34 on Tuesdays beginning at 6:30 P.M. As space is limited, call on Monday to reserve a chair.

Louis Licari Salon (693 Fifth Avenue, 15th Floor between 54th and 55th Streets—212–758–2090) does model cuts for $30, single process hair color for $40 and highlights for $60. Call for an appointment.

Oribe at the Elizabeth Arden Salon (691 Fifth Avenue between 54th and 55th Streets—212–319–3910) offers model services on Tuesdays (call that morning to schedule an appointment). Cuts are $20 and color or highlights are $40.

Oscar Blandi (The Plaza Hotel, 768 Fifth Avenue at 59th Street—212–593–7930) gives model cuts ($25) and color ($35) on Tuesdays at 7 P.M. Call Tuesday afternoon to schedule an appointment.

Oscar Bond Salon Spa (42 Wooster Street between Broome and Grand Streets—212–334–3777) gives FREE model haircuts or coloring two to three times a week. Due to the overwhelming popularity of the price (FREE), they are backed up for eons. Don't be surprised when they tell you the next opening will be in about four months.

Vidal Sassoon for Men & Women (730 Fifth Avenue between 56th and 57th Streets—212–535–9200) has model cuts from $14 to $18. You must stop in Monday to Friday from 10 A.M. to 5 P.M. or Wednesday at 6:30 P.M. to schedule an appointment, as the staff needs to see the cut you want before scheduling you into one of their classes.

Don't let the downscale surroundings of the **RandeeElaine Salon for Men and Women** (180 Seventh Avenue near Perry Street—212–229–0399) dissuade you from using their services. This decidedly unglamorous place in the West Village can make you gorgeous for very little money. Overall, for some services I don't think there is another salon in the city that comes close to the low prices RandeeElaine charges. Where else can you get a one-hour full-body massage for $30, a manicure *and* pedicure for $15 and a one-hour facial for $25? Other low-priced services include: haircuts starting at $14, hair coloring starting at $25, "Painless" full-leg and bikini wax for $25, "Painless" chest or back wax for $15, butt wax for $10, full body wax for $59, eyelash and brow tint for $10, Parafango body wrap for $30, acne back treatments for $25 and electrolysis for $40 an hour. You can find discount coupons to the RandeeElaine Salon in *HX, MetroSourceNY* and *Next* magazines.

Of all the women I polled about their favorite inexpensive nail salon, **Shanel Nails** (748 Ninth Avenue between 50th and 51st Streets—212–397–5078) was the place named most. The consensus is that this tiny salon in Hell's Kitchen is clean, does great work and charges very low prices. Manicures here are just $6 (the cheapest in New York, according to my research) and pedicures $13. This full-service nail salon also offers a complete menu of waxing treatments at very reasonable prices.

BEST BARGAIN

The **Shiseido Studio** (155 Spring Street between West Broadway and Wooster Street—212–625–8820) in Soho has one of the city's best bargains: beauty treatments at no cost. This store, which proudly claims, "No cash registers," offers a choice of free private makeovers, facial treatments, facial massages and product samples as a marketing tool to introduce the Shiseido line to the public. As great as this offer sounds, you can only take advantage of it once a year and you need an appointment (which isn't that easy to get, es-

FREE SERVICES

pecially if you want your pores cleaned immediately—the wait can be as long as six weeks). The Studio does offer a free weekly series of skincare and makeup classes that you may attend as many times as you like, and a free virtual makeover, the "Beauty Navigator," which demonstrates what you would look like with different makeup applications.

BEST BARGAIN

An entire *Village Voice* issue devoted to Shopping in New York during 2002, dubbed **Yacha at the Essex Street Market** (120 Essex Street—212–388–0449) the city's "Best Barber." With such a glowing title, I trundled off to check him out. After passing fish and fruit stands, I found the gruff and imposing Yacha in a small, frill-free space. He's popular, so I had to wait. I told him what I wanted; he grumbled something back in an accent so thick that it was completely incomprehensible to me. I nodded, pretending to have understood him, and he began to cut. Twenty minutes later, he finished—the cut wasn't what I wanted at all, but it was great. The biggest surprise was the price—just $6. If I wasn't loyal to my barber, and the Essex Street Market was more convenient for me, I'd be a regular. Go with an open mind, as you will have no say in how your hair is cut!

INTERNET SERVICE PROVIDERS
(ISP<u>s</u>)

ANOTHER OF THE MANY great services the **Actors Federal Union** (165 West 46th Street, 14th Floor—212–869–8926 or 322 West 48th Street, see chapter on "Banking and Credit Cards") offers its members is the best deal I've seen for connecting to the World Wide Web. For $9.95 a month, with the first month free, the credit union gives you unlimited internet access, including four e-mail accounts, 24/7 technical support and up to 20 megabytes of web space. For more information, call the Credit Union or visit their online website at www.actorsfcu.net.

RCN Cable's (866–603–4471) "Resilink Gold" plan, in addition to its incomparable deal on cable TV, and local and long distance telephone already mentioned, offers high-speed internet access all for a reasonable monthly fee. The internet access portion of this "package" comprises unlimited, always-on access; 4 e-mail addresses that are accessible from anywhere; and access speeds which are much faster than dial-up services so that you can surf the net quickly and enjoy lightning-fast downloads. Call RCN for monthly rates. (For a more detailed description, see chapter on "Cable Television".)

Some of the better-known ISPs like AOL, MSN, Earthlink, AT&T, Prodigy and Compuserve, are all good and reliable, but their monthly charges ranging from $19.95 to $24.95, can damage a tight budget. Fortunately, there are several **ISPs that offer lower-price or totally free access to the net**. The tradeoff for the freebies is the placement of an annoying banner ad on your screen while you are using them. And, most of the free sites give you direct access for only 40 hours per month and usually kick you off the net after about fifteen minutes; if you need to be online for any length of time, you will probably have to dial up several times.

Low-priced Internet Service Providers (ranging in price between $8.95 and $15.95 per month) include:

> **www.Bluelight.com**
>
> **www.Juno.com**
>
> **www.Netzero.com**
>
> **www.worldshare.com**

Free ISPs include:

> **www.Freei.com**
>
> **www.address.com**
>
> **www.dotnow.com**
>
> **www.nocharge.com**

FREE DEAL

Note: Need to RECEIVE faxes but don't want to splurge on a fax machine. With a computer with an ISP link, you can **receive faxes at no charge**. Go to either **www.efax.com** or **www.onebox.com** and download the fax application. Once installed, you will be given a free fax number that enables you to receive faxes via your e-mail address, which you can print out if you need a hard copy. One caveat: Since these services are free, you will not be able to SEND faxes. To send as well as receive, you must pay a fee to upgrade your service, so that you have that capability.

ACCESSING THE INTERNET IF YOU DON'T OWN A COMPUTER

YOU DON'T OWN A COMPUTER but need to surf the web or check e-mail? Don't despair; there are ways to get online. First, most New York City libraries offer free internet connection. Access is limited however to half-hour segments and since it's first-come/first-served, there is almost always a wait for a terminal. A good alternative, though it will cost you, is to visit a cyber café (see list below). Prices at each average around $10 to $12 an hour with most serving food, beverages and even alcohol for an additional charge. The best bargains are **EasyEverything Internet Café** in the heart of Times' Square (234 West 42nd Street between Seventh and Eighth Avenues—212–398–0724 or 212–398–0775) where you can go online 24 hours a day for only $1; and any one of several **Burger King** restaurants where 20 minutes of internet usage is free with the purchase of a "Supersized Combo Meal." Other internet cafés:

→ **Alt.Coffee**: 139 Avenue A between St. Marks Place and East 9th Street—212–529–2233

→ **Cyber Café**: 250 West 49th Street between Broadway and Eighth Avenue—212–333–4109

→ **Cyberfelds**: 20 East 13th Street near Fifth Avenue—212–647–8830

→ **Internet Café at the New York Computer Place:** 247 East 57th Street at Second Avenue—212–872–1709

→ **New York Computer Café**: 247 East 57th Street between Second and Third Avenues—212–872–1704

→ **Void:** 16 Mercer Street between Grand and Canal Streets—212–941–6492

→ **Web2Zone**: 54 Cooper Square—212–614–7300

CABLE TELEVISION

AN INCOMPARABLE DEAL on cable TV service is **RCN Cable's** "Resilink Gold" package. The Cable TV portion of this package (see "Local Telephone" and "Internet Service Providers" sections for additional information) includes over 85 channels of basic cable TV programming, expanded HBO and Cinemax channels, 31 commercial-free CD-quality music channels and 5 Pay-Per-View channels. RCN's price for all these services might seem high, but if you break it down by service, you'll realize that you probably spend as much or more on the individual services. I paid an average of $173 a month (and that didn't include HBO!) for local and long-distance phone service, internet access and cable. With RCN's "Resilink Gold," I now save about $55 per month. For more information and rates, call RCN at 866–603–4471. Note: RCN wires haven't been laid in all of the city neighborhoods yet and some buildings may not have access so when you call for information, verify that RCN is in your building.

VIDEO AND DVD RENTAL

YOU WOULD EXPECT, in this arts and media capital, a variety of outstanding places to rent DVDs and videos and it does have everything from high-tech/low-charm mega-chains, to low-tech/high-expertise small specialty stores. Among the latter are even stores dedicated to a single genre such as Asian films or Indian "Bollywood" movies. Sure, the chains have put a lot of mom-and-pop shops out of business—a Blockbuster obliterated two of my neighborhood favorites in recent years—but others have not only survived but are thriving. The following compilation, based on price and selection, lists the city's better outlets for DVDs and videos.

With their huge selection of Shakespeare plays, live theater and BBC recordings, **Evergreen Video** (37 Carmine Street near Bedford Street—212–691–7362) is my favorite rental outlet. Evergreen has an immense selection, with specialized sections including "Cult Trash," "1960s Comedies," "Avant Garde Special Interest," "Musicals," "Film Noir," "Fantasy," "pre-1955 Afro-American," "War," "Foreign," "Dance." Daily rentals are $3.25 for the first night and $1.62 each night thereafter. Evergreen's best deal offers members 4 DVDs or videos for $12 plus tax with up to three days to view them. To rent, become a member. Membership is free, but your credit card number is kept on file in case of lost, damaged or unreturned merchandise.

Fliks Video's two city locations offer several prepayment rental plans that provide good value to members:

- → Bronze Plan—10 DVD or videos for $39.95 plus tax
- → Silver Plan—20 DVD or videos for $74.95 plus tax

→ Gold Plan—40 DVD or videos for $129.95 plus tax

→ Platinum Plan—100 DVD or videos for $279.95 plus tax

Each plan includes a free catalog that lists Fliks's inventory of over 25,000 films, fast free delivery to your door in a guaranteed 58 minutes or less, free pickup, two-day rentals, free next-day reservations, and free rental credits with early renewal. The scope of the selection here doesn't compare with places like TLA, World of Video and Movie Place, but there is something to be said for not having to leave your home to get a video or DVD.

175 West 72nd Street between Broadway and Columbus Avenues–212–721–0500

1093 Second Avenue between 57th and 58th Streets—212–752–3456

Kim's Video Stores In the East and West Villages and near Columbia University, have created an ultra-cool mini rental empire dealing in everything from alternative and independent to rare and irreverent film titles that cater to the tastes of urban hipsters. To appease the bourgeoisie (as well as the hipsters' occasional desire for the mundane), Kim's also shelves the requisite Hollywood hits. Categories include what you'd expect as well as atypical genres like "Blaxploitation," "Indie," "Queer," "Anime," "Avant Garde," "Shorts," and "Cult." VHS and DVD Catalog titles cost $1.25 same day (returned before midnight), $2.50 overnight, $3.75 for two nights or $5 for five nights; new releases cost $3.50 per night. To save money here join "KimMoney," their frequent renter's program: when you prepay for videos, you receive credit that is applied to future rentals (i.e. for every $20 you pre-pay, you are credited $25, for every $50 you pre-pay, you are credited $65, and so on. Each branch requires a separate membership.

→ **Mondo Kim's,** 6 St. Marks Place near Third Avenue—212–505–0311

→ **Kim's East**, 85 Avenue A between 5th and 6th Streets—212–529–3410

→ **Kim's Mediapolis,** 2906 Broadway at 113th Street—212–864–5321

→ **Kim's Underground**, 144 Bleecker Street at LaGuardia Place—212–260–1010

The expert staff of cinephiles at **Movie Place** (237 West 105th Street near Broadway—212–864–4620) makes this rickety shop a "must" for serious film aficionados. Although their selection doesn't have the breadth of other independents, and heavens forfend that they should become computerized, the knowledgeable and personable crew is unparalleled. No matter what you are looking for, they know whether they have it; name a film or genre you like, and they will rattle off a list of similar titles you are sure to enjoy. An overnight rental on tapes and DVDs is a moderately priced $4.62 plus tax. Movie Place has a very liberal prepayment plan by which you can rent 6 DVDs or videos for $26, 13 for $48 and 30 for $94. Better yet, plan members get a free film with each rental everyday. Other plan features include two-day rental policy, Sunday through Thursday; rentals on Friday are for three days, due back by closing Monday; and free pick-up and delivery between 86th and 120th Streets on the Upper West Side.

Many branches of the **New York Public Library** have a wide assortment of videos that you are allowed to borrow for up to a week. You are limited to five at a time. Like books, there is no charge for borrowing videos. The selection varies from branch to branch with the **Donnell branch** (West 53rd Street between Fifth and Sixth Avenues), having a tremendous choice of film categories, including documentaries, animated, foreign-language and television (look for the BBC's "Complete Works of William Shakespeare"). Other branches with well-stocked video sections are the **Mid-Manhattan**

(Fifth Avenue at 43rd Street) and the **Library for the Performing Arts** (Lincoln Center—111 Amsterdam Avenue at 66th Street—212-870-1630), which focuses on videos related to the performing arts.

Too bad I don't live on the East Side. If I did, I'd be at **New York Video** (949 First Avenue at 52nd Street—212-888-4545) all the time. This store has one of the city's best selections of DVDs and videos (only TLA's is bigger), and no place is better organized. Their entire inventory of titles is on convenient LP-sized cards in wooden bins that are divided into myriad categories and subcategories. Nowhere other than this store have I seen such specialized sections as "Monster," "Detective," "Hammer Horror," "Russ Meyer," "Serial Killer," "Courtroom," "Violence," "Mad Scientists," "Ed Wood" and "Slasher Flicks." Also, New York Video is the only store I'm aware of that organizes its classic film sections by actors and directors. All DVDs and videos are $3.99 plus tax for two nights, except children's titles under 60 minutes are $1.99 plus tax. For a dollar more on any Friday rental, you can keep the film until the following Monday.

TLA Video (52 West 8th Street between Fifth and Sixth Avenues—212-228-8282) in the West Village is a godsend for film buffs. One step inside and you'll agree that this store has the city's largest selection of DVDs and videos. And, the quality of the selection is substantial. Yes, there are the Hollywood blockbusters and new releases, but TLA focuses here on unconventional titles, and there are tons of them representing every genre of celluloid ever conceived. I'd venture to say that almost any domestic and foreign title you are looking for is carried by this wonderful store. If not, the knowledgeable and dedicated staff will know how to find it. New releases are $4.50 the first night, $2.50 each additional night; general releases are $3.75 the first three nights, $1.75 each day thereafter. TLA offers two ways to view films economically: a 3-For-2 Special—when you

BEST SELECTION

rent any three films and return them all together on time, you will be charged only for two; a pre-paid Discount Card allows 10 rentals for $35, 20 for $65 and 50 for $150.

The bulk of the enormous inventory at the large **Tower Record and Video** stores is general interest and Hollywood titles, which sticks to the usual genres: "Television," "Comedy," "Drama," "Foreign," etc. Tower has little in the way of cutting-edge or "out there" films, but more the safe and dependable titles like Blockbuster rather than those carried by the better independently-owned neighborhood dealers. However, one can't quibble with the prices, which are some of the best in the city—new releases are $2.99 per night while catalog titles are only $1.49 for three nights.

BEST BARGAIN

383 Lafayette Street—212–228–5100
1961 Broadway at 66th Street—212–799–2500
725 Fifth Avenue in Trump Tower—212–838–8110

Having survived both escalating real-estate prices in its ever-gentrifying neighborhood, and a bully Blockbuster that was for years located across the street, **Video Blitz** (267 West 17th Street, 2nd Floor—212–645–6410) continues to faithfully serve the home viewing needs of Chelsea-ites. Its large selection is mostly mainstream titles from the usual genres, with few surprises. The exception is its vast gay and lesbian section, probably the biggest in the city (no surprise there given Video Blitz's location and demographics); even the gay adult titles outnumber the straight three-to-one. New DVD and video releases are $4.30 per night; catalog titles are $4.30 per two nights. Video Blitz does have three low-priced rental specials: Tuesday and Wednesday rent any two movies for $5.40; Thursday rent any three movies for $8.60; on Friday, Saturday, Sunday, and Monday, catalog titles are two-for-one.

Video Café (697 Ninth Avenue at 48th Street—212–765–6165) offers free membership and a moderate $3.78 per night rental on new releases, $3.24 per three night rental on catalog titles (which are any videos that are not "new releases") and $2.16 per three night rental on children's movies. To save big bucks, look into Video Café's discount specials: Tuesday and Wednesday rent one movie and you get a second free; rent three movies in one day and you get a fourth one free; after every eleventh paid rental, the twelfth is free; prepay for 10 video rentals, new or catalog titles, and it costs $32.45, which includes free delivery.

Along with Evergreen, TLA and the two Kim's locations on Bleecker Street, **World of Video** (51 Greenwich Avenue—212-691-1281) contributes mightily to making the West Village the city's best neighborhood for video rentals. This great store has one of the largest selections of general-purpose videos and DVDs, drawn from just about every genre imaginable including documentaries, dance, opera, horror, western, PBS/A&E, musicals, classics, TV, stand-up comedy, comedy classics, gay and lesbian, cult, adult, and Shakespeare. This video store requires you to buy a membership, but as the saying goes, membership does have its privileges: the $19.99 per year gets you three free rentals plus special rental savings, sale discounts and other club extras. Members choose their price: movies for three days/two nights are $4.16; tapes returned early receive $1 off coupons good towards the next rental; pay for 25 videos or DVDs in advance at only $2.20 for each three day/two night rental; pay cash on Tuesdays and receive a second tape free.

DISCOUNT SERVICE PROVIDERS VIA THE INTERNET

THERE ARE TWO OUTSTANDING websites that help consumers comparison-shop for a variety of vital services ranging from cell phone to long distance, credit cards, home and auto insurance, utilities and much more. I have used these sites to research all kinds of services, and through them found my cellular phone and renter's insurance plans. With both, I got exactly what I was looking for at the lowest possible price.

The mission of **MyRatePlan** (www.myrateplan.com) is to ensure that users of their website get the best value for the services they use every day. MyRatePlan provides a comprehensive, unbiased online information resource to help consumers "cut through the fine print," and locate the lowest price for the services they need.

MyRatePlan, launched in 1999 as a comparison-shopping site for wireless phone plans and has since added several other services, such as long distance, travel, satellite TV, credit cards, package delivery, insurance, internet access, online stock brokers, mortgages and auto loans. The site's consumers are able to evaluate and select plans among a number of providers. When a plan is located that fits an individual's needs, MyRatePlan opens the necessary links to complete the purchase online.

The **LowerMyBills** (www.lowermybills.com) press release states that its website aims "simply to help every American household save money for the important things in life," and it does a very good job of fulfilling that goal. To comparison-shop at LowerMyBills, enter your zip code, e-mail address and monthly bill information. The site assesses your current services, reviews others in your area and searches for the cheapest price on everything from phone and utilities to insurance, mortgages, internet access, debt relief and home and auto loans. Once the site's calculators have finished searching the net, a list of offers pops up in order of cheapest to most expensive, based on your personal criteria. If it finds alternative providers that can give you a better deal, LowerMyBills will assist you in switching. Best of all, LowerMyBills is completely free to use.

PART III

Staying Healthy

MEDICAL

THE HEALTH COVERAGE WE GET through the entertainment industry unions is pretty good: 80 percent of most doctor's visits is paid for by our insurance, as are optician, dentist, psychotherapist, pharmaceutical and other medical-related fees. Almost 100 percent of emergency room charges and hospital stays are covered.

Not all performing artists are covered, however. Many are not members of any unions and are therefore ineligible. Others, in one union or another, may not qualify either because either they have not worked enough weeks or because they have not earned the prescribed minimum. This can be pretty scary.

Fortunately, uninsured performers do have access to affordable health care in this city. Moreover, there are low-rate health insurance alternatives for those who do not qualify for entertainment union coverage.

The **Callen-Lord Community Health Center** on 18th Street in Chelsea (356 West 18th Street—212-271-7200) has a sliding scale for the uninsured (office visits as little as $30, depending on your income) without the third world feel of many public clinics. A straight friend of mine who uses this clinic says, "They are particularly interested in serving the gay and lesbian community, but do not inquire as to your preference. I have used them several times."

D•O•C•S, which is affiliated with Beth Israel Medical Center, is both a "walk-in" and a "by appointment" health clinic that charges uninsured patients very modest rates. A typical office visit for the uninsured is around $100, with most D•O•C•S services ranging anywhere from $80 to $290. The great thing about this clinic is that before they treat you, they do an evaluation and let you know exactly the amount of the visit; this insures that there are no surprises as you are leaving their offices. [For those who are covered, D•O•C•S accepts most insurance policies.] D•O•C•S is open seven days a week and most evenings has extended hours. Its three locations are:

> 55 East 34th Street between Madison and Park
>   Avenues—212–252–6000
> 1555 Third Avenue at 88th Street—212–828–2300
> 202 West 23rd Street at Seventh Avenue—212–352–2600

The **Gay Men's Health Crisis/Geffen Clinic** (125 West 24th Street between Sixth and Seventh Avenues, 6th Floor—212–367–1100) offering screenings for HIV and syphilis, charges on a sliding scale that ranges from $30 to $100. On Fridays, they have a "walk-in" program when screenings are only $15.

For almost twenty years **The Miller Health Care Institute for the Performing Arts at St. Luke's/Roosevelt Hospital** (425 West 59th Street between Ninth and Tenth Avenues, Suite 6—212–523–6200) has been providing affordable general and specialized medical care for performing artists as well as those in allied professions such as teachers, coaches, designers, writers, directors and production crews. Designed for and dedicated to the specific health needs of performing artists, the Miller Institute is also sensitive to the performer's budgetary constrictions—uninsured and underinsured patients are offered quality care on a sliding scale. The Institute also accepts Medicare and has several grants to expand access to their specialty programs. Institute services encompass everything from routine checkups and diagnosis and treatment of acute and chronic medical problems to specialized care like acupuncture, psychotherapy, dance medicine, speech therapy, physical rehabilitation, orthopedics, massage therapy and nutrition. Unique to the Institute are its voice laboratory to examine ailing vocal chords; a physical therapy gym with a sprung dance floor, ballet barres and mirrors; and a performance evaluation studio to examine musicians' performance problems and progress. Patients are seen by appointment only, but some slots are open every day for those with urgent medical problems.

The **New York City Department of Health** (212–427–5120) offers free and confidential HIV and STD testing at several locations throughout the city. The Department of Health also sponsors free safe-sex seminars, and for those who test positive, free counseling and doctor referrals. Call for locations and testing times.

The **Park Med Eastern Women's Center** (38 East 30th Street between Madison Avenue and Park Avenue South—212–686–6066) offers urine pregnancy tests free, blood pregnancy tests for $20 and full OB-GYN examinations for $100. Appointments are necessary for examinations; you may "walk-in" for pregnancy test.

Founded in 1996 by Dr. Barry Kohn and sponsored by The Actors' Fund (see "Getting Help" chapter) and Broadway Cares/Equity Fights AIDS, **Physician Volunteers for the Arts** (The Aurora, 475 West 57th Street, 2nd Floor—212–489–2020, ext. 140) is a free medical clinic providing quality health care for all uninsured and underinsured entertainment professionals. Twenty physicians, two podiatrists and a physical therapist all volunteer their time to provide a wide spectrum of medical services. Specialty care is also available for allergy, dermatology, gastroenterology, gynecology, internal medicine, immunology, liver disease, podiatry, pulmonology and psychiatry. In cases where a specialty consultation is necessary, Physician Volunteers for the Arts physicians refer patients to The Miller Institute (see above), or to New York Presbyterian Hospital for a flat fee of $40. Additional free Physician Volunteers for the Arts services include: ongoing information on wellness issues; quarterly blood pressure and cholesterol screenings; pap smear and cervical cultures; annual health fairs; flu Shots; women's health fair; mammograms; bone density testing; colon rectal cancer screening; PSA blood levels; electrocardiograms. To make an appointment, call Monday to Friday between 9:30 A.M. and 5 P.M.

Planned Parenthood of New York City offers family planning counseling and treatment of a wide array of gynecological needs including abortion, contraception, HIV testing and STD detection and treatment. All Planned Parenthood services are inexpensively priced (HIV and STD testing and birth control is free to students under 20, pregnancy testing is free to all) and discretion is assured. Call for more information on services or to make an appointment.

> Margaret Sanger Center, 26 Bleecker Street at Mott
>   Street—212–274–7200
> 44 Court Street, Brooklyn—718–243–0506
> 349 East 149th Street between Morris and Courtlandt
>   Streets, Bronx—212–965–7000

The **Ryan/Chelsea-Clinton Community Health Center** (645 Tenth Avenue at 46th Street—877-227-9266) opened in 2002 and offers primary care physicians and a complete range of health care services to members of the Midtown West community charged on a sliding scale. All members of the community are eligible for care at the Health Center, including low-income, medically underserved and uninsured patients, as well as those who are covered by Medicare and Medicaid. The uninsured pay a minimum of $29 per visit; depending on income, the most a patient would be expected to pay is $90, which includes X-rays, tests and blood work. Patients able to pay on the day of services are given a 30 percent discount. Uninsured patients are eligible for the Center's pharmacy plan, where they may purchase medication with only a $5 co-payment. The Center offers liberal payment plans for those who cannot pay on day of services. If, for any reason, the Center cannot treat a patient, they will refer the patient to one of their city affiliates. If hospital care is needed, the Center will refer the patient to St. Luke's/Roosevelt.

Young Men's Clinic (21 Audubon Street at 166th Street—212–342–5204), a joint project of Columbia University's Mailman School of Public Health and New York Presbyterian Hospital, offers free medical care to low-income young men under 30 and those who lack insurance. Although the clinic does offer complete health care including physicals, its primary goal is to treat sexual and reproductive health needs.

DENTAL

The **New York College of Dentistry** (345 East 24th Street between First and Second Avenues—212–998–9872) offers a full-service dental clinic and emergency dental care for those who are not covered by insurance or cannot afford private-practice dentist fees. For a one-time registration fee of $85 and office charges that are at least 25 percent lower than regular dental fees, an NYCD final-year student will examine your teeth and do any work that is needed. Not to worry, these students are expertly trained and are always overseen by an experienced dental professional. As the clinic understandably gets quite busy, make sure to go early.

CHIROPRACTIC AND ACUPUNCTURE

Dr. Craig Fishel at the **New York Chiropractic and Wellness Center** (115 East 57th Street at Lexington Avenue, 14th Floor—212–980–5444) offers chiropractic care to uninsured performing artists on a sliding scale. The initial office visit, which includes consultation, examination, X-ray, diagnosis and treatment, is $100. Office visits for the uninsured after the initial visit start at just $25 and include a full body adjustment and other treatments as necessary. If you are in need of acute care, New York Chiropractic and Wellness will charge you $150 per month, no matter how many visits you need in a four-week cycle; e.g., you can go five times a week for a month and still only pay a total of $150.

The **Pacific College of Oriental Medicine** (915 Broadway between 20th and 21st Streets—212–982–4600) instructs students in the healing art of acupuncture. To provide practical, hands-on training for its students, the College offers the general public an inexpensive acupuncture clinic. At $25 per visit for the first three visits, and free thereafter, Pacific College students, under faculty supervision, perform one-hour acupuncture sessions. If you are a little squeamish about a student sticking you (and you needn't be as all students at the clinic are highly trained and have reached a level of qualification before they are allowed to treat patients), you may have treatments by one of the college's faculty-practitioners at $60 for the first visit and $40 for all follow-up visits.

PRESCRIPTION DRUGS AND TOILETRIES

For uninsured actors in need of **prescription medication**, the best way I know to save on the high cost of drugs is to shop at www.drugstore.com. Prescriptions at this site cost about half what you'd pay at a pharmacy, and there is no tax or shipping fees.

In New York City, there are no discount pharmacies or drugstores. Let me rephrase that, although several drugstore and pharmacy chains like Duane Reade, Rite Aid and CVS would argue that they are indeed discount retailers, none really have everyday low prices. I'm not saying that they don't have discount prices; they all certainly have sales, specials and coupon offers to pull people into their stores. Almost everything these retailers sell however, except of course prescriptions, can be found at the general merchandise discount stores like Kmart, Conway and the rest, for less money. (For a list of these retailers, see chapter on "General Merchandise Discounts Stores.")

Duane Reade, which has a huge city presence, does exonerate itself with its **Dollar Rewards Club Card**. This free club offers members discounts on featured toiletries, sundries and other items each week, which can save you money. Pick up a Dollar Rewards Club application at any Duane Reade store.

THERAPY

New York is the greatest city in the world. It's also the toughest. The city is expensive, overcrowded, fast-paced, brusque . . . all the things that people who have lived here for any length of time ostensibly come to love. But it takes courage, tenacity, confidence, cunning and a bit of an edge to settle here comfortably. Often, city life reminds me of the lyrics from Boy George's song "Karma Chameleon": "Every day is like survival."

Dare I mention our crazy profession? In our business, we endure more rejection and disappointment than any other. One day we can be starring in a Broadway play or appearing on a TV show, the next we are scrambling for work. Not only that, every audition is the equivalent of a job interview and every day we are told, "No," sometimes more than once. Actually, getting the job, given how many people we are competing with, is the exception, not the rule.

So, how do we keep it together in this insane city and business? Therapy seems to help lots of New Yorkers, me included. To some, therapy is ridiculous, unnecessary, inconceivable, even a dirty word. However, it can be a real boon for us. Therapy can help us put our lives in perspective; it can give us an outlet to vent, to cry, to complain, to meditate, to ruminate, to sort through the past, to plan the future. It is a way to unload without burdening (or revealing too much to) our friends and family. Probably most beneficial, it is a safe place where we can speak freely and candidly to a caring professional who can help us assess our lives and behavior, and hopefully point us in the right direction.

Therapy comes at a high price, though. New Yorkers all over the city are paying their "shrinks" anywhere from $90 to $200 dollars for a 45-minute session. For those of us on a budget, those sums are an impossibility, making therapy feel more like a luxury than a necessity.

Fortunately, there are organizations that offer therapy priced on a sliding scale to low- and moderate-income individuals. These groups understand the importance of therapy for the entire New York community, not just the wealthy. They are devoted to helping us survive, reach our potentials, and live freer, happier lives. Of the several organizations that charge on a sliding scale, the five I mention I have either had direct contact with, or have come highly recommended by friends and colleagues.

Community Guidance (133 East 73rd Street between Park and Lexington Avenues—212–988–4800) was founded in 1953 with the idea that fees for therapy should be set on a sliding scale, based on a patient's means and income. Initially, you do an intake with a Community Guidance psychologist who asks you to discuss your background and the things you would like to work on. At this interview, you may request the kind of therapist you would like (man, woman, gay, straight) and your session rate is determined. Within a week or so, you are assigned to one of the group's therapists, all of whom are psychologists or certified social workers with advanced degrees. You meet the therapist in his or her private office. If at any time you feel the match is not a good one, you may request to be reassigned. Rates start at $35.

Identity House (39 West 14th Street, between Fifth and Sixth Avenues, Suite 205—212–243–8181), a nonprofit organization of caring volunteers provides counseling services and support to New York City's gay, lesbian, bisexual and transgendered communities. Founded as a safe place to explore issues of sexual identity and to help those who are struggling with sexuality, alienation, relationships and family, Identity House offers a wide range of services including counseling by professional psychotherapists, therapy referrals, discussion groups, conferences and workshops and nonclinical support services. The organization's walk-in center (open Monday, Tuesday and Friday from 6 P.M. to 9 P.M. and Sunday from 2 P.M. to 5 P.M.) provides peer counselors who themselves have confronted issues of personal identity, to discuss any concerns you may have; if necessary they make referrals. No appointment is necessary; a $20 donation is requested at the time of services, but no one is turned away if they cannot make the contribution.

The National Institute for the Psychotherapies (NIP) (330 West 58th Street between Eighth and Ninth Avenues— 212–582–1566) is a four-year post-graduate training facility for licensed mental health professionals. As part of their training, the therapists are required to see patients under the auspices of the Institute; NIP offers the New York community the services of these professionals on a sliding scale based on income and expenses. Initially, the patient is required to do an intake screening with a Ph.D. After an initial consultation with a therapist to determine the specific needs of the person, NIP will assign him/her to a therapist. If the consumer feels the match is not a good one, he/she can request to be reassigned. A friend of mine, who found his therapist through NIP, says, "Therapy is more an art than a science, so if you smell shit, yell shit!" Sliding scale fees start at $45, although fees for full-time students and the unemployed start at $25. Therapeutic sessions may take place either at NIP's facilities, or in the therapist's private office elsewhere in the metropolitan area, depending on the patient's needs and therapist availability.

The **Village Psychotherapy Referral Service** (80 East 11th Street at Broadway, Suite 643—212–460–5617) offers a wide array of psychotherapeutic, psychological and psychiatric services, including individual, couple and group psychotherapy. VPRS experts in child, adolescent and family therapy provide counseling as well as parenting and educational (psychological testing, etc.) services. All VPRS clinicians are certified, highly trained and experienced in working with a variety of populations, including fine and performing artists, gays and lesbians, children and young adults, and educators. All fees are based upon ability to pay (sliding scale). Call for an initial consultation when a member of the VPRS staff will assess your needs and match you with a specialist.

As a community mental health facility for over forty years, the **Washington Square Institute for Psychotherapy & Mental Health** (41 East 11th Street—212–477–2600) provides psychological services to middle income individuals and families. The Washington Square Institute emphasizes understanding their patients' present difficulties in light of past personal history and in helping them use this knowledge to achieve mastery over their lives. To enable their staff to arrive at the most appropriate plan of treatment for the patient, the Institute requires three intake sessions—an initial interview, a psychiatric evaluation and conference, and a treatment planning interview—which are charged at around $50 for each session. Once these sessions are complete, the patient is matched with a therapist, assigned a specific 45-minute period for treatment, and informed what the subsequent session rates will be. These rates are determined on a sliding scale from $35 to $100. All therapeutic sessions are held at Washington Square Institute's East Village location. To ensure continued quality of care throughout treatment, Washington Square Institute's Treatment Center views all patients as patients of the entire Institute, not only of a particular therapist. Should a patient wish to change therapists, or if for any reason the patient's therapist leaves, the Institute finds another suitable and qualified staff member to continue treatment. Washington Square Institute also offers group therapy, couples counseling and medication services.

Two **city hospitals** provide therapy and treatment at free walk-in clinics for those who are unable to pay. The clinics are staffed by professional therapists and treat a variety of problems including eating disorders, anxiety, depression and substance abuse. For more information and hours of operation, call:

Mt. Sinai Hospital: Fifth Avenue and 100th Street
Compulsive, Impulsive and Anxiety Disorders Program—
212–241–8304

NYS Psychiatric Institute at Columbia Presbyterian Medical Center: 1051 Riverside Drive at 168th Street
Depression Evaluation—212–543–5734
Eating Disorders—212–543–5316
Substance Abuse—212–923–3031

In an immediate crisis, there are several free **help lines** you can call. Most of those working the phone lines are trained in suicide prevention as well as in counseling for sex and crime victims, depression and personal problems.

AIDS Hotline—212–676–2550 / 212–447–8200

Alcohol & Substance Abuse Info Line—800–274–2042, 24 hours

Center for Inner Resources Development—
212–734–5876, 24 hours

Crime Victims' Hotline—212–577–7777, 24 hours

Help Line—212–532–2400, 24 hours

The Samaritans—212–673–3000, 24 hours.

Sex Crimes Report Line—212–267–7273, 24 hours

Established by the New York City Department of Health in conjunction with the Mental Health Association, **Lifenet** offers mental health counseling, information and a referral Line in English, Spanish and Chinese to assist those who are experiencing emotional distress in the aftermath of the World Trade Center disaster. 24 hours per day, 7 days a week.

For English Speakers—212–995–5824
For Spanish Speakers—877–248–3373
For Chinese Speakers—877–990–8585

MASSAGE

FOUNDED IN 1916, the **Swedish Institute College of Massage** (226 West 26th Street between Seventh and Eighth Avenues—212-924-5900) is considered one of the preeminent massage techniques schools in the country and has graduated thousands of students who have gone on to practice. The Swedish Institute's mission is "to create a safe and challenging environment for training students in the most current, practical, theoretical, scientific and ethical foundations of Western and Eastern holistic health care so that graduates are able to find and perform therapeutic work in a variety of settings." To provide practical training for its students, the Institute offers the general public two different inexpensive massage clinics where students, under faculty supervision, perform one-hour massage sessions:

→ **Stress Reduction Clinic:** meets for six weekend sessions and offers a basic full-body massage utilizing Swedish and Shiatsu techniques. The cost for the clinic is $125 for six sessions, which works out at a little over $20 per session.

→ **Therapeutic Massage Clinic:** explores the application of both Eastern and Western techniques to assess and devise treatment for a variety of conditions and patterns of disharmony. For this clinic, you must provide written approval from your doctor that you have no "contraindications for massage therapy." The twelve week session costs $225, $220 for seniors over 65.

To enroll in either clinic, call the number above and request an application.

Although the **Randee Elaine Salon** (180 Seventh Avenue South near Perry Street—212–229–0399) is a little on the dowdy side, the services it provides are all very good and very cheap (see chapter on "Personal Appearance"). Their massage therapists are mostly hefty Russian men and women with very strong hands who can break up almost any knot you've got. You'll stay relaxed when you receive their bill—only $30 for a one-hour massage if you use a Randee Elaine Salon coupon, which can be found in most gay periodicals like Metro Source, HX and Next. You need to make an appointment for massages.

OPTICIANS

White Cat Vision has two locations throughout the city and is probably the least expensive place in New York to buy eyeglasses. They stock a great selection of designer frames by Calvin Klein, Kenneth Cole, Fendi, Dior, and others, all starting at around $30. Most styles are very modern and fashion-forward. White Cat gives eye examinations, has a doctor on the premises and sells contact lenses. Locations:

> 22 East 14th Street between Fifth Avenue and Broadway—
> 646–336–9500
> 1475 Second Avenue at 77th Street—212–472–3030

For Eyes Optical Company (420 Lexington Avenue—212–697–8888) carries an almost similar inventory to the one at most eyeglass chains like Cohen's Fashion Optical, Pearle Vision and Lenscrafters, but undersells its competitors by anywhere from 10 to 30 percent. If you see something you like elsewhere and can't find it at For Eyes, they can probably order it for you and you'll still pay less.

HEALTH INSURANCE

BECAUSE MANY PERFORMERS do not receive health insurance through employment and do not qualify for needs-based insurance, they frequently fall through the cracks. In response to this crisis, the National Endowment for the Arts, in partnership with the Actors' Fund of America, have established the **Artists' Health Insurance Resource Center**. The AHIRC assists the arts community nationwide in accessing information about health insurance options. Go to the Actors' Fund website at www.actorsfund.org, where you'll find information about several government-subsidized programs and consumer organizations that offer quality affordable health-care coverage options. The information available includes: guides to purchasing insurance; artists' groups offering health insurance; a list of free and sliding scale clinics; health care options for the uninsured and underinsured; sources of emergency financial aid for medical/hospital bills; plans for the self-employed; access to group health insurance; and guides to gaining disease-specific assistance. Individuals may also receive health insurance advice and counseling through the Actors' Fund offices (729 Seventh Avenue at 49th Street, 10th floor—212–221–7300—see my discussion of the Actors' Fund in the "Getting Help" chapter) or through the AHIRC toll free helpline—800–798–8447.

Healthstat (330 West 24th Street between Ninth and Tenth Avenues—888–NYC–6116), administered by the Mayor's Office of Health Insurance Access (MOHIA), works to enroll those who are eligible (yearly income may be no more than a prescribed maximum—call for details) in one of several free public health insurance programs. To qualify, you must show documents that verify your financial status, such as pay stubs, bank statements, a copy of your lease and other pertinent information. Healthstat also helps those with low incomes, but who make too much to qualify for the free insurance, to obtain low-cost coverage.

For **assistance with medical bills during times of financial hardship**, refer to the "Getting Help" chapter. There you will find an all-inclusive list of unions, guilds and organizations that provide monetary aid to performing artists in emergency situations.

PART IV

Personal and Professional Resources

Getting Help

GIVEN THE UNPREDICTABILITY of our employment, our lives and our health, we may find we need assistance with financial difficulties as well as housing, legal matters, childcare, health and insurance concerns, chemical dependency, senior and disabled care, and career transition. Fortunately, there are organizations and programs established to provide free, compassionate, confidential assistance to all professionals in the entertainment community.

Actors' Equity Association (165 West 46th Street at Broadway—212–869–8530) assists members with up to $300 for general living expenses such as rent, food, utilities and medical expenses. To be eligible, you must be a member in good standing and have at least three years of Equity earnings.

A few years ago I had hurt my back and was laid up for several weeks. I saw a series of specialists, surgeons and physical therapists and received conflicting diagnoses. I had to have X-rays and a very expensive MRI; my treatment called for three pricey nerve root blocks. With each consultation and treatment, my medical debt soared to unmanageable levels. Ultimately, my back problems were healed so that I could walk and work again, but I was left with crippling debt, even after my insurance paid the portion of the bills they deemed "reasonable and customary." I was scared and did not know where to turn. Then, a friend told me about the program overseen by **The Actors' Fund of America** that was established to help members of the entertainment industry who find themselves in crisis. The benevolence from this organization helped me reduce my

PRICELESS RESOURCE

otherwise bankrupting medical debt; they also referred me to AFTRA, which assisted with my bills as well.

Founded in 1882, The Actors' Fund (729 Seventh Avenue at 49th Street, 10th Floor—212-221-7300) is the only national, nonprofit human service organization that provides for the welfare of all entertainment professionals—designers, writers, sound technicians, musicians, dancers, administrators, directors, film editors, stagehands, as well as actors. Professionals in film, television, radio, theater, dance and music all are eligible for The Actors' Fund services in times of need. To apply for assistance or to utilize the services of the Actors' Fund, you must document earnings made as a performer or in a performing related field. The many confidential programs the Actors' Fund oversees to address the needs of the acting community include social services, vocational counseling, financial assistance, supportive housing and medical care.

The **Actors' Fund social services**, developed and administered by a staff of social workers, include:

→ **Entertainment Industry Assistance Program**—offering counseling on a broad range of issues from career transitions to the challenges of aging in the entertainment industry and family and work matters. This program provides advocacy and referral on housing, legal, childcare, and health services needs; assists financially on an emergency basis for living and health expenses; schedules workshops throughout the year on such topics as budgeting, securing affordable housing, debt management, investments, taxes and estate planning.

→ **Chemical Dependency Program**—helping individuals and families address substance abuse and addiction with the goal of achieving and maintaining sobriety.

→ **Mental Health Services**—offering psychological evaluation, crisis intervention and counseling as well as referrals to clinics, hospitals, and sliding scale or reduced rate psychotherapists who are familiar with the needs of the entertainment industry.

→ **Phyllis Newman Women's Health Initiative**— providing counseling, support services and financial assistance toward health care and insurance costs for women who are coping with significant health problems. (See "Medical" chapter and my discussion of Physician Volunteers for the Arts for information on free mammograms and gynecological exams.)

→ **AIDS Initiative**, with the generous support of **Broadway Cares/Equity Fights AIDS**—providing care management, counseling, support groups, referral, emergency and ongoing financial assistance for medical treatment, housing and other basic needs for persons with HIV/AIDS and their loved ones.

→ **Senior Care Program** helps industry members in their "golden" years by providing information on community resources for medical/dental care, housing, assisted living and skilled care. The Actors' Fund social workers also provide elder-care counseling and support services for families and make home and hospital visits to coordinate health maintenance.

→ **Disabled Care Program**—providing support for those who are living with short- and long-term illness or disability.

The **Actors' Fund Health Services** include:

→ **Artists' Health Insurance Resource Center (AHIRC)** (see the "Medical" chapter).

→ **Physician Volunteers for the Arts** (see the "Medical" chapter).

The **Actors' Fund Employment and Training Services** include:

→ **AIDS Training and Education Project**—assisting AIDS Initiative clients who wish to explore transitioning to work, school and volunteering.

→ **Act II**—addressing the specific career training needs of entertainment professionals over 50.

The **Actors' Fund Supportive Housing programs** include:

→ **Affordable Housing Residences**—oversees The Aurora building (see chapter on "Finding a Home").

→ **Actors Fund Homes**—providing assisted living and skilled nursing care for retired entertainment professionals and their immediate family members in a comfortable environment.

American Guild of Musical Artists (AGMA) Relief Fund (1727 Broadway at 55th Street—212-265-3687) provides monetary assistance to members who are needy, aged, infirm or unable to meet financial obligations. The Relief Fund also assists members in need of counseling, medical or legal referrals.

American Guild of Variety Artists (AGVA) Fund (363 Seventh Avenue at 30th Street, 17th Floor—212-675-1003) offers financial aid to members who are ill, elderly or indigent to pay for rent, utilities and medical bills.

The **Episcopalian Actors' Guild of America, Inc.** (1 East 29th Street between Fifth and Madison Avenues—212-685-2927) offers emergency financial aid to performing arts professionals to help cover rent, utilities, union dues, moving and storage fees and medical expenses. You don't need to be an Episcopalian to apply, but you must be a working member of the theatrical profession (union membership is not necessary) and first go through the application process at your parent union and/or other agencies like The Actors' Fund to be eligible for grants from the Guild. Call the Guild for full eligibility requirements.

Screen Actors Guild Foundation (360 Madison Avenue at East 45th Street—212–944–1030) provides emergency assistance to cover rent/mortgage, utilities and car insurance/car payments for paid-up members who are sick, needy, indigent or aged. The SAG Foundation also assists members with medical expenses if they have no medical coverage.

The **Theatre Authority Fund** at **AFTRA** (260 Madison Avenue between East 38th and 39th Streets, 7th Floor—212–532–0800) assists any paid-up AFTRA member who is in need of financial help. Theatre Authority Fund grants are for living expenses only (rent, utilities, food, travel, medical, etc.). Members applying for assistance must show just cause why they are in need of financial help. Maximum assistance per year is $1,000, but there is no limit on how many times a member may apply.

The **Unemployment and Workers' Compensation Office** at **Actors' Equity Association** (165 West 46th Street—212–869–8530, ext. 327) is a little-known division of AEA, which can be a real lifesaver for members who have trouble collecting unemployment or been hurt while working. The office counsels and advises members on initial unemployment insurance filings and trouble-shoots on pending claims.

Twice this office has intervened on my behalf when the New York State Department of Labor delayed my claim; each time, their call resulted in the immediate disbursal of my benefits. The Unemployment and Workers' Compensation Office has a comprehensive understanding of the differing unemployment laws in all fifty states (since we work all over the country) and can answer questions regarding Combined Wage Claims, Interstate Claims, Interstate Combined Wage Claims, eligibility and requirements.

In connection with workers' compensation claims, the office advises and assists members in obtaining information on coverage. They trouble-shoot if an injured member's lost time benefits are held up, and keep an updated file on compensation coverage for individual theaters and shows. Also, in tandem with the Equity League Health Trust Fund, the office provides a Supplemental Workers' Compensation Plan for performers who are injured on the job and who lose time and salary as a result. To qualify for this benefit, you must be eligible and apply for workers' compensation. If you qualify for workers' compensation, the Fund gives additional compensation. Call for more information.

ACTING AND PERFORMANCE RELATED UNIONS, GUILDS AND ORGANIZATIONS

ACTING UNIONS

Actors' Equity Association
165 West 46th Street
New York, NY 10036
212–869–8530

American Federation of Television and Radio Actors
260 Madison Avenue, 7th Floor
New York, NY 10016
212–532–0800

American Guild of Musical Artists
1430 Broadway
New York, NY 10019
212–265–3687

American Guild of Variety Artists
363 Seventh Avenue, 17th Floor
New York, NY 10001
212–675–1003

Screen Actors Guild
1515 Broadway, 44th Floor
New York, NY 10036
212–944–1030

PERFORMANCE RELATED UNIONS, GUILDS AND ORGANIZATIONS

The Actors' Fund of America
729 Seventh Avenue, 10th Floor
New York, NY 10019
212–221–7300

American Federation of Musicians
1501 Broadway
New York, NY 10036
212–869–1330

Associated Actors and Artistes of America
165 West 46th Street, Room 500
New York, NY 10036
212–869–0358

Association of Theatrical Press Agents and Managers
165 West 46th Street, Suite 700
New York, NY 10036
212–719–3666

Directors Guild of America
110 West 57th Street
New York, NY 10019
212–581–0370

Dramatists Guild of America
1501 Broadway, Suite 701
New York, NY 10036
212–398–9366

Hebrew Actors Union
31 East 7th Street
New York, NY 10003
212–674–1923

Hispanic Organization of Latin Actors (HOLA)
107 Suffolk Street, Suite 302
New York, NY 10002
212–253–1015

International Alliance of Theatrical Stage Employees (IATSE)
1430 Broadway, 20th Floor
New York, NY 10018
212–730–1770

International Photographers of Motion Pictures Industries
80 Eighth Avenue, 14th Floor
New York, NY 10011
212–647–7300

League of Independent Stuntplayers
P.O. Box 196
Madison Square Station
New York, NY 10159

League of Professional Theatre Women
226 West 47th Street
New York, NY 10036
212–744–6003

National Association of Broadcast Employees and Technicians (NABET)
80 West End Avenue, 5th Floor
New York, NY 10023
212–757–7191

Police Actors Association
P.O. Box 20952
New York, NY 10009
212–995–9632

Society of Stage Directors and Choreographers (SSDC)
1501 Broadway, #1701
New York, NY 10036
212–391–1070

Writers Guild of America (WGA)
555 West 57th Street, Suite 1230
New York, NY 10019
212–767–7800

United Scenic Artists
29 West 38th Street, 15th Floor
New York, NY 10018
212–581–0300

Investing Information

Gary Ginsberg of Royal Alliance Associates, Inc. NASD, SIPC has an office at the Actors Federal Credit Union (165 West 46th Street, 4th Floor—212–869–8926, ext. 315), and helps actors understand the importance of beginning an investment program and the intricacies involved. As Gary says, "We applaud and respect actors for their capacity to be creative. They are trained to nurture right-brained thinking—to be free of the bounds of conventional thought. Yet, one of the most undeniable practical concerns of modern life is the left-brained necessity of 'personal finance,' and actors generally are not taught how to manage money. The ultimate irony of leading a creative life is that actors MUST address the financial aspect of their lives. They run their own business and typically will not have a 401 (k), corporate savings plan, substantive pension, or even health or life insurance, which is often provided by an employer. If an actor does not take care of his or her own finances, no one is going to do it for them."

Through his services, Gary helps performing artists evaluate their personal financial situation, and then educates them on what investment options correlate directly to their financial goals and risk tolerance. Gary believes that the only way to achieve these goals is by understanding that investing for the future is not a one-time event, but rather a lifelong process, which should be reviewed on an ongoing basis when goals, risks, taxes, financial circumstances, or investment allocations change.

For a lot of actors, taking the first step is the hardest. Gary constantly hears, "I can't afford it right now. I don't have enough at the end of the month to invest." Gary replies, "Change your attitude! If you don't start at the level you are at today, you will never start." His philosophy is, instead of looking at monthly investments as a luxury, **pay yourself first.** The first check you write each month should be to yourself; when you get into this habit you will become an investor for life. He adds, "Act once a month as if you're left-brained and financial freedom is a goal you can reach!" Gary holds his office at AFCU on Tuesdays and Thursdays. You must call for an appointment.

LAWYERS

A TIME MAY COME when you will need a lawyer, but won't be able to afford exorbitant legal fees. A few alternatives offer legal assistance either at no cost or at greatly reduced rates:

> Established for the exclusive use of members of participating AFL-CIO unions and their families, **Union Plus Legal Services** provides free or low-cost legal assistance to members of Equity. Call or go by the Equity offices (165 West 46th Street, 15th Floor—212–869–8530) and ask for a list of participating Union Plus lawyers in the New York Metropolitan area.

> Benefits through Union Plus include:

> → **Free 30-minute consultation** by phone or at the attorney's office on any personal legal matter you choose. There is no limit on the number of consultations, provided each is about a separate matter.

> → **Free review of important documents** such as leases, insurance policies, etc., followed by an oral explanation of the terms of these documents. Note: Written evaluations are **not** part of this service, nor are documents written by you or for use in a business capacity.

> → **Free follow-up services** by phone or letter to help you resolve a problem or dispute you may have.

> → **Confidentiality:** only your attorney knows you are using the program.

→ **30 percent discount** on more complex legal matters. In a contingent fee case (where the lawyer's fee comes out of any recovery or award you obtain), or on a business matter, a smaller discount may apply. Otherwise, flat fees usually apply to commonly needed services.

→ **Written agreement on all fees** to prevent any financial surprises.

All lawyers participating in the Union Plus program are selected for their involvement in the labor movement and their interest in serving union members. They have agreed to provide all program benefits (both free and discounted), to keep each member fully informed of the status of his or her case, and to abide by the administrative responsibilities required of them.

To insure your satisfaction with the program and the quality of its participating attorneys, Union Plus asks you to evaluate the services of your lawyer. Should you disagree with your lawyer regarding fees or other matters, Union Plus tries to resolve the dispute through informal mediation, or, if necessary, arbitration. Note: Because this is a union program, matters involving any union-related organization or official are not included. Furthermore, a Union Plus attorney may refuse to take any case as he or she so chooses.

Each year, **Volunteer Lawyers for the Arts (VLA)** (1 East 53rd Street, 6th Floor—212-319-2787) provides pro bono and low-cost legal services to over 5,000 members of the creative community in the greater New York Metropolitan area. Since 1969, the group has assisted artists with mediation services, educational programs and publications, advocacy, legal advice, professional business counseling, and representation. Included in VLA's many services are:

→ **Art Law Line**, a free legal hotline

→ **Pro bono placements** for low-income artists and non-profit arts organizations with volunteer attorneys from the area's finest law firms

→ **Low-cost membership** ($25 for full-time students, $75 for individuals and $200 for nonprofit arts organizations) entitling members to half-hour appointments with highly qualified volunteer attorneys to address arts-related legal issues at the group's bi-monthly clinics. Membership also covers discounts on seminars, workshops, publications and MediateArt Services; invitations to all Member Events; VLA Newsletter; access to the Speaker's Bureau and VLA's Board Bank; and discounts on pro bono consultations for those who meet VLA's Financial Eligibility Guidelines.

→ **Workshops** on specific legal topics related to the arts, such as:

• Nonprofit Incorporation and Tax Exempt Status

• Artists Rights and New Technology

• Starting and Operating a For-Profit Business

• Starting and Operating an Independent Record Label

• Contract Basics For Arts and Entertainment Professionals

• Copyright Basics

• Mediation Training

→ **Assistance with Nonprofit Incorporation**

Telephone for more information on VLA's services and membership or for a schedule of workshops.

If you have questions or need help with problems of discrimination in the workplace or housing due to sexual orientation or HIV/AIDS, contact the **Lambda Legal Help Line** (212–809–8585) for free guidance on rights and recourse. Lambda's Help Line is open on weekdays from 9 A.M. to 5:30 P.M.

The **Metropolitan Council on Housing Help Line** (212–979–0611) is set up to answer any questions you may have regarding apartments, leases, landlords, renter's rights, etc. This free service, staffed by legal professionals, can be accessed on Mondays, Wednesdays and Fridays from 1:30 P.M. to 5 P.M.

TAX PREPARATION

FOR OVER 25 YEARS, **VITA (Volunteer Income Tax Assistance)** has been offering free support to Actors Equity, SAG and AFTRA members in the preparation of their individual federal and state income tax returns. Located in the Actors Equity building (165 West 46th Street, 14th Floor—212-921-2548), VITA is an Internal Revenue Service program supported by the SAG and Equity Foundations and the New York local of AFTRA. VITA volunteer tax-preparers are all fellow union members whom the IRS trains to assist in the preparation of basic tax returns.

During tax season (the first Monday in February through the last Friday in April), VITA's office is open Mondays, Wednesdays, Thursdays and Fridays from 11 A.M. to 5 P.M. It is best to make an appointment; go to the VITA office on Opening Day (the first Monday in February) with a paid-up union card. Otherwise, If you don't have an appointment, you can come in as a "walk-in," but you are attended to on a first-come/first-served basis. (Of the more than 1700 people who have their taxes prepared by VITA each season, only about 330 make appointments.) Whether or not you make an appointment, you must go to the VITA office in person, show your Equity, SAG or AFTRA card and pick up a packet of worksheets prior to having your taxes done.

VITA does offer year-round assistance to union members regarding income tax questions (provisions in contracts, etc.), those having trouble understanding IRS correspondence or who have been audited. Its off-season hours are July through January on Wednesdays only from 11 A.M. to 4 P.M.

VITA reminds all those who utilize its services that "since neither the volunteers nor their sponsoring unions receive remuneration for the service, they are not legally liable for the return in any way. Responsibility for the accuracy and completeness of the return rests solely with the person(s) filing the return. Should the return be audited by the I.R.S., there is no guarantee that the VITA volunteer who assisted in its preparation will be available for help."

If you are unwilling either to wait on the hours-long line at VITA on the first Monday in February or to risk not getting a first-come/first served appointment, **Marc Bernstein** (250 West 57th Street, Suite 2403—212-582-3133) is a great alternative. Marc has been in the business of actors' taxes for 22 years, during tax season writes a weekly column on the subject for *Backstage*, and prepares the returns of hundreds of actors each year. Unlike VITA, Marc's services are not gratis, but he charges fair prices and works miracles for all who utilize his services. A friend of mine says, "He's not dirt cheap, but I've used him for 10 years and whether I've made no money or a lot of money (relatively speaking), he always saves me money." I've been a client of Marc's since 1984 and I've been so pleased with the work he's done for me that, if I could, I'd have the man canonized. Call early in the year for an appointment as he books up quickly. Fees are based on the complexity of the return.

For a good start to help yourself in preparing a tax return, check out CPA Peter Jason Riley's *The New Tax Guide for Artists of Every Persuasion* (Limelight Editions). This invaluable short reference book gives an overview of various types of income and expenses, and focuses on the deductions allowed by the IRS and the unique tax situations encountered by artists, including actors, singers, dancers, directors, visual artists, writers and musicians. Riley also details how performing artists can maximize deductions, reduce taxes, prepare for an audit, choose a tax advisor, set up a business entity and plan for retirement. Most helpful is the inclusion of spreadsheets for notating monthly and out-of-town expenses, earned income and claimed exemptions. As Riley says, the goal of his book is to help "make the tax preparation process less onerous and most importantly SAVE TAX DOLLARS!"

Author's Note: This book is tax-deductible!

TAX WRITE-OFFS

I'M NO LONGER SURPRISED by the number of actors, especially those fresh out of acting school, who know little or nothing about their income taxes, deductions, or even filing a claim. Consequently, I've been saying for years that every actor-training program in the nation should offer a "Business of 'Show Business'" course to discuss tax matters. We actors need to have a clear understanding of the income tax deductions we are entitled to *and how to take them*, because we can significantly reduce our tax burden and perhaps save ourselves hundreds, even thousands, of dollars annually.

An income tax deduction is the amount the government allows us to subtract from our overall annual tax bill. These deductions are calculated from the dollars we spend looking for work and marketing ourselves, but may include our out-of-town expenses, traditional IRA contributions, union dues, and charitable donations among many others.

A comprehensive list follows of the deductions actors are usually eligible to take. Be diligent and disciplined in keeping records, saving receipts, and logging daily business expenses in a journal, and you can save more money. But also, find a tax person who specializes in actors' taxes, because that person will have an understanding of the many and varied deductions we are allowed and knows how to navigate the individual tax rules and regulations of all 50 states (remember we work all over the country); it is almost always more financially advantageous to hire a tax-preparer than to do it yourself or have them done at a tax assembly-line outfit like H&R Block. (See chapter on "Tax-Preparation.")

USUAL WRITE-OFFS:

→ **Accompanist and Audition Expenses**

→ **Advertising and Publicity:** head shots, resumes, guides like *The Players' Guide* or *Academy Players Directory,* promotional theater tickets for agents, producers and directors for plays that you are in

→ **Agents' Commissions and Manager's Fees**

→ **Alimony**

→ **Answering Service**

→ **Audio/Video Equipment**

→ **Blank Video/Audio Tapes to Record Programs for Research**

→ **Books (Research)**—Including this book!

→ **Cable, Studio and Equipment Rental**

→ **Cable TV**

→ **CD's, Videos and Audio Tapes (Research):** purchase and rental

→ **Charitable Contributions:** monetary contributions, donations of items other than cash or checks (i.e., clothing, books, furniture, etc.—for these donations, you must get a receipt from the charitable organization if the value of the donation exceeds $500 and provide a photocopy of receipt for the IRS)

→ **Child and Dependent Care:** the amount incurred by you and your spouse for such care so that you can work or look for work. The I.R.S. requires the social security number or employer ID number for each individual or childcare facility employed

→ **Coaching, Classes and Lessons**

→ **Computer Services:** cost of computer services to create documents such as resumes, mailing labels, marketing materials, etc.

→ **Dancewear and Costumes/Wardrobe:** for clothing items used solely for theatrical purposes (i.e. a clown costume, a Renaissance costume), and that cannot be considered as "street clothing." Note: You need to prove this in case of an audit.

→ **Equipment Repairs and Maintenance:** cost of repairs and maintenance of equipment like televisions, VCRs, computers, tape recorders, CD players, stereos and DVD players

→ **Gifts for People in the Business:** a maximum of $25 per person per year

→ **Medical Expenses:** only Unreimbursed Medical Expenses and Health Insurance Premiums. For this deduction, you must show that you spent a certain percentage of your annual income on this category.

→ **Monthly Internet Connection** (Research and Promotion)

→ **Mortgage Interest:** the amount of interest you paid on your mortgage. For co-ops, this includes the amount of maintenance deemed deductible as interest by the co-op board. Co-op owners can enter the number of shares they own.

→ **Musical Arrangements**

→ **Office Supplies, Stationery and Postage**

→ **Pager or Beeper Service**

→ **Piano Tuning**

→ **Professional, Legal or Copyright fees**

→ **Professional Makeup, Wigs and Hair Care:** show that these items are used solely for performing purposes

→ **Real Estate Tax:** if you own a home, condominium or co-op, the amount of real estate tax you pay. For co-op owners, this includes the amount of maintenance the co-op board deems deductible as real estate tax

→ **Rehearsal Studio Rental**

→ **Restaurant Entertaining**—"wining and dining" of performing arts professionals such as directors, agents, casting people, etc.

→ **Scripts, Scores and Plays**

→ **Student Loan Interest**

→ **Tax Preparation**

→ **Telephone:** business long distance, pay phone calls, percentage of business-related cell phone calls, percentage of home phone

→ **Theatrical Props:** you must show that this purchase or rental was solely for theatrical use

→ **Tickets for Viewing Theater and Film (Research)**

→ **Tips and Gratuities:** to dressers, hair and makeup people, theater doormen, etc.

→ **Trade Publications:** *Backstage, American Theatre, Daily* and *Weekly Variety, The Ross Reports,* etc.

→ **Traditional IRA Contribution:** Up to $3,000 contribution annually is tax-free provided your earnings did not exceed a federally prescribed amount. Note: The prescribed maximums change yearly, so consult your tax person before contributing.

→ **Transportation for Seeking Employment**: includes taxis, subways, buses, etc.

→ **Travel Expenses for Out-of-Town Auditions:** transportation, lodging, auto rental and gas, food, laundry and dry cleaning, local transportation, local telephone and long-distance business calls. If you use your own car, list the total mileage accrued during the business part of your trip.

→ **Travel Expenses Incurred While Working Out-of-Town:** transportation, lodging, auto rental and gas, food, laundry and dry cleaning, local transportation, local telephone and long-distance business calls. If you use your own car, list the total mileage accrued during your business trip.

→ **Union Dues:** basic dues, initiation fees and 2 percent assessment to Actors' Equity Association

→ **Video Tape Rentals**

COMPUTER TRAINING

AS ACTORS, WE DON'T NEED TO KNOW how to operate a computer, right? Just a couple of years ago, I agreed with that sentiment, was computer illiterate and proud of it. Claiming that my brain was just too full to make room for the computer stuff I'd have to retain, I resisted getting a computer. What a difference two years makes. Today, I would not know how to survive without it. My entire life is on my computer: everything from my personal finances to resumes, teaching materials to address books, stationery, press, personal and business correspondence to pictures, even this book, all live on my hard drive.

I think that owning a computer (and knowing how to use it) is almost as important as owning a phone. Not only does it allow actors to communicate with the world via e-mail, but it can also be our most valuable marketing tool. With a computer, we can create our acting resume, stationery, press releases, mass mailings and mail merges, agent queries, business cards and address books. We can download plays via the internet, research playwrights, actors, directors, theaters, and even receive audition sides on it.

Moreover, computer skills are in demand and companies throw lots of money at those who can do data entry or web design, use Excel spreadsheets or PowerPoint presentations and create Word documents. Between acting jobs, sitting at a computer terminal does a lot less wear-and-tear on the soul and body (and often pays more) than waiting tables. Fortunately, there are two resources that train performing artists, at no charge, how to operate these terrifying but wonderful machines:

The **Actors' Work Program** (729 Seventh Avenue between 48th and 49th Streets, 11th Floor—212–354–5480) schedules several no-cost computer skills courses. To enroll, you need to be a member of one of the entertainment industry unions in good standing and to have attended a Monday afternoon orientation meeting. Program courses include:

- → **Basic Computer Fundamentals:** gives AWP members with little or no computer experience fundamental knowledge, such as computer terminology, creating and saving a file and printing a document.

- → **Keyboard Skills Class:** improves members' keyboard skills and speed. The class meets for nine hours a week for three weeks.

- → **Microsoft Word:** a five-week, three sessions per week intensive class, which develops members' skills using word software and general office work. Prerequisite: typing speed of 50 words per minute and a basic computer skills test.

- → **Microsoft Excel and PowerPoint:** a three-week, three sessions per week class, in which members learn how to create and manipulate spreadsheets, and develop a PowerPoint presentation. Prerequisite: typing speed of 50 words per minute and a basic computer skills test.

- → **Advanced Microsoft Word and Excel for Pitchbook Work:** a three-week, three sessions per week class, which teaches Word applications operators need to create documents bankers and stockbrokers use to sell products or services.

- → **Advanced PowerPoint:** a two-week, three sessions per week class, which teaches advanced techniques for PowerPoint presentations.

Call the Actors' Work Program and speak to a career counselor about enrolling in these free classes.

The **Consortium for Worker Education** (275 Seventh Avenue, 16th Floor—212-647-1900, ext. 332) offers free access to computers to practice Microsoft Word, Excel, PowerPoint, Access, typing skills and computer-based training programs. A computer lab facilitator is present at all times to answer any questions you may have. No prior reservations are necessary and, although the lab is on a first-come/first-served basis, there is generally no problem getting a computer. The Consortium conducts half-hour mini-computer workshops on a variety of subjects, everything from how to set margins to how to buy a computer. To utilize this facility, you must be a member of one of the entertainment industry unions, the Actors' Fund or the Actors' Work Program (see chapter on "Meaningful Interim Work and Career Transition").

MEANINGFUL INTERIM WORK AND CAREER TRANSITION

MEETING WITH A FRIEND RECENTLY whom I had not seen in several months, it wasn't long into our reunion when she asked me the inevitable actor-question, "What are you working on now?" My reply: "Well (ahem), I'm between jobs." Without missing a beat, she said, "No, you are between successes."

I liked the implication of that statement. So much of an actor's career is about looking for work, being unemployed, and trying to keep sane during those periods when we are "at large." Adopting the idea of going from success to success acts as a positive buffer to the inevitable downtime we have in our profession.

With nothing else to do that is at all meaningful, except look for the next acting job, that downtime can be brutal. Our egos take a battering; we question our talent, our place and ourselves in the business. And yet, our rent and bills must be paid and we must eat. So, we engage in survival work we hate, which exhausts us emotionally and physically and bashes our egos that much more. And then, of course, we get that acting job and are back on top of the world . . . this is an actor's never-ending cycle.

Well, the cycle need not be so dire; there are outlets for us that provide a community around the process of supporting ourselves when we are "between successes." These outlet organizations firmly believe that theater artists can develop parallel talents so that our survival work can excite us as much and be as creative and meaningful as our chosen craft. At the same time, they help the performing artist who has decided to leave the acting profession make a dignified transition among a group of supportive and creative people. If you have ever wondered, "Who am I when I'm not working? How will I manage my time when I'm not working?

Who will I be in the future?" these organizations can definitely help you:

The **Actors Work Program** (729 Seventh Avenue between 48th and 49th Street, 11th Floor—212–354–5480) is one of the best actor support services organizations in the country. The Actors' Work Program, a program under The Actors' Fund of America, has a free, full-service career counseling, education and training center for all members of the entertainment industry unions. Members are offered an opportunity to develop the skills needed to secure meaningful remunerative work while "between successes," or to explore changing career paths.

The Program operates from the idea that all actors possess many talents and skills that are invaluable to the business world and other professions, and helps acting professionals recognize these skills, obtain new ones and prepare for satisfying and financially rewarding employment. Its many no-cost services include:

→ **Individual Career Counseling:** to develop the AWP member's individual career plans

→ **Resume and Interview Workshop:** personalized help with resume preparation, interview techniques and job search strategies

→ **Career Search Spotlight and Other Seminars:** introduces an array of sideline career options including computers, teaching and entrepreneurial ventures; sponsors "career nights," which present a variety of additional fields of interest; offers seminars on returning to school, time management, careers in training, substitute teaching, small business practices, interviewing skills, salaries and other relevant topics

→ **Willard Swire Computer Lab Tutorials:** where members can practice their computer/typing skills and gain access to the Internet for job search and career exploration

→ **Classes:** includes computer (keyboard, Word, Excel and PowerPoint—see chapter on "Computer Training"), proofreading, English as a Second Language, teacher preparation, Arts-In-Education, and community support worker

→ **Tuition Grants:** helps eligible members access tuition assistance for training programs

→ **"Drop-In" Job Search Seminars:** Wednesday afternoon seminars help members who are between acting jobs explore and consider sideline work by sharing listings of current job openings

→ **Job Bulletin Board:** an ever-changing list of currently available job offerings—most for people with skills in computers, proofreading, English as a Second Language, etc.

You must be a member of an entertainment industry union and must attend one of their weekly orientation meetings to take advantage of the Actors' Work Program's many services. Orientations take place every Monday from 12:15 P.M. to 2 P.M. and give an overview of AWP's programs. At this time, any basic questions you may have about the Program will be answered and you will be scheduled for an individual appointment with Program counselor. To get started, call their number or drop in on one of the Monday orientations.

In 1985, **Career Transition for Dancers (CTFD)** (The Caroline and Theodore Newhouse Center for Dancers, 200 West 57th Street, Suite 808—212–581–7043) was founded to "empower current and former professional dancers with the knowledge and skills necessary to clearly define their career possibilities after dance, and to provide resources necessary to help make these possibilities a reality." CTFD gives dancers tools to help them decide what they want to do after their dance careers have ended and assists them in making a meaningful transition. CTFD's free services and programs include:

→ **Career Counseling:** a variety of one-to-one and career counseling programs for eligible dancers to use at every stage of their transition process

→ **Scholarships:** grants to retiring dancers so that they may initiate an academic or retraining process in the pursuit of undergraduate, graduate and professional degrees as well as skill and vocational certificates

→ **"Career Conversations":** a series of seminars and workshops on career planning topics and the transition process

→ **"Career Line":** a nationwide toll-free counseling and referral hotline for dancers outside the New York and Los Angeles metropolitan areas

→ **Resources:** an ever-changing and expanding array of reference guides, periodicals and other materials, both on-line and off, for dancers to utilize in their transition process

Career Transition for Dancers' services and programs are available to current and former dancers from all disciplines who can demonstrate they earned their livelihood from performing as dancers. Note: Income earned as a choreographer or dance instructor is not applicable. Call for full eligibility requirements and further information on membership.

RESEARCH ASSISTANCE

FOLLOWING ITS THREE-YEAR RENOVATION, the **Lincoln Center Library for the Performing Arts** (Lincoln Center—111 Amsterdam Avenue at 66th Street—212–870–1630) finally reopened in 2002 and performers throughout the city are rejoicing. With outstanding research and circulating collections covering all the performing arts from music to dance, theater and film, this place is for us. The library's 9 million holdings include books, recordings, videos, sheet music, correspondence, programs, set and costume renderings, scale models, and photographs. Want to read John Gielgud's autobiography? It's here. Want a copy of Tony Kushner's *Angels In America*? It's here. Want to hear a recording of Rex Harrison playing Benedick? It's here. Want to know what Frank Rich said about *Sweeney Todd*? It's here. Want to view John Barton's "Playing Shakespeare" television series? You can do it here.

The Theatre on Film and Tape division is the best part of the library for me. It holds taped or acquired recordings of thousands of live performances from Broadway, off-Broadway and regional theaters. These have been archived and are available to view. Space is limited, so you must call in advance to reserve the play you'd like to see; expect to wait about two weeks for an opening. Depending on monitor availability, the Theatre on Film and Tape division often allows walk-ins.

Flanked by huge windows that create a feeling of openness and light, the library's renovated reading rooms have several listening units at which users may review CDs and cassette tapes, 200 public-access computers, a sea of desks with electric outlets to plug in laptops, and hundreds of ergonomically designed Aeron chairs which, when compared with the utilitarian upright wooden seats of our youth, make research a luxury. What's more, the library has a state-of-the-art technology training center that offers classes and resources on research in the performing arts and an updated material retrieval system that allows for simultaneous access to its four research collections.

The Performing Arts Library hosts frequent and free exhibits on the life and work of distinguished actors, choreographers, directors, composers, designers, playwrights, singers, dancers and musicians. This is the best performing arts reference resource in the city, perhaps the world, so USE IT! Its four collections are:

Dance—212–870–1657

Music—212–870–1650

Rodgers & Hammerstein Archives of Recorded Sound—
    212–870–1663

Theatre on Film and Tape—212–870–1642

A great resource for actors, and one of my favorite museums is The **Museum of Television and Radio** (25 West 52nd Street between Fifth and Sixth Avenues—212–621–6800). The museum's collection contains more than 95,000 TV and radio programs made over the past 70 years. A computerized catalogue system with an enormous database allows the public to review the museum's collection of programs ranging from news to commercials to comedies to dramas and variety shows. I have found it especially helpful as a research tool when I am preparing an audition or role: using its vast database I have viewed everything from TV documentaries about Nazi Germany to portions of "Your Show of Shows" and BBC productions of Shakespeare plays. Throughout the year the museum hosts several film series that focus on topics of social, historical, popular or artistic interest. Ask for a schedule at the front counter. (For more information, see chapter on "Museums.") Note: You are limited to four hours of viewing/listening time per day.

Rehearsal Spaces

Until the real estate boom of the mid 1980s, there were several rehearsal studios around town that offered decent accommodations where cash-conscious actors could vocalize, rehearse scenes and monologues and work on auditions for as little as five or six dollars an hour. Today, there are few spaces, and most are miserably inadequate or prohibitively expensive. A couple of organizations remain sensitive to performers' needs and budgets:

BEST BARGAIN

New York Spaces has 35 clean, bright and spacious studios in three locations throughout the city, many ranging in price from $11 to $25 per hour. All of the rooms have windows and some are equipped with pianos and with phone lines for internet connections. You must call New York Spaces's central booking office at 212–799–5433 to reserve a room. Locations and hours are:

Eighth Avenue Studios
939 Eighth Avenue (between 55th and 56th Streets)
Suite 307
212–397–0039
Monday—Friday, 9 A.M. to 11 P.M.
Saturday and Sunday, 10 A.M. to 9 P.M.

Ripley Grier Studios
520 Eighth Avenue (between 36th and 37th Streets)
Suite 16
212–643–9985
Monday—Friday, 9 A.M. to 11 P.M.
Saturday and Sunday, 10 A.M. to 11 P.M.

West 72nd Street Studios
131 West 72nd Street
212–799–5433
Monday—Friday, 9 A.M. to 11 P.M.
Saturday and Sunday, 10 A.M. to 9 P.M.

Located in a landmark building in Chelsea, **Cap21 Studios** (18 West 18th Street, between Fifth and Sixth Avenues— 212–807–0202) has many clean, well-lit and comfortable rooms at rates that won't break the bank. Cap21's smallest rooms start at $15 per hour; they do offer discounts to non-profit organizations and companies. All rooms have pianos, the building is totally handicap accessible, and there are showers and changing rooms. To make reservations, contact the Facilities Manager at 212–807–0202. Hours of operation: Monday—Friday, 9 A.M. to 10 P.M.; Saturday and Sunday, 10 A.M. to 6 P.M.

RESTROOMS

IT WAS NEVER MY INTENTION to include a chapter about bathrooms in New York, but as I shared my plans for this book with friends and colleagues, the overwhelming response was, "Tell us where there are toilets that are available to the public!"

We actors traverse every nook and cranny of this city in the pursuit of work, often in neighborhoods we know nothing about, and occasionally need to use the facilities. You soon find that New York is bereft of public toilets and you have to be creative in a bathroom search. Some simple planning and logical sleuthing, however, will keep bladders empty, hair combed neatly and makeup perfectly applied.

The golden rule for gaining access to restrooms in restaurants, hotels and stores is never to ask if you may use the facilities. Only tourists ask, and the answer will always be "no." Pretend like you are a patron/guest and go for it. (Warning: no matter how badly you need to go, don't do as a friend of mine did and pee against a tree in Central Park. No sooner was his fly zipped than he was collared by two policemen and taken to jail. He spent 40 harrowing hours becoming acquainted with the city's netherworld from which he was not allowed to use a phone for hours, so that neither his wife nor the theater company with which he was rehearsing a play—he was on his lunch break—knew where he was; he was fed bologna sandwiches for breakfast, lunch and dinner and never slept more than 20 minutes at a time.)

For me, the city's large **bookstores** have the best restrooms. In almost every part of Manhattan there is either a **Barnes & Noble** or **Borders Books** and the facilities in each are usually clean and not far from the front door. Best yet, you don't need a

key and no one knows if you are there solely to use the water-
works or to buy books:

Barnes & Noble—
4 Astor Place at Broadway
396 Avenue of the Americas at 8th Street
33 East 17th Street at Union Square
105 Fifth Avenue at 18th Street
675 Sixth Avenue at 21st Street
901 Sixth Avenue at 32nd Street
385 Fifth Avenue at 36th Street
750 Third Avenue at East 47th Street
600 Fifth Avenue at 48th Street
160 East 54th Street at Third Avenue
1972 Broadway at 66th Street
2289 Broadway at 82nd Street
1280 Lexington Avenue at 86th Street
240 East 86th Street between Second and Third Avenues

Borders Books—
461 Park Avenue at 57th Street
550 Second Avenue at 30th Street

Most, if not all of the **fast food restaurants** like **McDonald's,
Burger King, Wendy's, Au Bon Pain, Ranch One**, **Boston
Market** and **Popeye's** have public facilities. Designated for "Customers Only" they often need a key to be opened. To gain entrance, act like a customer and pretend that you have just finished
your happy meal. If it is obvious that you have not dined there and
your need to go has reached emergency status, buy the cheapest
thing on the menu and demand the damned key!

The first thing to do if you need to make a pit stop is look for a
hotel. Almost all of Manhattan's neighborhoods have at least one
medium to large hotel with public facilities located on or near the
ground floor. None have a policing system to keep nonguests from

using the facilities, so you won't be hassled, and in most the restrooms are impeccably clean.

Other **large retailers** like **Kmart**, **Bed, Bath & Beyond**, and **Old Navy** also have public restrooms . . . .

Kmart:
>One Pennsylvania Plaza on 34th Street at Seventh Avenue
>770 Broadway at Astor Place

Bed, Bath & Beyond:
>620 Avenue of the Americas at 19th Street
>61st Street and First Avenue

Old Navy:
>610 Avenue of the Americas at 18th Street
>300 West 125th Street
>150 West 34th Street between Sixth and Seventh Avenues
>503 Broadway between Spring and Broome Streets

Manhattan's three **main transportation hubs** (Grand Central Terminal, Penn Station, and Port Authority Bus Terminal) all have toilets for the general public. The facilities at **Penn Station** (Seventh to Eighth Avenues between 30th and 32nd Streets) and **Grand Central** (42nd Street and Park Avenue) are large, clean, safe and centrally located. All I can say about the bathrooms at the **Port Authority** (Eighth to Ninth Avenues at 41st Street) is "yikes!" But, if you gotta go, you gotta go.

In each of the **major department stores,** there are at least a couple of men's and women's restrooms located on different floors. The larger the store, the more restrooms it has. These stores are scattered around three New York neighborhoods so that you are covered while you are in any of these areas:

>**Barney's**—Madison Avenue at 61st Street
>**Henri Bendel**—Fifth Avenue at 56th Street

Bergdorf Goodman—Fifth Avenue at 58th Street
Bloomingdale's—Lexington Avenue at 59th Street
Lord & Taylor—Fifth Avenue between 38th and 39th Streets
Macy's—34th Street between Sixth and Seventh Avenues
Saks Fifth Avenue—Fifth Avenue between 49th and 50th
  Streets
Takashimaya—Fifth Avenue between 49th and 50th Streets

In **Midtown**, where we do most of our auditioning, there are lots of bathroom options. The facilities in the **Actors' Equity Second Floor Members' Lounge** (165 West 46th Street) are the most convenient. If you wish to avoid a sea of people you know who will all want to tell you what they are up to and ask you the inevitable, "So, what are you doing?" stay away. Other bathrooms in the neighborhood are in the **Virgin Mega Store** on Broadway between 46th and 47th Streets in Times Square and several of the lower floors of the **Marriott Marquis Hotel** (across from the Virgin Mega Store). The beautiful and very trendy bathrooms at the **Paramount Hotel** (235 West 46th Street) are convenient at about 40 yards from the hotel's front door and are a narcissist's wet dream—all mirrors and reflecting surfaces. **ESPN Zone** (4 Times Square, 42nd Street and Broadway—212–921–3776) is the only place where, while sitting on the john, you may watch your favorite sports game. ESPN TV is screened on monitors right there in each stall.

Four of the city **parks** actually have public facilities. None will ever win awards for cleanliness, but they are convenient, safe and handy in times of need. You will find public park facilities in:

Washington Square Park—Thompson Street at Washington
  Square
Tompkins Park—Avenue A at 9th Street
Bryant Park—Sixth Avenue between 41st and 42nd Streets
Central Park—Near the Delacorte Theatre at the West 81st
  Street entrance

Public and government buildings such as **libraries, court-houses, unemployment offices** and the like all have restrooms that are available to the public.

Most New Yorkers' favorite pastime is to grumble over the obscene number of **Starbucks** there are in this city. But complain as we may, Starbucks offers one great service to all New Yorkers: public restrooms. Since Starbucks is everywhere, we need never worry about finding a place to go. The next time you need to use a facility and don't know where one is, stop anyone on the street and ask for the nearest Starbucks. Ten to one there is one within spitting distance. The restrooms, of course, are for "Patrons Only" and may require a key. Have the attitude that you will be dropping a couple of gold bricks for a cup of joe just as soon as you "wash your hands" and you won't be hassled.

PART V

Shopping

PROVISIONS

ALTHOUGH TINY IN SIZE, **Baldwin Fish Market** (1584 First Avenue between 82nd and 83rd Streets—212–737–4100) offers big savings on a variety of fresh seafood and fish. Some of the catch you can reel in at low prices at this Upper East Side emporium includes mussels for $2.50 per pound, cod for $5.99 per pound, squid for $4.99 per pound, Cherrystone or Little Neck clams for $7 per pound, and salmon steaks or Canadian salmon fillets for $7.99 per pound. If you have a yen for sushi, you can sate it at Baldwin's raw bar located at the rear of the store. Baldwin Fish Market offers free delivery to area residents.

Bell Bates Natural Food Market (97 Reade Street—212–267–4300), which has been serving Tribeca since 1885, carries a hefty variety of provisions and products at discounted prices. The aisles of this pristine, well-stocked store are brimming with inexpensive vitamins, homeopathic remedies, protein powders, organic household cleaners, natural cosmetics, herbal and sports supplements, organic produce, gourmet teas and coffees, natural foods and bulk items (see chapter on "Vitamins"). Some of the impressive deals I found on a recent visit include three packages of De Boles organic pasta for $4.19; two Genisoy Protein Bars for $2; Erewhon Instant Oatmeal for $1.99; Garden of Eatin' 7.5-ounce bag of tortilla chips for $1.99; 32-ounce carton of Rice Dream for $1.79; three Fantastic Foods 2.4-ounce Soup Cups for $3.29; 32-ounce R.W. Knudsen Very Veggie Juice for $1.99; Lightlife Smart Bacon for $2.69; and Boca Burger Meatless Patties for $2.99. Bell Bates also prepares delicious, healthy foods in its deli and has a juice bar and all natural salad bar.

Although fresh ravioli is the house specialty at **Bruno The King of Ravioli**, Bruno also makes and sells a wide variety of other pastas, delicacies and sweets. The prices at this purveyor of all things Italian are affordable, with a box of 40 ricotta-filled ravioli (a meal for three people) starting at just $3.99. And, twice each week Bruno's discounts selected ravioli for a savings of a dollar or more. Their many Ravioli choices include seafood, "Tex Mex," smoked salmon and cheese, pumpkin, artichoke, shitake mushroom with Marsala wine, and lobster. Other homemade pastas include manicotti, fettuccini, linguine, taglierini, gnocchi, cannelloni, stuffed shells, cavatelli (my favorite) and tortellini. For those who are watching their weight or cholesterol, Bruno's makes several pastas that have no eggs, no cheese, and are low in fat. Bruno's also features several "Heat 'N Eat" take-home dinners that they sell by the pound (starting at $2.89), as well as salads, olives, cheeses, gelato, fresh sausage, bread, specialty meats, a large selection of their own sauces (starting at $3.99 a pint, $4.99 a quart) and much more.

2204 Broadway, between 78th and 79th Streets—212–580–8150
249 Eighth Avenue between 22nd and 23rd Streets—
  212–627–0767
387 Second Avenue between 22nd and 23rd Street—
  212–685–7666

East Village Cheese Store (40 Third Avenue between 9th and 10th Streets—212–477–2601) has tremendously low prices, perhaps the city's lowest, on an abundance of imported and domestic cheeses. To insure their low-price-leader status, East Village Cheese has weekly "Superspecials," in which up to fifteen cheeses sell for only $2.99 a pound. Havarti, smoked Gouda, English Five County cheddar, ricotta salata and Israeli yogurt cheese were among those recently designated as "Superspecials." The bargains here don't end with cheese. This shop carries lots of meats, breads, sweets, savories, pâtés, crackers, coffees, teas, pastas, olives, jams and beverages at nadir prices.

134 • AN ACTOR PREPARES.... TO LIVE IN NEW YORK CITY

Ask just about any New Yorker to name their favorite supermarket, and nine times out of ten you'll hear **Fairway Fruits and Vegetables** (2127 Broadway at 74th Street—212-595-1794). For good reason . . . For freshness, variety and price, no other grocery store in the city comes close. Fairway has everyday low prices and special sales on unparalleled selections in every one of its huge departments, which include produce, bread, dairy, prepared foods, baked goods, beverages, cheese, olives, condiments, water, canned goods, fish and seafood, meat, coffee, tea, bulk food, olive oil and sushi. Upstairs is an enormous area where Fairway sells reasonably priced vitamins, supplements and organic and health foods. Caution: this popular store is not for the claustrophobic or those who can't endure aggressive crowds. Although Fairway is a big place, its maze like aisles are cramped with goods, forcing the pushy masses to constantly jockey for position. Be especially aware of seemingly sweet little old ladies who wield shopping carts as if they were lethal weapons. Open 24 hours, 7 days a week. Note: To avoid huge crowds and long checkout lines, don't even think about shopping at Fairway on weekends or after work.

BEST BARGAIN

For value and selection, the city's number one food retailer is **Fairway's Outlet** (2328 Twelfth Avenue at 132nd Street—212-234-3883). Housed in a huge dilapidated building on the Hudson River in Harlem, this warehouse store is literally packed to the rafters with an awesome array of provisions; the produce and refrigerated sections alone are larger than most Manhattan supermarkets. For those who have been to the Upper Westside Fairway, it's hard to imagine that this outpost store could stock a larger inventory (or that any place could for that matter), but they do. And, no market has better prices. Fairway Outlet's motto is, "Wholesale prices for the retail customer." After just one visit, you'll see what they mean. The tradeoff (there's always a tradeoff) is this market is not easy to get to or leave from; it's a several block walk to the 1 and 9 subway and not many cabs pass this remote location, making it imperative that you have a car. Fortunately, Fairway provides free parking.

Though not expressly an inexpensive market, the **Food Empo-rium** chain offers shoppers several ways to save money on their grocery bills. Food Emporium features two different "house brands" ("America's Choice" and "Master's Choice"), basically generic versions of name-brand grocery items, for about a third less than those originals. It has several weekly sales on a vast array of items and additional reductions for members in its Gold Points Reward Network. There is no charge to sign up for a member card. Gold Points sale items change weekly and can save you hundreds of dollars each year. Often, the only things I will put in my shopping cart are those that are on sale through the Gold Points card. Food Emporium has a huge presence throughout the city. All stores are mostly clean, well stocked and feature lots of specialty foods like coffees, cheeses and caviar. Each store also has a fresh fish and seafood section, salad bar, deli, bakery, and heav ing produce section. Check your phone book for the closest of its 23 New York locations.

All five metropolitan area **The Health Nuts** stores have compet-itive pricing and monthly sales on all kinds of healthy, organic and natural foods, products and cosmetics, as well as a large variety of vitamins, supplements and herbal and homeopathic remedies. Seen recently: Boca Veggie Burgers for $2.99 (regularly $4.29), Westsoy Organic Soy Beverage for 99¢ (regularly $1.99), Old Won sex Instant Oatmeal for 99¢ (regularly $1.99), Westbrae organic beans for 99¢ (regularly $1.59), Muir Glen organic pasta sauce for $2.69 (regularly $3.99) and Santa Cruz organic applesauce for $1.99 (regularly $3.59). If you need an immediate boost, The Health Nuts has a juice bar where they will make your favorite fruit and vegetable concoctions.

1208 Second Avenue at 63rd Street—212–593–0116
835 Second Avenue at 45th Street—212–490–2979
2141 Broadway at 75th Street—212–724–1972
2611 Broadway at 99th Street—212–678–0054
Bay Terrace Shopping Center, Bayside, Queens—
    718–225–8164

I wish I could wholeheartedly endorse the popular natural foods store **Healthy Pleasures** (93 University Place between 11ᵗʰ and 12ᵗʰ Streets—212–353–3663), but it barely meets my criteria for inexpensive grocery shopping. Most of the items here are downright pricey, with protein bars higher than almost anywhere in the city and a salad bar that is a real wallet buster. Healthy Pleasures acquits itself (and therefore makes it into this book) with its frequent promotions and sales. Especially good are vitamin and cereal specials that are often Two-for-One. (See the chapter on "Vitamins and Supplements.") Also, if you bring them $1,000 worth of Healthy Pleasure receipts, you will be rewarded with a gift certificate for $50.

Who would've thought that in the very expensive Chelsea Market (where a cookie goes for as much as $12, a loaf of bread can be $6, a quart of "designer" milk sells for $2.75 and 16 ounces of juice—albeit fresh squeezed—is $3.50), you can actually find unfathomably cheap produce? Well, you can at **Manhattan Fruit Exchange** (448 West 16ᵗʰ Street at Ninth Avenue—212–989–2444). This retailer charges prices for a cornucopia of beautiful, fresh fruits and vegetables that are barely above wholesale. Some examples: grape tomatoes—89¢ a pint (usually $2.50 in most supermarkets); Rome apples—99¢ a pound; red cabbage—39¢ a pound; plum tomatoes—99¢ a pound; jumbo yams—39¢ a pound; red potatoes—2 pounds for $2; Spanish or yellow onions—49¢ a pound; mesclun salad—$3.99 a pound (usually $7.99); greenleaf lettuce—99¢ a head; cucumbers—3 for $1; and a six ounce carton of mushrooms—$1. Manhattan Fruit Exchange has great prices on other foods like milk, cheese, juices, gourmet-flavored coffees (at a very low $4.59 a pound) and bulk nuts, dried fruits and candies.

The venerable (and venerated) **Murray's Cheese Shop** (257 Bleecker Street near Seventh Avenue—212–243–3289) in the West Village has excellent prices and weekly sales on a staggering variety of domestic and imported cheeses. Besides the stuff that clots arteries and increases cholesterol, look for Murray's good selection of affordable breads, crackers, olives (ranging from $4.99 to $7.99

per pound), pastas, vinegars and olive oils (a one-liter bottle of Murray's "Private Stock" Extra Virgin is $8.99). Recent deals on cheeses included domestic feta and pecorino romano at $4.99 per pound; homemade mozzarella, which they boast is the best in the city, at $5.99 a pound; Brie 60% at $3.99 a pound; Cupid's Choice camembert (in honor of Valentine's Day) at $4.99 each; and a goat's milk Coeur du Gilbert cheese at $5.99.

Although not a food store per se, **National Wholesale Liquidators** (632 Broadway, between Bleecker and Houston Streets— 212-979-2400), which sells brand-name manufacturer's overstocks and seconds, carries nonperishable food items at very low prices. You can find candy, dried fruits, nuts, preserves, canned, packaged and jarred goods, tea and coffee, all at about 40 percent less than you'd pay at your neighborhood grocery store. On a recent tour, I found 2-liter bottles of soda for 50¢, 2-pound tubs of dried apricots for $1.88, 16-ounce jars of honey for $1.59, 20-count English Breakfast teabags for 99¢, 1-liter bottles of mountain spring water for 44¢ and 6-ounce jars of marinated artichoke hearts for 79¢. Best yet, unlike most other closeout stores, all National Wholesale Liquidators' overstocks and seconds (which does not mean bad quality—it may mean that a label is misspelled) are in pristine condition and don't have dubious expiration dates. (See chapter on "General Merchandise Stores").

Along a 20-block stretch of **Ninth Avenue between 37th and 57th Streets**, are an inordinate number of **low-priced grocery stores, butchers, fish and seafood merchants, specialty food shops** and **produce dealers**. This agglomeration of provisions purveyors, probably the city's largest, is a blessing to those who live in the neighborhood (like me), but also draws tightwad gourmands from all over both for its quality foods and its prices. Based on inventory and savings, the following are my picks for the Ninth Avenue/Hell's Kitchen area's best and least expensive food retailers:

Bereft of charm (this place is a dive), the **Big Apple Meat Market** (573 Ninth Avenue, between 41st and 42nd Streets—

212–563–2555) has unbelievably cheap prices on a variety of
fresh meats, groceries and household goods. Some great savings include USDA prime boneless beef pot roast—$1.78 a
pound; leg of lamb—$1.98 a pound; sirloin steak—$2.18 a
pound; veal shoulder cutlets—$4.98 a pound; fresh Perdue sea-
soned roasting chickens—58¢ a pound; 6-ounce container of
Axelrod yogurt—45¢; 12-ounce bag of Lender's bagels—99¢;
White Rose bath tissue—50¢; 10-ounce box of Cheerios—
$2.59; and ground beef chuck—$1.28 a pound. For a real *The
Cook, The Thief, His Wife and Her Lover* kind of experience (or
to cool off in the summer), be sure to walk into the meat section, a huge walk-through refrigerated area where butchers,
who are bundled in several layers of clothing covered by blood-
soaked aprons, are carving up giant slabs of beef.

Central Fish Company (527 Ninth Avenue between 39th and
40th Streets—212–279–2317) and **Sea Breeze Seafood** (541
Ninth Avenue at 40th Street—212–563–7537), a block apart,
are two of the best and least expensive places in the city to buy
just about anything that lives in water. "Fresh" doesn't begin
to describe the quality of the goods at either store; the fish are
so fresh that they're practically still flapping. Both have titanic
selections and minisubmarine-size prices. Last time I looked at
Central, salmon fillets were $3.99 a pound, sea bass was $2.99
a pound, tilapia was $1.99 a pound, red snapper was $4.99 a
pound and bay scallops were $3.99 a pound. Sea Breeze had
mackerel at 99¢ a pound, sea scallops at $5.49 a pound, sea
trout at $1.99 a pound and catfish at $1.49 a pound. The
unique feature at Central is its huge tanks that hold an orgy of
lobsters ($6.99 a pound, "special" lobsters—whatever that
means—3 pounds for $14.99). Sea Breeze specializes in a huge
assortment of sea creatures: clams, mussels, oysters, even sea
urchins. If you don't see what you want at one place, you're
sure to find it at the other.

Almost a century before Starbucks besieged our fair city, **Empire Coffee and Tea** (568 Ninth Avenue between 41st and

42nd Street—212–586–1717) was vending goods to the residents of Hell's Kitchen. Still going strong, Empire is a great alternative to the slickness and high prices of the leviathan mega-chain. This laid-back, friendly neighborhood shop has an abundance of aromatic, flavorful and fresh teas and coffees at reasonable prices. The prices of their stock of custom-roasted coffees from light and dark roasts, special blends, flavored to decaffeinated range between $7 and $9 per pound. A large selection of loose and bag teas includes Pin Head Gun Powder Green, Pan Fried Green, Kenya Black, Chunmee Green, Lapsang Souchong and Licorice Spice. If you need coffee/tea paraphernalia like mugs, teapots, coffee makers, filters, canisters and grinders Empire also carries a small supply. Why not try a cup of java while you're there; Empire has several flavors brewing.

International Grocery (543 Ninth Avenue between 40th and 41st Streets—212–279–5514) is beloved by professional and amateur chefs alike for its giveaway prices on a vast selection of bulk foods. This unique food store, which specializes in Greek, Italian and Spanish products, has dozens of bins filled to overflowing with the freshest of items, including a variety of rices, flour, grains, pastas, couscous, dried fruits, beans, condiments, nuts, olives, spices and herbs. International Grocery discounts a large array of olive oils, coffees ($5 a pound for regular, $6 for water process decaf), cheeses, specialty meats, Middle Eastern delicacies like hummus and baba ganoush, and canned and packaged goods. Halvah lovers rejoice . . . International Grocery sells myriad flavors of what one friend calls, "the best and freshest in the city" at cheap prices.

Mazzella's Market (692 Ninth Avenue, between 47th and 48th Streets—212–586–0368) is primarily a produce wholesaler but sells a small array of reasonably priced fruits and vegetables to the public out of crates on the sidewalk in front of their warehouse. The selection here isn't nearly as good as the nearby Stiles Farmer's Market (see page 141), but can be a convenient place to grab a few things on the run.

Ninth Avenue Cheese Market has low prices on a mouth-watering selection of cheeses from around the world, as well as a host of other rations like bulk items, prepared foods, sauces, spreads, breads, candies, condiments, olives and olive oils. They also carry teas and an array of flavored coffee beans (which they will grind to your specifications) for just $5.99 a pound. Ninth Avenue Cheese makes the city's most delicious gourmet sandwiches stuffed with the likes of smoked mozzarella and eggplant, chicken tarragon, brie and sundried tomatoes, grilled vegetables and turkey pastrami, for an amazing $3.99 each. Not in the mood for a sandwich? Try their homemade soup bar ($1.99 for a quart container) or salad bar ($4.95 with a choice of fresh greens and four vegetable toppings). Besides their everyday low prices, Ninth Avenue Cheese has frequent sales and specials.

> 615 Ninth Avenue, between 43rd and 44th Streets—
>   212–397–4700
> 856 Ninth Avenue, between 55th and 56th Streets—
>   212–581–8282

The year-round **Ninth Avenue Farmer's Market** at 57th Street is minuscule, seven or eight vendors in the spring/summer/fall, only a couple in the winter, but you can buy a variety of goods at very low prices. Besides seasonal fruits, vegetables, herbs and plants that are grown at metro-area farms, the market features homemade baked goods like breads, pies and cookies as well as locally made cheeses and honey. The Ninth Avenue Farmer's Market operates on Wednesdays and Saturdays from 8 A.M. to 6 P.M.

The intoxicating, sweet aromas wafting from the **Pozzo Pastry Shop** (690 Ninth Avenue between 47th and 48th Streets— 212–265–7530) lure even the most calorie-conscious passersby to partake of the their fresh baked goods. Unlike most "baked on the premises" bakeries, Pozzo is incredibly cheap. Nowhere else that I'm aware of can you buy fresh made 10-inch pies (apple, lemon meringue, pecan throughout the year, pumpkin and mince during the holidays) for only $8, 6-inch cheesecakes for $6.50, and 9-inch cheesecakes for $9.50. Pozzo makes delicious 7-inch pound cakes and flavored loaf cakes (chocolate chip, black forest, banana nut, cranberry walnut and cinnamon pecan) for a whopping $3. Need a cake for a special occasion? Pozzo does custom orders with a variety of flavors and icings starting at $15.50. Note: Don't buy at Pozzo on Mondays or you might get dry leftovers—they are closed on Sundays.

By far the cheapest places in all New York to buy fruits and vegetables are the **Stiles Farmer's Markets.** Two of the three Hell's Kitchen markets are set in small circus-tent structures—one across from the Port Authority at the entrance to the Lincoln Tunnel between 41st and 42nd Street—212–967–4918, the other beside a parking lot on 52nd Street between Eighth and Ninth Avenues—212–582–3088. Both operate year-round (the tents are heated in winter, dress lightly in the summer) and have unbelievable prices on a fairly standard array of items; the prices are so good that I have friends who live as far away as Inwood who come to Midtown twice a week specifically to shop at Stiles. You'll encounter bananas for 39¢ a pound, five ears of corn for $1, asparagus for $1.50 a pound, two pounds of Anjou pears for $1.50, New onions as well as red and Idaho potatoes all at 99¢ for three pounds, mesclun greens for an astounding $3.99 a pound (compare that with $7.99 at Whole Foods!), gourmet coffee beans you grind yourself for $3.99 a pound, romaine lettuce 75¢ a head, celery 50¢ a bunch, a bag of baby carrots for $1 and mixed nuts for $2.99 a pound. Stiles carries a good selection of bread, pasta and eggs that are often fresher than those in supermarkets. I always walk out of Stiles' Market with two large grocery bags heaping with produce, for which I never spend more than $10. The third

BEST BARGAIN

Stiles location is at 569 Ninth Avenue between 36th and 37th Street—212–695–6213.

For Brooklyn's tree-hugging, crunchy-granola lefties on a budget, **Park Slope Food Coop** (782 Union Street, Brooklyn—718–622–0560) is a "must-join" organization. This member-owned and-operated market offers a diverse assortment of products, with an emphasis on organic, minimally processed and healthful foods and on household supplies that are marked only slightly higher than wholesale cost. This environmentally conscious store obtains most of its goods from local, "earth-friendly" producers, avoids products "that depend on the exploitation of others," promotes recycling, and supports nontoxic, sustainable agriculture. Only members may shop here, but membership is open to all: simply pay a $25 joining fee, commit to working at the coop 2¾ hours per month, pay a $100 investment fee (payment plans are available) that is returned when a member leaves the coop, and attend a new member orientation meeting (held every Monday and Wednesday at 7:30 P.M. and the second Sunday of each month at 4 P.M.). The Park Slope Food Coop provides free childcare during shopping/working hours.

How has the unglamorous **Pioneer Supermarket** (289 Columbus Avenue at 75th Street—212–874–9506) managed to stay afloat amidst the proliferation of self-consciously trendy shops, boites and boutiques on Columbus Avenue? Undoubtedly Pioneer has an ironclad lease that locks them to this location 'til the end of time. A good thing for their customers; this bastion of old New York (well, 1960s New York) looks like it hasn't been renovated in 40 years (one glance at the tile floors and you will see what I mean) and has prices on several items that don't seem to have changed much in 40 years either. Recent Pioneer bargains included Just Pik't premium orange juice (half gallon) for $2.50; 3 pounds of bananas for $1; boneless sirloin steak for $2.99 a pound; a pint of Häagen Dazs ice cream or sorbet for $1.99; Perdue whole chicken legs for 69¢ a pound; 12-pack of Amstel or Heineken beer for

$10.99; whole pork loin for $1.99 a pound; 10 Temple oranges for $1; 32-ounce jar of White Rose mayonnaise for 99¢; and 2 one-pound packages of San Giorgio pastas for $1. The Columbus Avenue store isn't the only Pioneer round the city; check your phone book for the nearest location.

Porto Rico Importing Company at Bleecker Street between Sixth Avenue and McDougal Street (212–477–5421) has been caffeinating the city since 1907 and is a coffee and tea drinker's paradise. This West Village emporium offers its customers over one hundred kinds of coffee beans (which they will grind to specification), from the world over in a variety of blends, roasts, shades and flavors. To insure the highest quality and freshness, and to make good on their promise that their joe is "the best that money can buy," Porto Rico does its own roasting. The results: a flavorful and aromatic product that is far superior to Starbucks and the other chains, and, with prices that range from $5.99 to $7.99 a pound, also somewhat cheaper. For added savings, Porto Rico places a different coffee on special each week and two times yearly (October 22–31 and April 15–30) drastically reduces its most popular beans. Porto Rico has what seems like endless rows of canisters of loose teas from the most exotic of places, and all at excellent prices. Porto Rico has two other locations:

107 Thompson Street between Spring and Prince Streets—212–966–5758
40fi St. Marks Place near Second Avenue—212–533–1982

New York's biggest, best and oldest farmer's market is the **Union Square Greenmarket** (north end of Union Square at 17th Street between Broadway and Park Avenue South—212–477–3220). At this bustling market with its carnival-like atmosphere, you will find reasonably priced just-picked produce, as well as bargains on quality fish, baked goods, home-jarred preserves and honey, and plants and flowers. At the end of each market day, many vendors discount their goods by as much as 50 percent so they won't have to cart them home, although you won't find the more unusual produce left. Market hours are Mondays, Wednesdays, Fridays, and Saturdays from 7 A.M. to 6 P.M.

People in the know come from all over New York to buy their groceries at the **Westerly Natural Market** (911 Eighth Avenue on the Northwest corner of 54th Street—212-586-5262). This cramped store is packed to the ceiling, literally, with brand-name natural foods at the city's lowest prices. In addition to its everyday discounts, the Westerly also has monthly sales where items are so drastically reduced that it seems the store is practically paying you to shop there. It is not uncommon to find Tropicana Orange Juice on sale two half gallons for $5; Health Valley and Barbara's brand natural cereals for as low as $1.29; six-ounce Fantastic brand Chicken Flavor Rice Pilaf two for $1; or Newman's Own Chocolate Chip Cookies for $1.89. Be aware, though, fresh produce and meat are not inexpensive; I'm sure that if and when the store expands, those prices will come down too. The Westerly prides itself on offering its customers huge discounts on a vast selection of vitamins, herbs and homeopathic remedies as well as nutritional and sports supplements. Many, if not most, of the vitamins are "Buy One, Get One Free," protein bars cost half what you would pay at most other places and supplements sell at rock-bottom prices. The staff is always friendly and helpful and those overseeing the vitamin and supplement areas are definitely experts in their field.

Unless you live in the Meatpacking District, **Western Beef's** main Manhattan outlet (403 West 14th Street at Ninth Avenue—212-989-6572) on the far reaches of West 14th Street is quite a schlep. Not a problem. With the money you'll save shopping at this large warehouse-like store, you can afford a cab to get you home; hell, you can afford a car service! As you'd expect from the store's name and location, this place specializes in meat; what you might not expect is how cheap the prices are—practically wholesale. For example, recently whole fresh hams, split chicken breasts and boneless beef briskets were $1 a pound; combination end and center cut pork chops were $1.65 a pound; boneless beef eye round or bottom round steaks were $2.99 a pound; store-made ground turkey was 99¢ a pound; beef rib steak was $4.99 a pound; rib or loin lamb chops were $2.99, butcher trimmed beef round cutlets were $2.99, Italian style shoulder veal cutlets were $4.99; and London Broil was $1.69 a pound. I could go on and on listing the savings here, but you get the point. If I've left you with the impression that Western Beef is strictly a butcher's, my mistake. This is a full-service supermarket whose aisles are heaving with produce, frozen foods, canned goods, bread, dairy, household products, you name it—everything and more to stock the pantry and fridge. And, the prices on non-meat items are just as low, like plum tomatoes for 69¢ a pound, a 6-ounce can of Star-Kist Tuna for 60¢, 2 liters of Pepsi Cola for $1, four 16 ounce packages of Barilla pasta for $3 . . . like I said before, you get the point. Hail a cab and get thee to Western Beef. Residents of the Upper West Side and the boroughs will be happy to know that Western Beef has stores in their areas; consult your phone book for the nearest location.

Whenever I tell anyone that I am including **Whole Foods Market** (250 Seventh Avenue between 24th and 25th Streets—212-924-5969) in my discussion of inexpensively priced grocery stores, they almost always look at me as if I have lost my mind. Most everyone agrees that Whole Foods is the finest and most beautiful market in New York. All also agree that it is one of the city's most expensive. I cannot argue with the NY's "finest" assessment for it is indeed, for me, a pleasure dome of a supermarket—the aisles are artistically stacked and stocked with "healthy," "natural," "clean," "free range," " fresh" and " pure" foods. The store is bright, accessible and uncrowded. The employees are all cheerful, helpful and knowledgeable, and even the bright, attractive and interesting patrons look as if they were hand-chosen by Central Casting to enhance the store's already ideal ambience. It makes me happy to shop at Whole Foods; I've cured a case of the blues more than once by meandering up and down the glistening aisles. As for being one of the city's most expensive markets, I don't necessarily agree. Yeah, most items you can purchase elsewhere for a lot less money, but Whole Foods redeems itself with its many weekly sales and promotions. Recent specials included "Veri-Pure"

Puffed Honey Kashi cereal for $2.29 (regularly $3.39), "Magic Hat" beer 6 pack for $6.99 (regularly $8.99), "After the Fall" 32-ounce juices for $1.89 (regularly $2.29), "Lifestream" Frozen Waffles for $1.99 (regularly $2.69), and "Mi-Del" 10-ounce package of lemon snap cookies for $1.99 (regularly $2.69). In addition, Whole Foods markets its own brands at everyday discount prices, like its "365" brand soups for only $1.19, salad dressings for $1.79, cereals and peanut butter both always $1.99. A 14-ounce container of Whole Foods sesame sticks is always $2.99 and the same size container of banana chips is $2.29. The chain packages its own protein bars ("Verve" and "Everyday"), which are comparable to "Cliff Bars" and "Powerbars," for only 99¢ each. Whole Foods has lots of great prepared foods (which can be rather expensive), the most aesthetically pleasing produce section you've ever seen, an exquisite cheese section that always has specials, fresh baked breads and desserts, environment friendly cleaning products, luxurious natural toiletries, and a separate store next door devoted to vitamins, supplements, scents, aromatherapy, personal hygiene products and a plethora of products that other stores don't carry.

To many a city dweller, especially those who love to cook, **Zabar's** (2245 Broadway at 80th Street—212-787-2000) is as synonymous with New York as are the Empire State Building and the Statue of Liberty. A city icon, Zabar's is a veritable monument to great food and good dining and carries an awesome selection of the crème de la crème (as well as crème anglaise and crème fraîche) of imported and domestic food items. Whether it is coffee, cheese, charcuterie, olives, smoked fish, candy, Jewish delicacies, baked goods or prepared foods, Zabar's has the very best. Labeled by such superlatives, you'd think that the store would be expensive; for the quality and variety of its gourmet goods, Zabar's is actually relatively inexpensive. Watch for the special sales on a number of items each week.

SPIRITS, BEVERAGES AND BREWS

FOR BROOKLYNITES, or those who are willing to make the trip out to Cobble Hill, **American Beer Distributing Company** (256 Court Street at Butler Street—718–875–0226) offers outstanding selection, savings and service on beer, soda, water, sport drinks, and other beverages. This superstore stocks one of the area's largest assortments of beers, including domestic ales, lagers, microbrews, hard ciders, malt beverages, bocks, stouts, porters, wheat beers and barley wines. It also carries a huge variety of imported brews such as doppelbacks, amber and dark lagers, British ales, smoked beers, festival beers and malt liquors. Even teetotalers will want to shop here because almost every soda imaginable is in stock, as well as a wide range of carbonated and noncarbonated bottled waters, "New Age" beverages, syrups, teas and juices. Best of all, American Beer offers incredible everyday discounts over deli and supermarket prices, and weekly Super Sales and coupons for additional savings.

B & E Quality Beverage (511 West 23rd Street between Tenth and Eleventh Avenues—212–243–6559) is a discount retailer of almost every drinkable except wine and liquor. They carry a full compliment of sodas, waters, sports drinks, juices, and teas plus their wide selection of American microbrews and international beers, not only from countries you'd expect, but from many you wouldn't like Poland, Russia, Brazil, India, Korea, China, Thailand and Argentina. B & E specializes in inexpensively priced Belgian beers, and there are a lot. You'll also find a smattering of "seasonal" brews; one December visit discovered featured beers with names like "Winter Warmer," "Christmas Ale," "Winter Welcome" and "Delirium Noel." Speaking of novelty beers, B & E is one of the few stores I've seen that carries the 14 percent alcohol content "Samichlaus Bier," termed the "strongest beer in the world" by the Guinness Book of World Records ($4.50 for a 12-ounce bottle). Great beer deals include a six-pack of Tsingtao for $6.95, a six-pack of Sam Adams for $6.50, a case of Saranac for $19.95 and a six-pack of the New Orleans brewed Abita Ale for $7.95.

For price, selection and service, wine retailer **Best Cellars** (1291 Lexington Avenue at 87th Street—212–426–4200) is my favorite. Being completely ignorant about wines, selecting a suitable bottle is a grueling chore for me. Best Cellars takes the drudgery out of wine shopping by organizing its inventory by category, color and flavor. Whether I'm in the mood for a sparkling wine, a light red, a heavy white, a dessert wine, or anything in between, I go to the respective section and take my pick. Moreover, the staff is extremely knowledgeable and ready to offer insight and guidance in the selection process . . . not something you'd expect from a store where all bottles are under $10. That's right, *all* wines are priced under $10. Free tastings are held daily except Sunday, from 5 P.M. to 8 P.M.

In Chelsea, the small shop **Crossroads** (55 West 14th Street at Sixth Avenue—212–924–3060) is stacked from floor to ceiling with wine and liquor from all over the world. Crossroads cannot be categorized as a "cheap" liquor and wine outlet, but it does carry several good, inexpensive wines, such as Bogle Chardonnay—$8.99, Preece Sauvignon Blanc—$4.99, Livio Felluga Pinot Grigio—$14.99 and Rabbit Ridge Zinfandel—$8.79. On multiple purchases you find bargains—buy any six bottles that are tagged with an orange price sticker and you will receive a 10 percent discount; buy any twelve bottles for a 20 percent discount. There are occasional other liquor bargains. On a recent price-sniffing expedition, a "Magnum Madness" sale had Cutty Sark Whisky for $25.99, Jim Beam Bourbon for $18.99, Ron Rico Rum for $16.99, Georgi Vodka for $10.99 and Gilbey's Gin for $14.99. One visit and you'll understand why both *New York Magazine* and *New York Press* have named Crossroads the city's "Best Wine Shop."

Garnet Wines & Liquors (929 Lexington Avenue at 68th Street—212-772-3211) discounts wines from around the world and has something for every taste and budget. For imbibers who are exercising financial frugality, Garnet has hundreds of excellent vintages from Chile, Australia, California, Spain, New Zealand, New York, France, Italy and elsewhere at remarkably low prices. Among Garnet's bargains, I found Yellow Tail Shiraz for $5.49, Macon-Villages Chardonnay for $6.49, Hardys Nottage Hill Merlot for $7.99, Orvieto Classico for $6.49, Baron Herzog Chenin Blanc for $6.99 and Beringer White Zinfandel for $6.99. If you favor champagne, Garnet carries several inexpensively priced brands like Chandon Brut for $12.99, Freixenet for $7.99, Charles Lafitte for $15.99 and Piper Sonoma for $11.99.

The expert staff at **Nancy's Wine For Foods** (313 Columbus Avenue at 75th Street—212-877-4040) is trained to assist consumers in making informed decisions about what to serve with any type of meal. Nancy's specializes in small batch wines and imports from Germany (with over 100 Rieslings), but does feature an impressive selection of international, sparkling, dessert and "weird and wondrous" wines. If you think that a store with such specialties and service would be expensive, you'd be wrong—Nancy's features over 180 bottles of good wines for under $10.

New York Beverage (207 East 123rd Street, between 2nd and 3rd Avenues—212-831-4000) boasts that it offers the largest and finest selection of beverages available anywhere in New York, and all at discount prices. One visit to their Harlem warehouse and you'll have to agree. New York Beverage's remarkable inventory of almost every beverage imaginable (except wine and liquor) includes a full range of domestic and imported beers and microbrews, sodas, waters (sparkling and non-sparkling), mixers, juices and ciders. Since New York Beverage is a warehouse, you'll pay warehouse prices, which means huge savings over your supermarket or deli. If you are worried about how to transport your potables home, don't—the company offers reliable home and office delivery for a nominal price. Too lazy to make the trip uptown? No problem: phone orders are also available. Check the website (www.newyorkbeverage.com) for a complete list of products.

The lowest prices in town on wine and liquor are at **Warehouse Wine and Spirits** (735 Broadway between Waverly and 8th Street—212-982-7770). This megastore stocks its shelves with about every kind of wine and brand of liquor out there, and at prices that no other retailer in the city can beat. For inexpensive, quality wines, choose from a huge selection for under $10. A good clearance section has wines starting at $4.99 a bottle, and by the case there is always 10 percent off. If you want the hard stuff, a wide range of liquors, from "call" to premium brands are sold here at bargain prices. Once you've entered Warehouse Wine and Spirits and seen their discounts, you will want to snap up all you can carry, but don't go crazy, remember bottles are heavy and you have to get them home. Okay, go crazy—if you spend $100 or more and live below 86th Street, Warehouse will deliver at no charge.

BEST BARGAIN

VITAMINS AND SUPPLEMENTS

Bell Bates Natural Food Market (97 Reade Street—212–267–4300), in Tribeca for one hundred years carries a plentiful selection of vitamins, minerals, homeopathic remedies, protein powders and herbal and sports supplements in addition to its discount-priced provisions. There is always a sale on many of these items. Recently, all Bell Bates own brand vitamins were 30 percent off and all Twinlab, Nature's Answers and Nature's Herbs vitamins and supplements were 25 percent off. Natrol Ester-C (500 mg.) with Bioflavanoids, regularly $41.59, was $24.95; a 36-pack of Alacer Emergen-C, regularly $14.95, were $8.97; Twinlab Daily One Caps, regularly $43.95, were $21.97; and Boericke and Tafel Echina-Spray, regularly $9.49, was $5.69.

General Nutrition Center (GNC) Stores, which carry most major brands of vitamins, performance supplements, diet pills, herbs, fat-burners, etc., is by no means cheap. At best, this natural health chain can be considered moderately priced. What they have going for them, besides location (29 stores in Manhattan), is their GNC Gold Card. Using the Gold Card, which costs $15 per year, 20 percent is deducted from any purchase you make on the first Tuesday of each month. Weekly promotional sales on various items, all EAS products always discounted 20 percent, and all GNC brand products always "Buy-One-Get-The-Second-At-50 percent-Off" help keep prices lower. There are myriad GNC stores in all five boroughs; consult your phone book for the nearest location.

Using the same policy as for their provisions, **The Health Nuts** stores price competitively and set monthly sales on their large variety of vitamins, supplements and herbal and homeopathic remedies. Recent bargains included 30 percent off the entire lines of vitamins by Twinlab, Natrol, The Health Nuts, Schiff, Nature's Answers and Nature's Herbs. A 36 pack of Alacer Emergen-C was $8.97 (regularly $14.95); 60 Oreganol gel caps were $19.97 (regularly $33.29); 32 ounces of Naturade Aloe Vera gel was $10.47 (regularly $17.45); 100 tablets of Hylands Calms Forte was $5.31 (regularly $7.59) and 250 capsules of Modern Products Swiss Kriss was $5.99 (regularly $9.99). Monthly specials include protein bars and powders, sports and nutrition supplements and diet aids.

> 1208 Second Avenue at 63rd Street—212–593–0116
> 835 Second Avenue at 45th Street—212–490–2979
> 2141 Broadway at 75th Street—212–724–1972
> 2611 Broadway at 99th Street—212–678–0054
> Bay Terrace Shopping Center, Bayside, Queens—
>   718–225–8164

Many health food stores profess to have the largest selection of vitamins and nutritional supplements in the city, but I think **Healthy Pleasures** in the East Village (93 University Place—212–353–3663) really does. The shelves are stocked so high with the many formulations, brands, types and sizes that library ladders are in place to help you get to the products that are out of reach. The enormity of the inventory can be a little daunting. I often stand agape in the aisles, puzzling over, among other things, what the real benefit of "time-release" over "non-time-release" is. My choice is based ultimately on which products are on sale. Fortunately, Healthy Pleasures is always having a Two-for-One special on one or another of its vitamins, herbs and supplements. (See my discussion of Healthy Pleasures in the chapter on "Provisions.") The staff here knows their products, and if you are afraid of heights, they will climb the ladders for you.

The Vitamin Shoppe always discounts name brand and its own brand products 20–40 percent off suggested retail prices. The store's selection of health products is huge and includes vitamins (of course), supplements, herbs, teas, alternative and homeopathic remedies, nutrition and sports bars, bodybuilding supplements, books and personal care products and appliances. Besides shopping at its 27 stores citywide, you can also order by phone (1–800–223–1216), by fax (1–800–852–7153), by mail, or on the web (www.vitaminshoppe.com); its monthly catalog is chock-full of discounts and specials. On top of their everyday low prices, The Vitamin Shoppe maintains a "Frequent Buyer" program that rewards customers with points (one point for every dollar that you spend) to be used for credit toward future purchases. Check your local listings for the nearest Vitamin Shoppe location.

Go to the **Westerly Natural Market** (911 Eighth Avenue at 54th Street—212–586–5262) for its huge discounts on a vast selection of vitamins, herbs and homeopathic remedies as well as nutritional and sports supplements. Many, if not most, of the vitamins are "Buy One, Get One Free," protein bars cost half what you would pay at most other places and supplements sell at rock-bottom prices. The staff is always friendly and helpful and those overseeing the vitamin and supplement areas are definitely experts in their field. (See chapter on "Provisions.")

BEST BARGAIN

CLOTHING

THE BARGAIN WOMEN'S CLOTHING shop **Backwoods** (315 West 57th Street between 8th and 9th Avenues—212–459–2975) is a favorite of several of my actress friends. Most everything in this small store is priced from $10 to $30. Those who love Backwoods characterize the merchandise as "funky," "chic" and "cheap" and they rave about the quality, selection and helpful sales staff. Backwoods stock changes frequently so there's always something new to see and buy.

BEST MARK-DOWNS

For timeless and tasteful men's and women's clothing, **Banana Republic** offers some of the best bargains to be had in the city. No, I haven't lost my marbles. Despite the perception that Banana Republic is an upscale clothier, you can find cheap prices. I'll explain . . . every five to six weeks they introduce new inventory, which means they have to clear the shelves of the old. That "old" merchandise is marked down by 20 percent to 30 percent. The longer these unsold goods stay in the store, the more they are reduced. My entire wardrobe, (and I mean everything), is Banana Republic merchandise, and I've never paid full price for any of it. How do I do this? Make frequent trips into the stores, scope out what you want, calculate about when it will go on sale and return at that time. My system has never failed me and among my incredible buys are two all-wool Italian suits at less than $200 each; lots of long sleeve stretch shirts for $9.99; a great pair of shoes that always receive compliments for $49.99; tons of all-wool and cotton sweaters for under $20; countless crisp and colorful cotton dress shirts for $19.99; and several Italian made silk ties for $7.99. Everything you'll need can be found under one roof, from cashmere, cotton and merino wool sweaters, rubber rain jackets, overcoats, suits, dresses, coordinates, khakis, dress shirts, blouses, skirts, leather pants and jackets, trousers, tee-shirts, underwear, accessories, bags and jewelry. The merchandise design for men and women are mostly simple and classic (with the slight edge and influence of European designers like Helmut Lang and Prada), making them ideal duds to wear to auditions. Check your phone book for the nearest location.

Every summer and winter, no fashion-conscious, bargain-hunting New Yorker would dare miss the ritual of **Barney's Warehouse Sale.** Thousands descend on Barney's Chelsea Co-Op Store (236 West 18th Street between Seventh and Eighth Avenues—212-826-8900) where the sale takes place, to devour as much low-priced high fashion as they can. During the sale merchandise can be 50 to 80 percent off Barney's regular prices. One caveat however: 80 percent savings sounds great, but Barney's is an expensive store and that percentage on a $2,000 suit or a $3,000 dress means the item is still a lot of money. For the diligent, some deals are still to be had, especially on accessories. It's not unheard of to find designer belts, ties, scarves and even some bags for as low as $20. Even if you have no intention of buying, the Barney's sale is something every New Yorker should experience once. The warehouse becomes a war zone where rapacious shoppers grab, push, shove, bicker, toss and sometimes come to blows over pieces of well-sewn cloth, providing enough spectacle to rival what it must have been like to sit in the Roman Coliseum during Caesar's time. The sales take place in February and August; call store for details or watch the "City" section of *The New York Times* and sales section of *Time Out*.

Bolton's, whose motto is "If you've seen it before, you've seen it for more," carries women's clothing and accessories at discount prices. You won't find many designer items here, but there are lots of brand-name goods that are attractive and affordable. A 100 percent silk blouse was just $19.99; a sweater by Rafaela was $12.99; and Harvé Benard wool separates were $29.99 for the skirt, $39.99

for the pants and $59.99 for the jacket. For very good end-of-season clearances Bolton's discounts merchandise by up to 50 percent. Check your local listings for the nearest Bolton's location.

No, the **Burlington Coat Factory** (707 Sixth Avenue—212–229–1300) chain doesn't sell just coats, even though they do carry a lot of them, and many by leading designers like Calvin Klein, Nautica, Kenneth Cole, Liz Claiborne and Jones of New York. The rest of this designer discount chain's inventory doesn't really have a lot in the way of designer items, and the ones they have aren't that fetching (one of the reasons designer discount stores exist is to sell the stuff that other retailers couldn't!). On basic, non-trendy, mainstream, brand-name apparel for men, women, children and infants, you'll find good reductions as well as in their shoe and handbag departments. If you don't mind last season's styles, you will find something you like at a great price.

Canal Jean Co. (504 Broadway near Spring Street—212–226–3663) has really low prices on a large variety of fun, casual clothes like jeans, tee-shirts, lingerie, accessories, underwear and socks, bags, jewelry, shoes, vintage clothing, leather coats and pants and club wear. Innumerable designer and brand-name products can be found here, with Levi's having the most conspicuous presence. Canal's colorful, hip and sexy merchandise is definitely suited to the young—they do a booming business with the students from nearby N.Y.U.—but the young-at-heart are sure to find some good buys as well. Check out the basement bargain area for some of the lowest priced garments in the city—literally thousands of pieces of new, used, closeout and irregular items, all for $10 or less, as well as several 99¢ bins.

For hardcore shoppers, serious bargain hunters and tourists in the know, **Century 21** is a favorite destination. (It does not advertise.) Here you can find top name brand and designer men's and women's fashions at fractions of their original prices. Imagine a large department store in which their entire inventory of cutting edge, of-the-moment clothing is on sale *all the time*—that's Century 21. Like any department store, Century 21 carries other merchandise like accessories, cosmetics, fragrances, sunglasses, housewares and electronics at its discount prices.

22 Cortlandt Street at Chambers Street—212-227-9092
472 86th Street, Bay Ridge, Brooklyn—718-748-3266

Whether you have kids yet or just need gifts, the national chain **The Children's Place,** is one of the city's best outlets to buy inexpensive baby and children's clothing and accessories that are both durable and adorable. The merchandise here is similar to what Baby Gap and Gap Kids is doing, but always a few dollars less expensive. The Children's Place has frequent sales for even greater savings. Check local listings for the nearest Children's Place location.

The cheap general merchandise store, **Conway,** has a handful of locations throughout Manhattan and the other four boroughs where you can find low-end items at very low prices. For many of my friends, Conway is a favorite haunt for truly cheap cotton shirts, accessories, socks and underwear, knockoff purses and summer clothing. Consult your phone book for the nearest location.

Discount retailer, **Daffy's,** has great bargains on both designer and non-designer clothing and accessories for men, women and children. Most of what you will find are current season fashions with prices up to 60 percent less than you'd pay at a regular retail store. On top of their everyday low prices, Daffy's has frequent holiday and clearance markdowns. Several of my friends love this place for its selection and bargains, and do the bulk of their apparel shopping in it. I've never had any luck at Daffy's, but have to admit, I've not spent much time here. The jumbled piles of strewn clothing and picked-over racks quickly make me nervous and I end up fleeing after a couple of minutes. If the aesthetics of shopping aren't your concern, you'll do just fine here. Check your phone book for the nearest location.

Domsey's (431 Broadway at Hughes Street, Williamsburg, Brooklyn—718–384–6000), the Goliath of discount vintage clothing stores, carries piles and piles of every imaginable item of used clothing. With a little persistence and a lot of time, you can find some real treasures in this vast warehouse store. Domsey's even has huge "Buck-a-Pound" bins where, although you're not likely to find runway worthy fashions, you will find plenty of stuff to wear when you paint your apartment.

Like T.J. Maxx, Burlington Coat Factory and Daffy's, **Filene's Basement** is a designer discount retailer where you'll have to do a lot of sniffing and snooping to suss out the good stuff. But fear not, there is good stuff to be had if you are willing to work. Besides reasonable prices, Filene's also has periodic clearance sales where unsold merchandise is further reduced.

620 Sixth Avenue at 18th Street—212–620–3100
2220 Broadway at 79th Street—212–873–8000

Find Outlet specializes in women's very modish designer labels and high-end previous season stock at 50 to 80 percent off the original prices. Think of this store as a remarkably inexpensive outlet for pleasingly hip clothes, shoes and accessories. New stock arrives almost every day, so call or stop in whenever you are in the neighborhood. Two locations:

229 Mott Street between Prince & Springs Streets—
212–226–5167
361 West 17th Street at Ninth Avenue—212–243–3177

I am amazed, given that I regard myself as a know-it-all of cheap anything in the city, that until very recently, I had never heard of **Gabay's** (225 First Avenue at 13th Street—212–254–3180). This popular Lower East Side establishment has been attracting crowds for years with its unbelievable prices on an eclectic collection of exclusive designer handbags, shoes and men's and women's clothing. When I say designer, I mean designer . . . most of the stuff here is the crème de la crème of the fashion world, such as Fendi, Kate

Spade, Loro Piana, Giorgio Armani, Chanel, Calvin Klein, Ralph Lauren, Ermengildo Zegna and Donna Karan. Most of Gabay's inventory consists of irregulars and seconds from tony department stores (almost everything I saw on my most recent visit still had Bergdorf Goodman sales tags) but is in impeccable condition. Please keep in mind when I say "unbelievable prices," I mean unbelievable given what the original prices on these items were. Although Gabay's charges anywhere from 40 percent to 75 percent below retail, prices here are not cut-rate. Go often as the merchandise changes nearly every day.

Although **The Gap** is probably the country's most prominent retail clothing chain (God knows they are in New York) it does have attractive, comfortable, well-made and reasonably priced merchandise for men, women, children and infants. When it comes to quality, style and cost, The Gap bridges "the gap" between the more upscale goods at Banana Republic and the downscale ones at Old Navy (no surprise there since all three are operated by the same parent corporation). In addition to its affordable prices, The Gap, like its siblings, constantly introduces merchandise to its line, which means frequent sales and clearances to make way for the new stuff. For the Gap nearest you, consult your phone book, or spit in any direction—you're bound to hit one!

With several enormous stores in Manhattan, Harlem, Queens and Brooklyn that seem to have materialized out of nowhere (are there more on the way?) the Swedish clothing super-retailer **H&M** has planted firm roots in the city and made living here that much sweeter. Why? On everything from cool men's and women's business attire to hip club clothes, fun party frocks, relaxed casual duds and trendy designer knockoffs, H&M's prices are the city's lowest. This arbiter of "fashion and quality at the best price" also has incredibly low prices on a great selection of undergarments, accessories, bags, makeup, jewelry and women's plus sizes. H&M's inventory is the kind of stuff you see being worn by the city's beautiful people—you know, the folks who are immediately whisked past the velvet ropes at happening clubs, or who have runway-side seats at the hottest new designers' shows. Apparently everyone wants to dress like the beautiful, as these stores are always mobbed (the wait to get into dressing rooms can sometimes take an hour or more). For H&M's savings, style and selection, it is worth enduring the throngs. Check your local listing for the nearest location.

If you have a penchant for glitter, sequins, feathers or fake fur, you will feel right at home at **Joyce Leslie.** At these emporiums of in-expensive, hot and trendy junior fashions, you can assemble a funky outfit for a night on the town, or a "trailer trash" costume for the annual Greenwich Village Halloween parade. This isn't the place you'd go to fit yourself out for temp jobs or to meet the in-laws, and with its decidedly youthful bent, not your store if you're pushing 30. There are racks and racks of cheap denim and poly-ester, as well as spangly tops for $9.99, low-cut and tight-fitting cable weave sweaters for $12.99, and jeans with revealing lace seams for $24.99. Besides its everyday low prices, Joyce Leslie has frequent sales. Check your phone book for the nearest location.

Although **Loehmann's** (101 Seventh Avenue at 16th Street—212–352–0856 and 2807 East 21st Street, Brooklyn—718–368–1256) is categorized as a designer discount store, for quality, selection, serv-ice and goods, it is a step above the others. Here you will find the best of both household names and less mainstream designers of men's and women's fresh, hip and happening clothing. Prices on their high-end items are cheaper than department and specialty stores and boutiques, but they are not cheap. Your Loehmann's purchase will be a splurge, but worth it if you are in the market for top quality, style and value.

For basic athletic clothing, shoes and equipment, there is no better place than **Modell's**. If you are in the market for the most recent aerodynamic running shoe, or the most sought after warm-up suit, you won't find it here. What you will find is last season's hot shoe as well as team jerseys and functional, if perhaps styleless, sports clothing at savings of 50 percent and more. Recently, men's and women's Fila warm-up suits were $25, regularly $39.99; Adidas long-sleeve tees were $9.99 (regularly $19.99); men's Champion fleece turtlenecks were $10 (regularly $35); Nike Air Integrity walking shoes were $32.50 (regularly $64.99); Adidas women's tennis shoes were $32.50 (regularly $64.99); and Timberland men's waterproof Chukka Field Boots were $59.99 (regularly $119.99). Modell's also carries discount sports equipment—a Wilson All-Pro basketball was $5 (regularly $19.99); an Ab Slide was $19.99 (regularly $39.99); and those popular but impractical urban scooters were only $10 each. To keep customers coming back, Modell's offers free membership in their MVP (Modell's Value Plan) Club—for each purchase you make, you will collect points that are turned into reward gift certificates. Modell's has a low price guarantee that promises if you find the same item at another store for less, they will beat the price and refund 25 percent of the difference.

200 Broadway at Fulton Street—212–964–4007
51 East 42nd Street at Vanderbilt Avenue—212–661–4242
901 Sixth Avenue at 33rd Street—212–594–1830
1535 Third Avenue at 86th Street—212–996–3800

Nice Price (493 Columbus Avenue between 83rd and 84th Streets—212–362–1020), owned and operated by the people who run SSS Sample Sales (see chapter on "Sample Sales"), offers the latest women's top designer fashions at savings from 50 percent to 80 percent below retail prices. With such great bargains, this is an ideal place to assemble a wardrobe of very nice, stylish audition clothing that will say, "I am successful" the minute you walk in the room.

For great looking, dependable and affordable clothing to knock around in, there is no better place than **Old Navy**. Brought to you by the same people who operate The Gap and Banana Republic, Old Navy specializes in cheap cool-casual. Their huge array of merchandise includes khakis, painters pants, pajamas, jeans, sweaters, shirts, skirts, dresses, shorts, bathing suits, athletic wear, tee-shirts, hats, accessories and jewelry as well as their signature items like cargo pants and colorful fleece tops and Tech vests. They not only have exceptionally low regular prices, but also weekly specials, coupon sales and end-of-season blowouts where all unsold items go for next to nothing. Check your phone book for the nearest location.

The **Orchard Street Shopping District** (Orchard Street and the surrounding area between East Houston and Canal Streets) on the Lower East Side has been designated New York's "Historic Bargain District," and the title is fitting. This area, which has been the bargain center of the city for the last hundred years, is a mecca for inexpensive designer apparel and much more. For maps and more information about the district, contact the Lower East Side Business Improvement District (261 Broome Street, New York, NY 10002—212–226–9010). Note: Some of the stores in the District take only cash.

Rags-a-Go-Go's vintage apparel store is teeming with second-hand clothing, shoes and accessories, all at thrift shop prices. A lot of the stuff it carries is pretty basic (tee-shirts, jeans, sweaters), but there is a good share of hip to outré styles that will definitely make a fashion statement (what that statement will be is up to you). Although the goods here are secondhand, most if not all are in excellent condition.

218 West 14th Street near Seventh Avenue—646–486–4011

Strawberry, a New York institution since 1932, carries a huge selection of inexpensive junior, young missy and children's clothing, shoes and accessories. You won't find much in the way of designer duds or brand-names, but the stuff here is stylish and appealing to young folk. Check your phone book for the nearest location.

If separating the wheat from the chaff is your desire for an alternative profession (in case this acting thing doesn't work out), you'll love **T.J. Maxx** (620 Avenue of the Americas—212–229–0875). This discounter of name brands from previous seasons has a lot of junk to sift through; aisles and racks and shelves of it. For the assiduous, however, there are huge rewards: lots of designer and retail names like Donna Karan, Calvin Klein, Express, Givenchy, Chaps and Polo Ralph Lauren, Gap, Old Navy, Nautica and more, for very little money. This is a particularly good place to buy underwear and socks: a 3-pack of Calvin Klein tighty-whities is $14.99; a 3-pack of Gold-Toe athletic socks is $4.99 and dress socks by either Dockers or Geoffrey Beene are three for $7.50. The discounts on women's underthings are just as good.

For city guys on a budget, who don't mind looking like they live in the suburbs, **Today's Man** is the store for them. This retailer of bland, low-style (and no-style) men's fashions has lots of basic sweaters, shirts, suits, shoes and casual wear at low prices. At Today's Man, it's possible to find a neutral colored dress shirt for around $25; a suit, albeit a little boxy, for about $300; and a pair of those wingtips like dad used to wear for around $80. Need I tell you that none of my gay friends go near this place?

529 Fifth Avenue at 44th Street—212–557–3111
625 Sixth Avenue at 18th Street—212–924–0200

The inexpensive, armed-services-inspired goods at **Uncle Sam's Army Navy** (37 West 8th Street between Fifth and Sixth Avenues—212–674–2222) appeal less to military buffs and war re-enactors than they do to club kids. Sure, they have camouflage, but in shades of shimmering blue, which is guaranteed to garner attention on the dance floor. The many bargains at Uncle Sam's include Dickie work pants for $4; vintage leather jackets for around $100; flight jackets for $49.95; Ralph Lauren vintage military pants at $8 and shirts at $4 to $8; and $1 military badge bins. For $8, Uncle Sam's will make you a set of personalized dog tags . . . you need never forget your name again.

In the Spring 2002 season, camouflage pants and tee-shirts were all the rage on the runways. Little did the fashionistas know that **Weiss & Mahoney** (142 Fifth Avenue near 19th Street—212–675–1915) has been doing camouflage for years, and for a lot less ($9.99 for tees, $25 for pants) than that with a designer imprimatur. Besides the camouflage, this emporium, which bills itself as, "the peaceful army navy store," carries a lot of what you'd expect at great prices. Dickie work pants were $20; jungle boots were $20; field jackets were $65; down jackets were $99.49; leather combat boots were $40; Carhartt work dungarees were $22; and all union suits, Timex watches and Columbia winter wear was 25 percent off regular prices.

Zara, a Spanish owned retailer with stores throughout the world, has very low prices on modish men's and women's clothing, shoes and accessories. Most of what you will find here are well-made knockoffs of leading European designers, without the designer price tag. If you are lucky enough to catch one of their end-of-season sales, you won't pay less anywhere else for some very nice clothes.

580 Broadway near Prince Street—212–343–1725
750 Lexington Avenue at 59th Street—212–754–1120
39 West 34th Street near Fifth Avenue—212–868–6551
101 Fifth Avenue near 17th Street—212–741–0555

SHOES

SHOES ARE PROBABLY THE MOST important item of clothing in our closets, especially since we traverse the city mostly on our feet. Our shoes need to be sturdy, well crafted, provide support and, New York being Fashion Central, have at least a little style. Therefore, shoe expense should be the one corner we are not willing to cut—not that it's easy to find good, cheap shoes.

Over breakfast with my agents a while back, I told them of my intention to write this book. They all thought it was a great idea, with my agent Nancy asking almost immediately, "Where can I get good shoes inexpensively?" I ahemmed a lot. I vamped. I sputtered. The truth is, I didn't know, because, there is no one store that carries great quality, fashionable shoes at discount prices year-round. Sure, there's the swath of 8th Street between Sixth Avenue and Broadway that is lined on both sides with shoe stores that do have periodic sales, but none are genuine discounters.

Fortunately, actors can augment the cost of shoes by taking advantage of the **Conrad Cantzen Memorial Shoe Fund** for performing artists. In 1945, actor Conrad Cantzen died and provided in his will that part of his estate be put into a fund toward allowing performers to buy a new pair of shoes annually. Cantzen believed that performers were more confident when auditioning in new shoes and that a good pair was necessary in an actor's daily round of auditions. Overseen by the Actors' Fund of America, the Cantzen Shoe Fund lets actors purchase a new pair of shoes from a shoe store for up to but not exceed $80. The applicant is then reimbursed up to, but not over $40. To apply to the Shoe Fund, the following requirements must be met:

OUTSTANDING DEAL

→ You are currently unemployed in the performing profession.

→ You are a current, paid-up member of a performing arts union.

→ It has been at least a year since you last applied.

If you can meet all the criteria, call or write the Actors' Fund (729 Seventh Avenue, 10th Floor, New York, NY 10019—212–221–7300) and request an application for the Conrad Cantzen Memorial Shoe Fund. Once you receive the application, fill it out, attach a copy of your current union card and the original printed store receipt for your shoes and send it back. After the application is approved, a check will be mailed to you in approximately 90 days. Note: The Shoe Fund cannot accept written credit-card receipts that do not have a breakdown of your purchase. Also, your shoes must be purchased within the year in which you are applying.

By polling friends, scoping out several retailers and scrutinizing my own shoe buying habits, I compiled some places where you can find shoes at discount prices:

As I already mentioned, I love **Banana Republic** (see my valentine to B.R. in the "Clothing" chapter). The Banana carries all kinds of well-made, very fashionable shoes that are knockoffs of up-to-the-minute styles, and most are manufactured in Italy. Yeah, they aren't cheap, but all eventually go on sale after they've been on the shelves for a few weeks. And, the sales are pretty spectacular. I have three pairs of Banana Republic shoes, none that I paid more than $49.99 for, and all are handsome, sturdy and comfortable. My favorite pair are complimented on all the time, and I am constantly asked, "Are those Prada?" The women I've talked to who purchase B.R. shoes on sale feel just as passionately as I do. Search the phone book for the seventeen Banana Republic locations.

Kenneth Cole began as strictly a shoe designer/retailer but has since branched out into all facets of clothing. K.C. still offers a huge selection of ridiculously fashionable but also practical Italian-made shoes. Like Banana Republic, these shoes are not cheap (some are downright expensive). However, about four times a year, they are greatly reduced to clear the way for the next season's styles. You'll find Kenneth Cole stores at:

353 Columbus Avenue at 77th Street—212–873–2061
597 Broadway near Houston Street—212–965–0283
95 Fifth Avenue at 17th Street—212–675–2550
107 East 42nd Street (Grand Central Terminal)—
    212–949–8079

Many of the **discount clothing stores**, including **Burlington Coat Factory, Century 21, Daffy's, Filene's Basement, Loehmann's, Syms** and **T.J. Maxx** (see "Clothing" chapter), carry shoes for men and women. The roster of designer and brand-names these stores carry is impressive. You'll find (deep breath) - Bass, Johnston & Murphy, Florsheim, Bostonian, Cole Haan, Bruno Magli, Giorgio Brutini, Sebago, Clarks, Hush Puppies, Sperry, Timberland, Reaction by Kenneth Cole, Steve Madden, Skechers, Enzo Angiolini, Nine West, Aerosoles, Adidas, Naturalizer, New Balance, Reebok, Avia, Liz Claiborne, Keds, Dexter, Rockport and Doc Martens among many others. Most styles are from previous seasons and are marked down by 30 percent or more from their original prices. Unfortunately, when I explored these stores, I found that there was a better range of styles in smaller sizes for men, larger sizes for women. Men take note, Loehmann's only sells women's shoes. Store locations:

Burlington Coat Factory:
    707 Sixth Avenue at 23rd Street—212–229–1300

Century 21:
    22 Cortlandt Street—212–227–9092
    472 86th Street, Bay Ridge, Brooklyn—718–748–3266

Daffy's:

111 Fifth Avenue at 18th Street—212–529–4477

462 Broadway at Grand Street—212–334–7444

335 Madison Avenue at 43rd Street—212–557–4422

125 East 57th Street between Park and Lexington Avenues—212– 376–4477

1311 Broadway at 34th Street—212–736–4477

Filene's Basement:

620 Sixth Avenue at 18th Street—212–620–3100

2220 Broadway at 79th Street—212–873–8000

Loehmann's:

101 Seventh Avenue at 17th Street—212–352–0856

2807 East 21st Street, Brooklyn—718–368–1256

Syms:

42 Trinity Place—212–797–1199

400 Park Avenue at 54th Street—212–317–8200

T.J. Maxx:

620 Avenue of the Americas at 19th Street— 212–229–0875

Most of the **discount stores on Canal Street** around Broadway and Lafayette (see chapter on "General Merchandise Stores") carry one kind of shoe or another. Some have "brand-name" athletic shoes (emphasis on the quotations); some carry the real thing, albeit from two or three seasons ago. You can also find dress and casual shoes made from all kinds of materials—leather, "pleather" and canvas. The design is mostly utilitarian and has circa 1977 Soviet-issue style. You trade style for drastically low prices and a mere several seasons durability.

Today, If my agent Nancy were to ask me where to buy good shoes inexpensively, **Eitan's Bootery** (23 East 33rd Street near Madison Avenue—212–725–6240) would be the first words out

BEST BARGAIN

of my mouth. Eitan's carries women's all-leather shoes and boots made exclusively in Italy or Brazil that are obscenely inexpensive. The day I was there, most pairs were on sale for $9.99 and up to $19.99. The highest-priced model was a whopping $29.99. The styles range from dressy to casual pumps, business heels to sandals. I did not see many brand-names (the only two I recognized were Caressa and Nine West), but most were very attractive and appeared to be extremely well made. If I were a woman, this is where I would buy all my shoes.

Find Outlet specializing in women's very modish designer merchandise and season-old stock, has only a sparse selection of shoes, but like everything else in this store, they are pleasingly hip and remarkably inexpensive. New items arrive almost every day, so call or stop in whenever you are in the neighborhood (see chapter on "Clothing"). Two locations:

229 Mott Street between Prince & Springs Streets—
    212–226–5167
361 West 17th Street at Ninth Avenue—212–243–3177

The **Historic Orchard Street Shopping District** (Orchard Street and the surrounding area between East Houston and Canal Streets) has 30 quality leather goods shops, most with extraordinary prices on a variety of shoe styles. Give yourself a few hours to check out all the leather vendors in the neighborhood before making your final decision and don't be afraid to haggle. For maps and more information about this bargain shopping area, contact the Lower East Side Business Improvement District (261 Broome Street, New York, NY 10002—212–226–9010). Note: A lot of the stores in this district only accept cash.

At **Make 10 Ladies and Gents Shoewear Warehouse Store** (44 West 39th Street between Fifth and Sixth Avenues—212–391–2926), you can find lots of great looking designer men's and women's shoes for as little as $12, with a large selection at $20. Unlike most warehouse stores that sell low to

BEST BARGAIN

unload undesirable merchandise, the shoes here are classic in style and very fashionable.

Parade of Shoes, with seven stores throughout the city, is a haven for bargain shoppers of women's shoes. Sorry guys, this chain only sells women's styles . . . however, for those of you who are looking for a pair of pumps—and you know who you are—I'm sure they would be only too happy to help. Of the women I queried about the quality and style of Parade of Shoes' inventory, the response was overwhelmingly positive for these well made, inexpensive copies of the most recent designs. The consensus is that you can't do better than Parade of Shoes for last-for-a-season knockoffs. One friend said, "They're surprisingly cute for so cheap." Your local listings will tell you where to find the nearest store.

The inventory of men's and women's shoes at **Payless Shoe Source** is not at all *au courant* among the fashionistas, or anyone with any sense of style for that matter. What this store does do well is price—their shoes are cheap, cheap, cheap! At Payless, the adage holds true, you really do "get what you pay for." Check your phone book for the nearest location.

At **Pearl River Mart** (see chapter on "General Merchandise Stores") there are several aisles of shoes, mostly of the slipper and thong variety, that look well constructed and are cheaply priced—some are decorated with brocade or needlepoint and some are silk. In a section of 100 percent leather-upper and athletic shoes for men and women, none are at all fashionable, but they look solid and are cheap. Two locations:

> 277 Canal Street at Broadway—212–431–4770
> 200 Grand Street—212–966–1010

For unbelievably low prices on fashionable men's and women's shoes, bypass the main sales area of **Shoe Mania** (853 Broadway at 14th Street—212–253–8744) and go straight upstairs.

There you'll find a staggering selection, most by famous designers like Kenneth Cole, Mephisto, Ecco, Rockport, Dansko, Timberland, Merrell, Diesel, Puma, Clarks, Skechers, Camper, Bacco Bucci, Durango and BCBG Max Azria, at a fraction of the price of the shoes downstairs. I have no idea why these shoes are so deeply discounted as most are stylish, well made and comfortable. Go often as the selection changes constantly.

Zara, the Spanish retailer with stores worldwide (see "Clothing" chapter) has a petite selection of shoes, all fashion-forward and all made in Europe. They are mostly modestly priced but at the end of each season are clearance-reduced, some for as low as $19.99. Zara store locations:

580 Broadway near Prince Street—212–343–1725
750 Lexington Avenue at 59th Street—212–754–1120
39 West 34th Street near Fifth Avenue—212–868–6551
101 Fifth Avenue near 17th Street—212–741–0555

HANDBAGS AND ACCESSORIES

THE BARGAIN WOMEN'S CLOTHING shop, **Backwoods** (315 West 57th Street between 8th and 9th Avenues—212–459–2975), that is a favorite of several of my actress friends carries belts, scarves, purses and other accessories for its usual $10 to $30 prices, sometimes less. The accessories are "funky," "chic" and "cheap" too. Backwoods stock changes frequently so there's always something new to see and buy.

For shoppers with a lot of good karma, perseverance and a willingness to dig through mounds of merchandise, excellent bargains, especially on accessories, are to be had at **Barney's Warehouse Sale** (236 West 18th Street between Seventh and Eighth Avenues—212–826–8900). During this semi-annual New York fashion ritual, it's possible to find high-end designer belts, bags, scarves and ties for as little as $20. The Barney's Warehouse Sale takes place every February and August; call store for details. (For more information about the Barney's sale, see the "Clothing" chapter.)

BEST BARGAIN

A good deal of the commerce on **Canal Street** (known affectionately as "Avenue of the Counterfeits") between Lafayette and West Broadway is the sale of designer knockoffs, or what the police would less subtly classify as "contraband merchandise." Here for about $15 to $35, you can buy ersatz designer bags with labels like "Kate Spade," "Gucci," "Louis Vuitton" and "Prada." The bags look like the real thing but cost about a tenth of what you'd pay for the real thing. Unfortunately, you do get what you pay for, so don't expect that these will last you more than a few months.

The big **chains Gap**, **Banana Republic**, **Zara**, and **Old Navy** all carry a huge, ever-changing assortment of well-made, attractive and functional accessories and bags. Old Navy has, by far, the best everyday prices on such items, but the others have frequent sales where you can pick up anything from wallets and key chains to belts, hats, scarves, briefcases, backpacks, small luggage and jewelry for a song. For more information on these retailers, refer to the chapter on "Clothing."

Many of the **discount clothing stores**, including **Burlington Coat Factory, Century 21, Daffy's, Filene's Basement, Loehmann's, Syms** and **T.J. Maxx** (see "Clothing" chapter) carry lots of designer and non-designer handbags, as well as belts, wallets and other accessories at low to moderate prices. Most are styles from a season or so ago but are marked down by at least 30 percent from their original prices. On a recent expedition to each of these stores, I found handsome handbags for as little as $15, leather wallets starting at $8 and belts at $10. Store locations:

Burlington Coat Factory:
   707 Sixth Avenue at 23rd Street—212–229–1300

Century 21:
   22 Cortlandt Street—212–227–9092
   472 86th Street, Bay Ridge, Brooklyn—718–748–3266

Daffy's:
   111 Fifth Avenue at 18th Street—212–529–4477
   462 Broadway at Grand Street—212–334–7444
   335 Madison Avenue at 43rd Street—212–557–4422
   125 East 57th Street between Park and Lexington
      Avenues—212– 376–4477
   1311 Broadway at 34th Street—212–736–4477

Filene's Basement:
   620 Sixth Avenue at 18th Street—212–620–3100
   2220 Broadway at 79th Street—212–873–8000

Loehmann's:

101 Seventh Avenue at 17th Street—212–352–0856

2807 East 21st Street, Brooklyn—718–368–1256

Syms:

42 Trinity Place—212–797–1199

400 Park Avenue at 54th Street—212–317–8200

T.J. Maxx:

620 Avenue of the Americas at 19th Street—212–229–0875

Find Outlet, that specializes in women's designer labels and high-end season-old stock at 50–80 percent off the original prices, carries a small selection of accessories. Like everything else in this store, the belts, handbags and scarves are pleasingly hip and remarkably inexpensive. New items arrive almost every day, so check regularly (see chapter on "Clothing"). Two locations:

229 Mott Street between Prince & Springs Streets—
     212–226–5167

361 West 17th Street at Ninth Avenue—212–243–3177

The goods at **Gift Show** (231 Canal Street between Centre and Baxter Streets—212–334–8760) are a step above those carried at the numerous Canal Street vendors of designer-impostor labeled handbags. For a few dollars more than its neighbors, Gift Show sells unique, better-made fakes that are fashionable, functional and will last almost as long as the originals.

Rhinestones are a girl's best friend at **Girlprops.com** (153 Prince Street near Broadway—212–505–7615 and 203 Spring Street at Sullivan Streets—212–625–8323). This very fun and very cheap accessory shop in Soho is packed with glittery and gleaming items for girls of all ages. Where else can you find fake fur hats, day-glo purses, faux leopard print gloves, rainbow hued boas, colored hair spray, wigs in wild shades like chartreuse and lavender, body glitter, fishnet leggings and tons of bejeweled belts, bobby pins, headbands, necklaces, bracelets and earrings, for prices that start as low as $1? There is a lot of kitsch here, but there's also a lot of stuff your mom would be happy to wear.

Great Value (23 East 33rd Street—212-889-5792) carries a huge assortment of belts, handbags, backpacks, canvas messenger bags, belts, wallets, leather watchbands, ties (which I don't recommend—UGLY!), sunglasses, costume jewelry and luggage, all at deep discount prices. "Designer handbags from New York, Italy, Spain and Paris" (as their sign outside says) start at about $30. Most everything here, besides the aforementioned ties, is of exceptional quality, style and price.

The Swedish chain **H&M** landed in New York and immediately won us over with its ultra-hip/cool/trendy clothes at ultra-cheap prices. This arbiter of "fashion and quality at the best price" has a huge line of inexpensive, stylish accessories for men and women that includes wallets, backpacks, fanny packs, handbags, sunglasses, jewelry, belts, gloves, hats, scarves and watches. Prices for many of these items start as low as $3 and don't go too much higher. (See my chapter on "Clothing.") Check your local listing for the nearest H&M location.

Beyond clothing and shoes, the **Historic Orchard Street Shopping District** (Orchard Street and the surrounding area between East Houston and Canal Streets) has 30 quality leather goods shops, most with extraordinary prices on a range of accessory items from hats and bags to purses, belts, and wallets. Allow time to check out all the leather vendors in the neighborhood before you make your final decision. On a recent foray into the area, I found well-made bags as low as $40. (See my chapter on "Clothing" for more information on this district.)

In tourist-heavy areas around the city, you will see groups of people who sell handbags right on the sidewalk. You may have seen them the last time you were on your way to Bloomingdale's, Carnegie Hall, a Broadway show or in Soho. While hawking their goods, they always seem to be a little distracted; don't mind them, they're just watching for approaching police. You see, these bags are all faux versions of very expensive designers brands like Calvin Klein, Liz Claiborne, Gucci, Kate Spade, Louis Vuitton, and Prada. As most are counterfeits, their quality is not great, but they look like the real thing, and isn't that all that matters? Prices range from $15 to $45 for these bags, whose real counterpart would go for ten times these prices. These guys "set up shop" all over town, but concentrate their presence in the tourist areas, usually right next to the merchants who are selling "designer" wristwatches and sunglasses. Note: These vendors only accept cash. (See my chapter on "Sunglasses.") The four areas where I've encountered them most frequently are:

→ the Upper East Side on Lexington Avenue around 60th Street in front of, or across the street from, Bloomingdale's

→ on lower Broadway, between Canal and Houston

→ on Seventh Avenue and Broadway in the theater district, especially an hour or so before a performance

→ around or in front of Carnegie Hall and the neighboring hotels

The **Sock Man** (27 St. Marks Place near Second Avenue— 212–529–0300) carries exactly what you'd expect—socks. His brands and styles range from athletic to business/casual and prints of every color, thickness and design you could possibly want, at prices that are easily half what you'd find at department stores. Besides your basic socks, he also carries anklets, tights, hosiery, garters, thigh-highs, leg warmers and toe socks in all sizes, for all ages.

Most of my socks come from the **sock vendor** at the Sunday **Greenflea Market at I.S. 44** (Columbus and 76th Street—

212–721–0900). He sells every style, color and brand imaginable at very reasonable prices. (See the chapter on "Flea Markets.")

For plain old white athletic socks, you can't beat the **sock guy** who sets up a card table on the west side of Ninth Avenue between 42nd and 43rd Streets every weekday from about 3 P.M. on. He has good quality merchandise (he also sells underwear) at unbelievable prices—3 pairs for $5 or six pairs of tube socks for $5.

The tiny East Village shop, **Tompkins Square Studio** (147 Avenue A between St. Marks Place and 7th Street—212–477–9578), has a huge array of handbags and purses at very low prices. Here you'll find cloth, leather or microfiber designer samples and closeouts for as low as $7 and no higher than $24. They also have a large selection of cheap, funky bags that are beaded or embroidered. Be sure to check out their popular line of campy change wallets (just $7) that have 3-D pictures of the Last Supper or Pope John Paul.

LEATHER GOODS

WHEN BUYING LEATHER, remember one rule—there is no shame in haggling. Leather dealers expect it. What a boon for consumers who hope to score some skin for very little scratch. (See "Haggling" chapter.)

Domsey's (431 Broadway at Hughes Street, Williamsburg, Brooklyn—718–384–6000), that vast warehouse of discount used clothing, carries lots of vintage leather jackets that are dirt-cheap. Because everything here is used, the selection and condition of a lot of the merchandise can be "iffy," but diligence is rewarded; the more you dig, the more likely you are to find a great, low-priced jacket. If you are at all allergic, take your Sudafed before going, as this place is dusty.

The city's **Garment District** (from 34th to 41st Streets between Seventh and Eighth Avenues) has innumerable leather goods shops whose windows are filled with "too-good-to-be-true" deals on all kinds of leather items. Sure, there's a lot of tacky stuff in those windows, but there are also some good-looking coats and jackets (with prices starting as low as $59.99) as well as handbags and shoes. The harder you look in this neighborhood, the more apt you are to find what you want; and the more open you are to haggling, the more likely you are to arrive at a very low price.

The **Historic Orchard Street Shopping District** (Orchard Street and the surrounding area between East Houston and Canal Streets) comes into its own with 30 quality leather goods shops, and most with extraordinary prices on a number of items from coats and jackets to skirts, pants, shoes, hats, bags, purses,

BEST BET

belts, wallets and other accessories. Take your time to check out all the leather vendors in the neighborhood. Choose your two or three favorite items and then haggle mercilessly with the proprietors (they all expect it) until you arrive at a price that you are willing to pay. (See "Clothing" chapter for information about the Orchard Street area.)

Leather Friends Jackets (142 Orchard Street—212–420–8038) sells its entire stock of men's and women's leather jackets for just $99.99. The jackets here are attractive, appear to be made of good leather and look like they are well crafted. Leather Friends also carries a wide range of bags (all sell for $50 each), belts and other fine leather accessories.

Several **shops on Broadway between 11th and Canal Streets** carry very fashionable leather goods at discount prices. These shops are not above haggling with you and will often reduce the price of an item even more if you pay cash. Wander up and down Broadway and comparison-shop before making your final purchase—this way you can pit one store against another ("So-and-so is selling the same jacket for $30 cheaper, can you do any better?"). It always works.

For only $99.99, **Urban Leather Outlet** (275 Seventh Avenue at 25th Street—212–727–7810) sells women's and men's fashionable leather and suede jackets in several styles including bombers, three-quarter lengths, and sport coats. There are leather jackets that start as low as $69.99, but trust me, you don't want to be seen in those. For the extra $30, you will be the height of fashion and look like you spent a lot more. Urban Leather Outlet also carries low-priced leather pants, hats, gloves, and summer sandals. The latter were on sale the day I was there at a very reasonable $9.99 a pair, or two pairs for $14.99. Look for Urban Leather Outlet's occasional ads in the *Village Voice* that offer discount coupons worth $25 to $50 off most merchandise for even greater savings.

MAKEUP

IN OUR BUSINESS, MAKEUP IS A MUST—and not just for women. On occasion, we men are also in need of a bit of "slap." Although the majority of male actors don't use makeup on stage anymore, there are times when it is called for—some character parts of course, but also when we have to look older (if you're 40 and playing Lear you'll be using makeup) or younger (40 and playing Romeo???); or, when we have to look better (Romeo) or worse (hopefully at 40 you don't look like Lear).

Too, there are those auditions and interviews when it is advantageous to disguise the previous night's drinking binge or the consumption of too much chocolate. I have a scar under my right eye, the result of being kicked in the face with an ice skate while playing hockey when I was 13 years old. In person, it is almost imperceptible. On camera however, it is quite prominent. Several years ago, my commercial agent, Tracy, noticed the scar and recommended a product that she said would conceal "problem areas" without being at all conspicuous. I dashed to The Makeup Center where they showed me the proper way to apply it with great results. Now I never go on a commercial audition without it. Lucky for us, there are all kinds of places in New York where women and men can buy quality theatrical and street makeup at great discount prices:

Because it caters to the theatrical industry and professional makeup artists, everything at **Alcone** (235 West 19th Street—212–633–0551) is always discounted. Alcone's great appeal is that it carries brands not found in any other stores, such as Visiora, RCMA and Kryolan, and has a website where anything from its stock can be ordered (www.alconeco.com). Alcone sells popular theatrical brands like Ben Nye and Mehron, as well as removers, sponges, powder puffs, and palettes. If it is special effects makeup you want, this is the place to go; Alcone has the definitive selection of latex, blood products, bruise kits and scar-making materials in the city. No proof of professional status is needed.

The **Aveda** beauty emporium in Soho (233 Spring Street between Varick Street and Avenue of the Americas—212-807-1492) carries its own exclusive line of makeup and hair-/body-/skin-care products, all engineered from plant and flower extracts. Many favor these products for their purity and for the absence of alcohol and other harsh chemicals. Aveda offers all eligible actors (you must present either a union card, picture and resume, portfolio or a composite card as well as a picture ID) a 30 percent discount for most purchases; not included in the discount are accessories, applicators, vitamins and candles. Although Aveda has several stores throughout the city, the 30 percent discount is only good at the Spring Street location.

The socially conscious **Body Shop** chain is world famous for giving a portion of their proceeds to help disadvantaged peoples and endangered areas like the South American rainforest. Their environment-friendly bath and beauty aids and makeup are already moderately priced, but often greatly reduced during sales and promotions. Eleven stores throughout Manhattan; check your phone book for the nearest location.

Just a hop and a skip from the theater district is **Cosmetic Market** (9 East 39th Street—212-725-3625), which has to be the city's cheapest place for both name brand and drugstore variety makeup. Although the goods at Cosmetic Market cannot be categorized as the most up-to-the-minute, must-have products, the selection is vast and eclectic and includes every kind of beauty item from makeup and perfume to creams, lo-

BEST BARGAIN

tions and grooming aids. Not everything here is perfect; some of the packaging is battered; many of the items are sloppily displayed and there seems to be a lot of discontinued merchandise; but with prices this low (lipsticks, nail polish and the like for as little as $1), who cares about displays or packaging? (Cosmetic Market carries a big assortment of gift items too like picture frames, books, candles, imported olive oil, dolls, Christmas ornaments, purses, dop kits and name brand candies like Droste, Guylian, Saronno, Perugina and Rocher, also at low prices.)

H&M, the cheap yet trendy Swedish clothing store (see chapter on "Clothing"), carries its own line of makeup. Like everything else here, H&M's quality for makeup is very good and the price very inexpensive. Check your local listing for the nearest location.

Not as generous as many of the other makeup stores in the city, **Bob Kelly Cosmetics** (151 West 46th Street, Room 902—212–819–0030, ext. 17) does offer actors a 10 percent discount off all Bob Kelly Theatrical professional makeup. This is the makeup you probably used when you started out as an actor, and there is still no better theatrical base or crème stick on the market. You must show your union card or picture and resume, to be eligible for the discount

On payment of an annual fee of $35, **MAC Cosmetics** stores offer performers a generous 30 percent discount on all products through their "Preferred Professionals" program. To be eligible, you must present photo identification and any two of the following: composite card, valid union card, head shot, program/press materials with name credit, contract on production company letterhead or crew/cast call list on production company letterhead. There are two MAC locations:

14 Christopher Street at Gay Street—212–243–4150
767 Fifth Avenue at 22nd Street—212–677–6611

The **Makeup Center** (150 West 55th Street—212–977–9494) stocks a large assortment of theatrical makeup by Ben Nye, Stein's and Mehron as well as a full line of special effects products such as bald caps, stage blood, blood capsules, crepe hair, latex and glitter. The Makeup Center features its own line of theatrical and regular makeup. By presenting a membership card from any of the acting unions, actors receive a 30 percent discount on all sales.

The French beauty chain **Sephora**, new in town, is already considered the best in Manhattan. Their signature black and white design and ambient lighting makes their stores very inviting, and they stock an extensive array of name-brand cosmetics as well as skin and hair care products. Sephora is not necessarily cheap, but their line of cosmetics is fairly inexpensive and I am told, very good. Seven locations citywide; check your listings for store nearest you.

SUNGLASSES

IF YOU WANT HIGH-QUALITY, stylish designer sunglasses that are the real thing, not what Canal Street and the guys in front of Bloomingdale's are hawking, with excellent UV protection, but you don't want to pay Saks Fifth Avenue prices, you cannot beat the selection at **Century 21** (see chapter on "Clothing"). You won't find $5 sunglasses here (unless there is a clearance sale), but for anywhere from $20 to $100, you will find great, sturdily constructed styles for less than half what you'd pay at the leading department stores.

> 22 Cortlandt Street at Chambers Street—212–227–9092
> 472 86th Street, Bay Ridge, Brooklyn—718–748–3266

BEST BARGAIN

At **H&M** (see chapter on "Clothing") you can find yourself some *way cool* sunglasses for prices that even the street vendors and Canal Street can't compete with. Starting as low as $3.49 a pair, you can find a multitude of shades that are probably a bit better constructed than the street variety. Check your local listing for the nearest H&M store locations.

Look for groups of **merchants in tourist-heavy areas** who sell sunglasses right on the sidewalk. You may have seen them on your way to Bloomingdale's, Carnegie Hall, a Broadway show or in Soho. They carry their goods in large squares of fabric. Why the fabric you wonder? Well not only is it used as a simple and tasteful background to display the sunglasses, but more importantly, it can be folded up in the blink of an eye if the vendor spots a cop in the vicinity. These sunglasses are all counterfeits of expensive designer brands like Armani, Calvin Klein, Claiborne, Gucci, Ray Ban and Bollé. In the nature of counterfeits, their quality is not great, but they look like the real thing, they come in cases that look like the real thing and they are real cheap, with prices anywhere from $10 to $25. You can usually find these guys selling their wares right next to the "designer" wristwatch and handbag sellers (see my chapter on "Handbags and Accessories"). These sellers "set up shop" all over town but tend to concentrate in tourist areas listed in the "Handbag" chapter.

The **stalls on St. Mark's Place** (between Second and Third Avenues) and many **busy street corners** are year-round sunglasses emporiums. For as little as $5, and depending on your taste, you can buy yourself, hip, conservative, or utilitarian sunglasses. Don't expect a lot of UV protection and don't expect that they will last very long, but hey, they are only $5. You are sure to find a pair that makes you look great, and let's face it, isn't that really more important than a few ultraviolet rays?

The **stalls and stores on Canal Street** are another good bet for finding cheap sunglasses. Here you will see a lot of the same goods as on St. Mark's Place and at the street fairs, and the bulk of what you find is counterfeit, laughably fake. It always amazes me that some of the Canal Street merchants have the *cojones* to represent such patently false junk as the true-blue, honest-to-God thing, when the plastic on the frames is flimsy, the logos appear to be haphazardly glued on to the temple-pieces, and the lenses are so fragile that they look like *they* need protection from the sun. If you can get past the cheapness and the fact that they probably provide less UV protection than if you were not wearing sunglasses at all, there are some fun styles to be found here for very little cash.

FURNITURE

SETTING UP A HOME IS A COSTLY but necessary nuisance. To exist with any semblance of comfort, we need a few basics like a bed, a chair, a bookcase, a table and something to throw some clothes into. Before laying out a lot of cash, I recommend two ways to acquire furniture that won't cost anything at all.

First, go hunt for discarded pieces. A favorite pastime of many New Yorkers is to comb through trash bins and stoop and curbside garbage piles for cast-off furniture. Believe it or not, there are a lot of treasures to be found on the street. Wander around the city on trash pickup day or the night before and take a good look at the garbage. Newcomers will be surprised at the incredible things New Yorkers throw away. Often these pieces are in impeccable condition—just no longer wanted by their original owners—and once they hit the street, they are fair game for the first to stake claim to them. Although reluctant to admit it, most young urbanites, myself included (when I *was* young), have, or have had, a piece or two of refuse furniture.

Second, network with friends and colleagues. In our cramped city quarters, people can't afford to hold onto furniture they don't need—they don't have space for it. So, mention to everyone you know that you're looking for furniture. You may find from among those you have alerted, some will be only too happy to part with what they no longer want or have room for. Over half of the contents of my first city apartment were hand-me-down pieces, and all served me well until I could afford the things I wanted.

If neither of these alternatives is appealing, or you've grown tired of living with other people's tastes, it's time to go shopping. Hopefully the following will help keep you from breaking the bank:

Greenpoint Used Clothing and Furniture Warehouse (460 Driggs Avenue between 10th and 11th Streets in Brooklyn—718–599–4017) is an enormous place stuffed to the rafters with, yes, you guessed it, used clothing and furniture. All kinds of gems are to be found here, most in very good shape and for very little money. If your thing is priceless antiques at bargain prices, go somewhere else (and if there is such a place, please tell me), but if you're in the market either for newish stuff or vintage pieces, you'll have lots to choose from. The inventory here changes constantly, so check in periodically.

IKEA (Elizabeth Center, New Jersey—908–289–4488), the Sweden based furniture company, with superstores throughout the world, is a godsend for dorm room dwellers, new homeowners and fresh-off-the-bus émigrés to the big city. IKEA's corporate philosophy is to offer a wide range of well designed, comfortable, functional and durable home furnishing products at prices so low that as many people as possible will be able to afford them. On this promise, IKEA delivers the goods. The IKEA store is a marvel of home furnishing products, a whopping 12,000 in all, with something for every room and every taste at prices that are unbelievably low. Hands down, this is the city's least expensive outlet for attractive, quality furniture. (Okay, there isn't actually a store in New York City, but a free IKEA shuttle bus leaves from and returns to the Port Authority bus station several times each Saturday and Sunday). How do they thrive selling stuff so cheap? They buy in bulk and require you to schlep it home and assemble it yourself. (Lugging some of that stuff on the bus isn't pretty. I once bought two 4-foot-tall bookcases that I had to drag home from the bus by myself . . . living two blocks from Port Authority does have its rewards!) But for the money you save, it's definitely worth it. That free IKEA shuttle departs every 30 minutes from 10 A.M. to 2:30 P.M. Saturdays and Sundays from Port Authority Bus Terminal, Gate 5, and returns every 30 minutes from 12 noon to 6 P.M. Call 800–Bus–IKEA for more information.

BEST BARGAIN

Props for Today (330 West 34th Street between Eighth and Ninth Avenues—212–244–9600) has an eclectic assortment of affordable furniture and decorative items ranging from over-sized and overstuffed sofas, to "shabby chic" sectionals, stark metal dining tables, Empire style chairs, pinecone shaped candles, Adirondack picture frames, classical busts, and gaudy gold mirrors. Why such a hodgepodge of goods and why so cheap? Props for Today's main business is renting out furnishings for photography, film and parties. Most of what you find here has been used in commercials, magazine ads, films shot in the area, and New York based TV shows and soaps. Once these props are no longer needed (the film has wrapped, the ad is shot, the TV show's designer gives the set a facelift), and Props for Today has determined they cannot be recycled, they end up in their retail outlet. Although a lot of the stuff is technically "used," it is in excellent condition. Better yet, it is priced to move. Who knows, you could walk away with Erica Kane's sofa, "Mango's" nightstand, or a chair that Starr Jones sat in. The inventory here is always changing, so you may want to stop in whenever you are in the neighborhood. Props for Today does hold occasional sales when they open their upstairs warehouse to the public; most of the contents are sold at unbelievable prices (call for dates or ask to be put on their mailing list).

Straight From the Crate's merchandise is ideal for people who are outfitting a new home on a budget. Although the stuff is glorified dorm room furniture, it is attractive, functional, sturdily built and inexpensive. You can furnish every room from this store's inventory of office furniture, dining tables, and all kinds of chairs, armoires, bookcases, entertainment centers, CD/DVD racks, coffee tables, futon frames and lamps. Recent bargains included a computer workstation on coasters for $149; a halogen torch lamp with bulb for $39; a 5-drawer dresser for $159; a 24-inch solid wood stool for $30; a 2-tier tech trolley for $69; and a 60-inch heavy steel CD rack for $99.

114 First Avenue at 61st Street—212–838–8486

261 Madison Avenue at 38th Street—212–867–4050

1251 Lexington Avenue between 84th and 85th Streets—
212–717–4227

161 West 72nd Street between Columbus and Amsterdam
Avenues—212–579–6494

464 Park Avenue South at 37th Street—212–725–5383

50 West 23rd Street between Fifth and Sixth Avenues—
212–243–1844

An ideal way to save money on furniture (and exercise some creativity at the same time) is to buy unfinished pieces and paint or varnish them yourself. Several stores in the city offer excellent savings on **unfinished furniture** for every room in your home, and have a variety of styles and woods to choose from. If you're useless with a paintbrush, for an extra charge, the furniture can be finished for you.

The mother of all unfinished furniture stores is **Gothic Cabinet Craft** with its 25 retail outlets throughout the five boroughs. Here you will find a huge selection of inexpensive tables, chairs, dressers, desks, bookcases, beds, entertainment centers, and even mattresses by Sealy and Serta. If you don't see what you want, Gothic can custombuild a piece to your specifications at an affordable price. Gothic's solid wood dressers start as low as $99; pine bookcases at $38; 3-drawer pine Captain's beds at $125 (birch are $229); pine platform beds at $89; and nightstands at $69. Gothic Cabinet Craft has periodic sales and more frequent coupon specials (look for their ads in *The Village Voice*). Consult your phone book for the nearest Gothic Cabinet Craft location.

Innovative Woodwork (355 Third Avenue at 26th Street—212–683–2127) claims that they stock the largest variety of unpainted solid wood furniture available for same day or next day delivery in New York. It is hard to imagine that they have a larger selection than Gothic Cabinet Craft, but as their prices are comparable, I will forgive them the hyperbole. Among the many bargains I saw on a recent trip to Innovative, a solid butcher-block drop-leaf dining table was $199; a 7-drawer Aspen wood dresser was $349; a solid pine storage chest was $119.99; and a 4-drawer desk was $229. They carry a large assortment of book-cases in a variety of sizes and woods (pine, maple and oak), and do custom orders at discounted prices.

Mike's Furniture Store (520 Amsterdam Avenue at 85th Street—212–873–1336) on the Upper West Side sells excel-lently crafted and reasonably priced finished and unfin-ished furniture, such as tables, chairs, bookcases, computer and entertainment centers, beds and wall units. Mike's car-ries a large group of furnishings for kids and babies. They also do special orders.

Although you probably won't be furnishing your new home from New York's premier (and expensive) furniture stores, like ABC Carpet and Home, Domain, Maurice Villency, Roche Bobois, E.J. Audi, and Palazzetti, these emporiums periodically hold **warehouse sales** where a lot of unsold and "as is" items go for a fraction of their list prices. To reach the warehouses, you usually have to schlep out to some obscure corner of Brooklyn, Queens or Long Island, but the savings are worth the trip and the quality is always very high. These sales are usually advertised in the "House & Home" or front-page sec-tions of *The New York Times*, but you can also call the store and inquire when they will be held.

ABC Carpet & Home: 888 Broadway at 19th Street—212–473–3000

E.J Audi: 160 Fifth Avenue at 21st Street—
212–337–0700

Roche Bobois: 200 Madison Avenue at 35th Street—
212–725–5513

Domain: 938 Broadway at 22nd Street—212–228–7450

Palazzetti: 515 Madison Avenue at 53rd Street—
212–832–1199

Maurice Villency: 949 Third Avenue at 57th Street—
212–725–4840

MATTRESSES

BUYING A MATTRESS IS NOT EASY. There are countless brands and models to choose from as well as stores that sell them. Furthermore, everyone claims to have the lowest prices, but it is nearly impossible to comparison shop. The same Serta model at Sleepy's is given a completely different name at Macys's and a different name again at 1–800–Mattres, and so on. Prices vary wildly from store to store. And then there are those constant nagging TV newsmagazine exposés about mattress retailers who are covering old mattresses with new fabric and selling them to unsuspecting consumers. What's a shopper to do?

First, steer clear of the 1–800–mattres merchants. I don't infer that they sell a shoddy product, or that they have exorbitant prices. Generally, the opposite is true. The problem with these phone retailers is, you don't know what you're getting. You must go into a store and try out several mattresses, to determine which is the most comfortable, which gives the best support, and which will help you get a good night's sleep.

Next, visit a few showrooms. Since it's impossible to comparison shop by make and model, you will have to do it by feel and comfort. Once you have narrowed down the two or three mattresses that suit you, don't be afraid to haggle—play one retailer against another. Tell the salesman at store B, "I like this bed, but a similar one at store A was $100 dollars cheaper. What can you do for me?" This may make you uncomfortable, but mattress salespeople expect it.

Finally, make sure you shop in stores that have some longevity in the business, a good selection of mattresses to choose from and positive customer feedback. The following merchants fall in this category and all offer bedding at affordable prices as well as free or cheap delivery and set-up.

Sleepy's, which has been in business for eighty years, claims to carry the world's largest selection of name brand mattresses at the lowest prices. They back up this statement with their "Incredible Price Guarantee" offer that if you find the same mattress for less, anywhere, Sleepy's guarantees to beat the price or you get your purchase free plus $500. As I note above, though, it is often difficult to prove this, as like mattresses are given different names at the various retailers. Sleepy's reassured me that they use "comparison charts" to determine which of their mattresses are comparable to those carried in other stores. In fact, Sleepy's doesn't beat Town Bedding (see below) when it comes to price (Sleepy's explains that Town Bedding models are mostly from last season, which is true enough, even though Town's merchandise is brand-new and top-of-the-line), but they come close. Sleepy's does outdo Town Bedding when it comes to selection and brands; they carry Aireloom, Serta, Sealy, Back Care, Kingsdown, Stearns & Foster, Spring Air, Simmons Beauty Rest, Masterpiece and Chatham & Wells. Besides their low prices and selection, Sleepy's offers customers "when you want it" delivery, removal of old bedding and a 60 day home trial exchange policy. Look in your phone book for the nearest of Sleepy's 16 city locations.

Located in the center of Chelsea's self-consciously glamorous emporiums, restaurants, cafes and male boutiques, **Town Bedding** (205 Eighth Avenue between 20th and 21st Streets— 212–243–0426) is an eyesore. What a dump! If you can get past Town Bedding's defiant lack of décor, organization and cleanliness, you can find yourself a great bed, futon or sofa bed for very little money. Town Bedding does not carry a lot of stock, but what they do carry (Serta, Simmons, Continental, Therapedic and Spring Air) is very good and much less expensive than their competitors. You can save literally $100 to

BEST BARGAIN

$200 on a mattress comparable to what you would find anywhere else. Town Bedding offers an unconditional money back guarantee on all its merchandise, provides free delivery in the five boroughs, and will remove your old bed at no charge. Better still, the salesmen could not be more laid back; actually, lethargic would be an apt description, the opposite of high-pressure salespeople.

If sleeping on a **futon** is your thing, there are many stores in the metropolitan area that carry this inexpensive option to conventional mattresses. Several advertise in *The Village Voice* and often have sales or offer discount coupons:

Canal Furniture (402 Broadway, one block north of Canal Street—212–925–5343) has four floors of futons and contemporary furniture at competitive prices.

Futon Furniture Center carries futons, frames, loft beds, tatami beds and thousands of covers. Five locations in Brooklyn and Manhattan:

    265 West 72nd Street near Broadway—212–712–2133
    373 Third Avenue at 27th Street—212–683–1717
    51 West 14th Street between Fifth and Sixth Avenues—
        212–727–1252
    37 West 14th Street between Fifth and Sixth Avenues—
        212–243–1774
    309 Vandervoort Avenue, Brooklyn—718–782–2557

Not only does **Futonland** have a large selection of frames, futons, covers, pillows and throws, they offer same-day delivery and free assembly. Three locations:

    730 Amsterdam Avenue between 95th and 96th Streets—
        212–663–8454
    89–12 Queens Boulevard, Queens—718–779–5766
    55–18 Myrtle Avenue, Queens—718–497–5181

Futon Plus (375 Broadway at White Street—212–941–1384) offers low-priced futons, frames and living room sets as well as same-day delivery and free assembly.

Futon Warehouse (113 University Place at 13th Street—212–473–6567), the store where there is "always a sale," advertises itself as having the largest selection of futons in New York. You'd be hard-pressed to argue with them. The stock here is immense. In addition to futons, they sell frames, covers, pillows, shelving, tables, chairs and bookcases; a clearance center is on their second level.

HOUSEWARES

LOCATED IN THE NEWLY SPRUCED UP meatpacking district, **Bodum Café and Home Store** (413–415 West 14th Street between Ninth and Tenth Avenues—800–232–6386) has to be the city's most whimsical housewares retailer. The shop's credo is, "Good design should not be expensive"; it could also be, "Good design should not be dull." There's nothing here that isn't brightly colored as well as being artfully designed, and completely practical. Best of all, this stuff is cheap: Bodum's famous Caffettiera coffee maker is $14.95; multihued tissue boxes are $4.95 to $5.95; wastebaskets start at $5.95; shopping trolleys are $9.95; beech paper towel holders are $9.95; nail brushes are $1.95; a set of four punch glasses are $4.95; and bast place mats are $1.95 each. If you need office supplies, look no further: you can pick up a lemon-colored paper-clip holder for $2.95, a cherry-hued stapler for $2.95, a blueberry pencil sharpener for $1.95 and a pomegranate tape dispenser for $1.95. The bathroom isn't forgotten with a huge line of gadgets and linens as well as closet organizing systems. Breeze through the back clearance area, which is swarming with extra-cheap home necessities, and once you've finished shopping, grab a cup of coffee and a nibble at the Bodum Café.

Catering to master chefs and civilian gourmands, **Broadway Panhandler** (477 Broome Street at Wooster Street—212–966–3434) carries the best tools of the cooking and baking trades. Appealing to such a discerning demographic, the inventory, unfortunately, is composed of mostly high-end items at high-end prices. But city foodies are in luck because there are constant sales, clearances and promotions where a large portion of the merchandise is discounted from 10 percent to 50 percent below regular prices.

As far as home necessities go, the inventories at **Filene's Basement** and **T.J. Maxx** are pretty slim pickings. If you're in the market for inexpensive home décor items, both are worth a browse. They do have vases, picture frames, pillows, candles and candleholders, as well as some not very useful stuff that someone with little taste thought was quite tasteful. T.J.'s has inexpensively priced bath towels (large bath sheets by Polo Home were only $7.99), and Filene's is noteworthy for its assortment of affordable glassware, stemware (some cut crystal) and dinnerware (a 20-piece place setting for four of "Blue Willow" china was only $29.99).

Filene's Basement:
620 Sixth Avenue at 18th Street—212–620–3100
2220 Broadway at 79th Street—212–873–8000

T.J. Maxx:
620 Avenue of the Americas at 19th Street—
212–229–0875)

Fishs Eddy's two New York locations feature inexpensive new and never used vintage china and glassware. Appealing to diners with a sense of humor, most of the stock here has been gathered from stores, restaurants, golf and country clubs, universities, ocean-liners, government institutions and manufacturers. I saw logos decorating a wide array of china recently that included "Petroleum Club of Maitland," "Migis Lodge on Sebago Lake," "Isla Del Sol Yacht and Country Club," and "Four Diamond Award Dinner—Black Point Inn Resort." Fishs Eddy also features sets of reasonably priced dishware with zany border patterns like a ticker tape, baseball lingo, the Manhattan skyline (including the World Trade Center), a checkerboard and the San Francisco skyline. This store's best bargains are on its basic white china: mugs are $1.50

each, bowls and dinner plates are $3.50, bread plates are $1.25 and cups are $1.95. Fishs Eddy locations:

889 Broadway at 19th Street—212–420–9020
2176 Broadway at 77th Street—212–873–8819

For myriad household items that you don't want to spend a lot on, check out the various cheap **general merchandise** and **99¢ stores** such as **Conway** or **Odd-Job.** (See "General Merchandise Stores" for a complete listing.)

Home To Go (89 Chambers Street) carries towels, sheets, pillows, curtains, tablecloths and place mats, items for the bathroom and some kitchen and cooking supplies at very cheap prices. Cotton bath towels start at 99¢, twin-size poly-cotton sheet sets start at $7.99.

The giant home furnishings superstore **IKEA** (Elizabeth Center, New Jersey—908–289–4488) has an enormous housewares section, which carries just about everything (except appliances) that a home would ever need. Like everything at IKEA, these home necessities, gadgets and decorative items are attractively designed, functional and incredibly inexpensive—probably the least expensive in New York (okay, as I already mentioned, IKEA isn't actually in New York, but you can get there easily by the free shuttle bus). For details on the IKEA bus, call 800–Bus–IKEA. (For more information on IKEA, see the "Furniture" chapter.)

Situated in the center of 14th Street's "Cheap Pan Alley," **Jonas Department Store** (40 West 14th Street between Fifth and Sixth Avenues—212–242–8253) carries an array of inexpensive household items. I wouldn't recommend using it to shop for small kitchen appliances, as the brands and prices here are only so-so. What you can find are cheap linens for the bed, bath and kitchen. Sheet sets start as low as $9.99; one entire wall is covered with not particularly eye-catching but definitely serviceable curtains and window treatments costing only a few dollars; hand towels start at 99¢ and bath towels about $4 each.

Kaufman Electrical Appliances (365 Grand Street between Essex and Norfolk Streets—212-475-8313), an obscure, dumpy little shop on the Lower East Side, has amazing prices on all kinds of small appliances. Some examples: a half-gallon PUR water filter was $15; a Toastmaster toaster was also $15; a Remington men's automatic precision personal groomer was $20; a mini Dirt Devil vacuum cleaner was $35; a Braun 10-cup coffee maker was $30; a Salton hot air popcorn maker was $14; a small Cuisinart food processor was $28; a Braun Oral-B plaque remover/automatic toothbrush was $25; and a cappuccino maker was $25. Kaufman also has a large selection of stainless steel flatware starting at $10 for a 20-piece set, and fine china place settings that sell at close to wholesale.

Kmart devotes thousands of square feet to inexpensive housewares, from kitchen gadgets and small appliances to bedding, linens, towels, cookware, glassware, dishes and curtains. What Kmart does really well, and sells at great prices, is their complete line of Martha Stewart products for the home. Martha's 100 percent cotton sheets and towels are the least expensive I've found, are excellent quality and are frequently put on sale for even greater savings. My entire apartment is painted with Martha Stewart brand paints purchased at Kmart. She offers hundreds of colors (256 to be exact), provides swatches that recommend which colors go well together and even a how-to book that demonstrates the proper way to paint a room. From my experience, the quality of the paint is very good; it has not faded, cracked or peeled, and it is washable. Best of all, it's really cheap and goes on sale all the time. Martha's latest Kmart venture is a line of inexpensive home organizers. Everything to get your office, kitchen, bathroom, closet and desk into Type A order can be found here, and all reasonably priced. (See "General Merchandise Stores.") Kmart store locations:

One Pennsylvania Plaza on 34th Street between Seventh
and Eighth Avenues—212–760–1188
770 Broadway at Astor Place—212–673–1540

The Bowery, between Grand and Delancey Streets, is the lighting center of the city. Here you will find dozens of retailers selling their wares at discount, contractor and even wholesale prices. My favorite is **Lighting by Gregory** (158 Bowery—212–226–1276). A huge 4-store complex staffed by helpful experts that carries (or can get for you very quickly) just about any brand or type of lighting fixture you desire. Their prices are several dollars below retail.

Contrary to what you might think, **Macy's** (151 West 34th Street between Sixth and Seventh Avenues—212–695–4400), the "biggest store in the world," has great prices on its huge assortment of kitchen tools and small appliances, pots and pans, baking utensils, vacuum cleaners, bathroom electronics, dinnerware, bed linens, curtains, towels and much more. Their seasonal and semi-annual sales where prices are slashed below anything you'd find at even the cheapest discount stores are especially good. My Proctor-Silex toaster, Mr. Coffee coffee maker and Sunbeam iron, all purchased on sale in the **Cellar** at Macy's, were only $9.99 each and have lasted for years. Recent Macy's bargains have been a 10-piece set of Teflon cookware including tea kettle and steamer for $59.99; tablecloths for $11.99; fan or ceramic heaters for $39.99; a Salton rice cooker for $14.99; king or queen sheet sets for $24.99; a 45-piece stainless steel dinner set for $34.99; a Hoover upright vacuum for $99.99 and bath towels for $3.99 each. Watch out for their frequent coupon sales that allow an additional savings of between 10 percent and 25 percent. Where Macy's really excels is in its customer service: the sales staff (admittedly when you can find them) is very knowledgeable and helpful, and the store has a liberal return policy. If you're going to buy a big-ticket item, open a Macy's charge account. On the first day that you use the card, Macy's gives you an additional 10 percent off. As a Macy's cardholder, you will have privileges like access to Customer Appreciation and preview sales, as well as receiving circulars announcing future promotions.

National Wholesale Liquidators (632 Broadway, between Bleecker and Houston Streets—212–979–2400) sells brand-name manufacturer's overstocks and seconds in its vast inventory of household basics, and all at discount prices. You can find everything from flatware and appliances to pots, pans, bedding, bath accessories, china, glasses and stemware, and home-furnishing items, marked down 20 to 40 percent off retail. I found a 4-Pack box of GE soft white lightbulbs for 99¢, a Goldstar microwave oven for $39.97, a Proctor-Silex toaster for $10.97, a seven-piece set of nonstick cookware for $19.97 and a Black & Decker cordless Dustbuster for $14.97. (See chapter on "General Merchandise Stores.")

Although the goliath chain **Pottery Barn** can never be accused of having cheap everyday prices, this purveyor of simple, tasteful housewares and furnishings does have frequent clearance sales when you can pick up stemware, dinnerware, silverware, vases, frames, rugs, linens, bedding, curtains, decorative items, candlesticks and holders, pillows, etc., for very little money. Two Pottery Barn locations:

600 Broadway at Houston—212–219–2420
1965 Broadway at 67th Street—212–579–8477

For price and selection, the housewares section at **Target** is unparalleled by any of the city's other general merchandise stores (except perhaps National Wholesale Liquidators—see above). I especially love their Michael Graves designed blenders, coffee pots, flatware, cooking utensils, toasters, alarm clocks, teakettles, picture frames, and knife sets. These ultra-hip domestic items are practical, stylish and designed with a sense of humor. For the bedroom and bathroom, Target features a large collection of inexpensive and moderately priced items. Unfortunately, there are only two Target stores in New York itself (New Jersey has two, but you need a car to go to either), and from Manhattan they are a pain in the ass to get to. If you are willing to make the trek, a wondrous world awaits you. Look for Target's periodic sales and specials circular inside the Sunday edition of the *New York Times*. (See chapter on "General Merchandise Stores.") Target locations:

13505 20th Avenue, Flushing, Queens—718–661–4346 (take the 7 train to the end of the line at Flushing/Main Street; from there, you have to take a bus. It's best to call store for details

Queens Place, Queens Boulevard and 55th Avenue, Elmhurst, Queens—718–760–5656 (E train to Woodhaven, G Train to Grand Avenue/Newton)

For anyone who likes to cook, **Zabar's** (2245 Broadway at 80th Street—212–787–2000) is a culinary haven. The second-floor housewares section of this revered Upper West Side institution has the city's largest and best selection of products, from adequate to top-of-the-line, that would ever be needed to outfit a kitchen. There is virtually every type, brand and price range of toaster, blender, mixer, processor, iron, pot, pan, dish, wok, colander, utensil, vacuum, dust buster, air purifier, space heater, humidifier, microwave, scale, coffee maker, water filter, cappuccino maker, mug, glass, pitcher, linen, bowl and hotplate—they even have an entire department devoted to knives for God's sake—available on the market, and most at very reasonable prices. Even their high-end inventory is several dollars cheaper than the competition. Better yet, Zabar's always puts a large portion of its stock on sale at jaw-dropping discounts.

ELECTRONICS

Canal Street in Chinatown is a bargain shopper's paradise where you will find row upon row of shops, storefronts and cubicles crammed with all kinds of electronic equipment. Know though, like most of the other merchandise in this area, the quality and legality of this stuff is dubious, and don't even think about getting a warranty. As the saying goes, "You pay your money and you take your chances!" If you need something temporary until you can afford what you really want, and dependability and durability aren't your first priorities, Canal Street is calling. (See chapter on "General Merchandise Stores.")

Crocodile Computers (360 Amsterdam Avenue between 77th and 78th Streets—212-769-3400) bills itself as New York's favorite source for new and used computer equipment. One step inside its cramped quarters and you'll know why—low prices. On new merchandise, Crocodile charges a few to several hundred dollars below most retailers and factory-direct companies like Dell and Gateway. On their refurbished and tip-top used equipment you can save big bucks. Crocodile's large stock of IBM and Macs, laptops and desktops is always in flux and unpredictable (the stuff here moves); you may need to call or visit several times before you find what you're looking for, especially if you are in the market for a used computer. Whether new or used, Crocodile guarantees its merchandise for 90 days, including parts and labor. Besides computers, Crocodile has a wide selection of inexpensive software, computer games, manuals, printers, keyboards, music software and recording equipment.

On three packed floors in midtown, **Datavision** (445 Fifth Avenue between 39th and 40th Streets—212-689-1111) carries about every electronic product known to man, and at very competitive prices. On a recent visit, Datavision was having an amazing sale on Sony Vaio computers with most discounted up to $200 below their list prices. Other great deals included Vivistar 50-pack 700 mb blank CDs for $9.99 (regularly $19.99); a Panasonic Fax machine with caller ID for $79.99 (regularly $89.99); a Compaq Presario desktop computer with Intel Pentium 4 processor and DVD for $1,249 (regularly $1,498); and an Evolution mp3 player for $99 (regularly $119). Depending on what you purchase and how much you spend, Datavision offers freebies like software, speakers, CD-R media, headsets, VCRs and gift certificates.

My favorite place in the city to buy electronics is **J & R Music World** (23 Park Row—212–732–8600). They've got it all—an incomparable and large selection of quality merchandise, low prices and frequent sales. Best of all, they will match or beat the price of any other store if you bring in an ad (this year I found a pair of Klipsch speakers at a competitor for $80 less than J & R; I told the J & R salesman who immediately offered them to me for $85 below his store's original price). Taking up an entire block across from City Hall, J & R's huge inventory encompasses every electronic product and accessory you can imagine, from notebooks and desktops to scanners, fax machines, internet appliances, printers, monitors, CD burners, peripherals, software, video games, mp3 players, sound cards, palm computers and handheld organizers, telephones, cordless phones, cell phones, home office equipment, DVD players, CD players, VCRs, minidisk players, videos and DVDs, CDs, televisions, camcorders, cameras, receivers and amplifiers, mini stereo systems, speakers, radios and clock radios, keyboards, personal care products, watches, and even some housewares. If you don't mind schlepping all the way downtown, you're sure to find what you are looking for at a great price. J & R delivers large items; rates for delivery are determined by weight.

Kmart has a small selection of low-end, frill-free electronic equipment at okay prices. For all their excellence in areas like their

Martha Stewart line, this isn't where I'd buy a stereo or television. On the other hand, if you're looking for an ordinary alarm clock, a disposable camera, a portable disk player to use at the gym or a serviceable boom box for next to no money, you'll do just fine here. Kmart store locations:

One Pennsylvania Plaza on 34th Street between Seventh and Eighth Avenues—212–760–1188

770 Broadway at Astor Place—212–673–1540

Recently voted "Best Discount Shopping" by the editors of *New York Magazine*'s "The Best of New York" issue, **National Wholesale Liquidators** (632 Broadway between Bleecker and Houston Streets—212–979–2400) is by far the city's superior discount merchandise store. Besides its other great deals, it carries a wide assortment of well-known electronics merchandise, marked 20 to 40 percent below retail. On a recent visit, I found both a Sharp 19-inch color TV and a Sharp DVD/Video/CD player for $139.97 each; a Conair Trimline phone for $5.97; an Emerson portable stereo CD player for $39.97; an AT&T digital answering machine for $24.97; and a Curtis portable AM/FM radio for $6.97. Unlike most other closeout and overstock specialists, everything on National Wholesale Liquidators' three floors is in perfect condition. (See chapter on "General Merchandise Stores.")

With a vast inventory, competitive prices and good warranty plans, **The Wiz** is an excellent option for buying electronics. What The Wiz doesn't do so well is customer service. I know next to nothing about electronics and yet whenever I go to one of these stores, I feel like I could give the salespeople some instruction. Consider yourself warned. They more than compensate for their mostly lackadaisical staff by holding frequent sales with discounts of up to 50 percent off regularly marked prices. Better yet, The Wiz promises to match or beat any of their competitors' advertised prices. Recent bargains included a Sony CD Walkman for $49.99, an Aiwa AM/FM alarm clock for $14.99, a Fuji 35-mm camera for $69.99, a

Panasonic Palmcorder for $299.99, a Daewoo DVD/CD player for $98.99, a Quasar VCR for $59.99 and a Toshiba 13-inch color TV for $99.99. To find out about their sales, look for The Wiz circulars in the Sunday *New York Times*. Check your local listings for The Wiz store nearest you.

BOOKS, PLAYS AND SCRIPTS

ONCE UPON A TIME, Manhattan was "Land O' Books." Almost every neighborhood in the city supported great small to medium-sized specialty, independent and mom-and-pop book peddlers doing their best to raise the literary standard of all New Yorkers. The demise of these stores began in the real estate boom of the 1980's, when greedy landlords gouged their tenants for everything they could, which put those who couldn't afford exorbitant rents out of business. Adding insult to injury, along came the corporate mega-bookstores (they know who they are), who, by under-pricing the competition, drove a final nail into the coffins of many of the long-gasping little guys. Although several of the great Manhattan bookstores are gone (when both Academy Books and Coliseum Books shuttered last year, I was inconsolable), there are still a number of wonderful places to acquire books, plays and scripts. Lucky for us who live on a budget, several are discount vendors.

None of the city's drama book dealers is an actual discounter, but I am including them in this chapter, as this book is intended for theater professionals and I feel it is important to tell where these places are and to describe each briefly. Moreover, the acting editions of plays are generally inexpensive—between $5 and $8—so, I'm not that far off the mark by including these in this discussion.

The 24-hour **Accidental Records** (131 Avenue A between St. Marks Place and 9th Street—212–995–2224) in the East Village sells a huge array of mostly new and used paperbacks at 30 percent to 40 percent off list price. A majority of the inventory here is modern fiction and as Accidental's owner, Craig Lopez, says, "they are primarily the books you always meant to read but never did." A word of caution—this place is a dump. The clutter of books, CDs and junk is overwhelming, partly because the books are not placed in any order and are, a first for me, stacked from floor to ceiling instead of shelved. These are minor irritations, however, since the helpful staff can locate just about anything in stock.

Located around the corner from Strand, **Alabaster Bookshop** (122 Fourth Avenue at 12th Street—212–982–3550) carries a variety of cheap used and rare titles. Particularly good is their selection of books on art, theater and film. On my last visit, Alabaster had a couple hundred Dramatist Playservice and Samuel French acting editions, clearly once part of the library of a theater professional. Be sure to rummage through the outdoor $2 carts where you're likely to find a must-have.

Applause Theater and Cinema Books (211 West 71st Street just off Broadway—212–496–7511) carries a small but adequate collection of scripts, screenplays and film and theater related books, periodicals and magazines. Unlike the city's other theatrical bookstores, Applause has an inventory of discounted used volumes, and occasionally reduces on select titles and has periodic sales. When I was there last, all hardcovers were 20 percent off.

The behemoth **Barnes and Noble** gives discounts of up to 40 percent off hardcover bestsellers, up to 30 percent off paperback bestsellers, and has numerous bargain racks of remaindered merchandise. Is it my imagination though, or have the discounts at this store diminished? It seems to me that while in the process of obliterating most of their competition, B & N offered consumers more generous savings. Coincidence? I'm not sure what to think, but feel compelled to put it out there. Discuss amongst yourselves. What's the use complaining? Kvetch as I do about their domination in the book market, I'd be lying if I said I didn't shop here. Consult your phone book for the nearest Barnes and Noble location, or see the chapter on "Restrooms."

The subterranean **Book Ark** (173 West 81st Street at Amsterdam Avenue—212–787–3914) sells, buys and trades quality used and rare hardcovers and paperbacks in all subjects including foreign titles. The selection here is small but good in all areas, with a respectable section of theater books and plays (acting editions are as cheap as a couple of bucks). Although this shop is housed in a low-ceilinged basement, there is always soothing new age music playing to enhance the browsing.

Borders Books (the city's second largest book retailer) offers discounts on bestsellers similar to those at Barnes & Noble (the city's largest book retailer).

461 Park Avenue at 57th Street—212–980–6785
576 Second Avenue at 32nd Street—212–685–3938

There are several **curbside book-peddlers** who set up tables throughout the city. They have a huge presence around Union Square and on the Upper West and Upper East Sides for their supply that seems to have mysteriously "fallen off of the back of trucks." Fortunately, we New Yorkers reap the benefits of these "accidents" by being charged about half the price that we'd pay for the same book if bought in a legitimate bookstore. Their supply is usually of the best-seller and coffee-table art-book variety, but they carry a lot of titles and the books are usually in mint condition.

Drama Books (250 West 40th Street between Seventh and Eighth Avenues—212–944–0595), by far the best theatrical bookstore in the city, perhaps the country, has gotten even better now that it has moved into new, more spacious quarters in the Garment District. If it is in print and has anything to do with the theater, you can find it here. Besides carrying just about any play ever published, Drama Books has a huge selection of books devoted to theater-related subjects, ranging from stage makeup and design to dialects, history and drama therapy. You'll find a very good assortment of books on film and

BEST STORE

video, as well as lots of industry newspapers and magazines, agent and casting-director mailing labels, and DVDs of acclaimed theatrical performances. The very helpful and friendly staff (I assume most are aspiring actors) are put through rigorous training. This store, which I consider "actor church," is a sanctuary for anyone who works in, or is passionate about, the theater.

Fifty percent of the profits from donated used books at **East Village Books** (101 St. Mark's Place between First Avenue and Avenue A—212–477–8647) supports local causes. Most of East Village's books are general interest and extremely cheap. The people working behind the counter are helpful but not intrusive and really know their stock. A bonus: If you are looking to make some fast scratch, East Village Books claims to pay the highest prices in the city for used books, CDs and tapes.

Gotham Book Mart (41 West 47th Street between Fifth and Sixth Avenues—212–719–4448), a New York landmark since 1920, carries a combination of new and used books and journals on literature, the arts, philosophy and myriad special interests. Famous for smuggling books into the U.S. by authors James Joyce, Henry Miller and D.H. Lawrence, when those authors' books were banned under inflexible obscenity laws, Gotham has been a pilgrimage destination for some of the greatest literary figures of the twentieth century, including Tennessee Williams, Noel Coward, Arthur Miller, Gertrude Stein, Nathaniel West, Thornton Wilder, Eugene O'Neill, Saul Bellow and T.S. Eliot. Although Gotham does not discount its new books, it reduces its large collection of used merchandise by 50 percent and more off original prices; acting editions of plays can start as low as $2. In fact, Gotham has huge reductions on its entire inventory of used film and drama books. On Gotham's "Buck and Below" wagons, books are as cheap as 10¢, and many are even free. A word of warning: although the staff is very knowledgeable, they are a surly bunch. I've been coming here for years and Gotham's gruffness has been as dependable as its selection and good prices. I imagine its want ads read, "Only the unpleasant need apply." Make sure to pop into Gotham's upstairs gallery, which features the works of the late illustrator Edward Gorey, as well as changing exhibitions. Note: The folks at Gotham have asked me to mention that after years at their historic Diamond District location, they have lost their lease and will be moving to a new home in the near future.

The diminutive, two-story emporium **Gryphon Bookshop** (2246 Broadway between 80th and 81st Streets—212–362–0706) is packed solid with cheap, mostly used and rare paperbacks and hardcovers. Books are everywhere, covering every surface, creating obstacles in the aisles and making it hard to negotiate the stairs. One man's clutter is a book lover's paradise. The helpful staff, who are undoubtedly responsible for the mess, knows their inventory inside and out—if they have what you are looking for, they will point you in the right direction. What you won't find here are scripts or theater/performing arts books. For those, check out the excellent selection at **Gryphon Record Shop** (233 West 72nd Street, between Broadway and West End Avenue—212–874–1588). The Gryphon Bookshop's outdoor bargain shelves have deals on all kinds of books you never wanted to read and probably never will, but are worth a look just the same.

At the **Housing Works Used Book Café** (126 Crosby Street between Prince and Houston Streets—212–334–3324) there is a very eclectic collection of books at rock-bottom prices. Unlike most of the city's used bookstores, a majority of the more than 55,000 volumes here are in new or nearly new condition. All proceeds from the Used Book Café benefit Housing Works, an organization that assists homeless people with AIDS. (See chapter on "Thrift Shops.")

Ivy's Books (2488 Broadway between 92nd and 93rd Streets— 212–362–8905) on the Upper West Side is the best organized and most inviting of the city's many new and used book emporiums. Besides its new and used titles, this quaint shop also sells rare books, including first editions, and vintage paperbacks, as well as cards, stationery and some gifts. Ivy's size doesn't allow for a large inventory, but it does a good job of stocking its shelves with the same gamut of topics and genres that are found at larger stores. Prices on used volumes are very low, and there is a nice array of inexpensive used theater books and scripts. Ivy's also has a cart of sale books on the sidewalk out front, often featuring acting editions, with titles never more than a couple of dollars.

I know most used bookstores wear their disarray as a badge of honor, but does **Mercer Street Books** (206 Mercer Street at Bleecker—212–505–8615) really have to be so slapdash? It feels like the store hasn't shelved a book properly in years. Interspersed among the mostly used fare are some new volumes and review copies, and if you are interested in art, theater or fiction, you're in luck as each of these areas has a great range of titles. Prices here are comparable to most of the other used book dealers around town. Now, if they'd only spruce the place up a bit. . . .

The entire inventory of **Murder Ink Books of Mystery and Suspense** (2486 Broadway between 92nd and 93rd Streets— 212–873–1908) is devoted to, well, mystery and suspense. Here you will find more new, used, rare and signed whodunits than you ever imagined existed; and since most are paperbacks, they are affordably priced. Murder Ink also has tons of out-of-print titles starting at just $4.99, and a great collection of vintage collectible paperbacks with provocative titles like *The Gallows in My Garden, Cry Hard, Cry Fast, The Only Girl in the Game,* and *Marihuana.*

Of course, the absolute cheapest way to get your hands on the books you want is to utilize the New York, Queens Borough and Brooklyn **Public Library Systems**. With great services, branches throughout the five boroughs and free membership, there is no reason not to join. And, most branches hold ongoing and occasional sales when hardback books go for about $1, paperbacks for 50¢. For more information, including locations, hours and services, call or go to their websites (for info regarding the New York Library of the Performing Arts, see my chapter on "Personal and Professional Resources"):

New York Public Library: www.nypl.org—212–930–0800
Brooklyn Public Library: www.brooklynpubliclibrary.org—
   718–230–2100
Queens Borough Public Library: www.queens.lib.ny.us—
   718–990–0700

Ruby's Book Sale (119 Chambers Street between West Broadway and Church Street—212–732–8676), which has deep discounts on new and used hardcovers and paperbacks, has an impressive section of low-priced reference and computer books and an assortment of art volumes that is comparable to the city's leading book retailers. Used paperbacks and backdate magazines are 50 percent off the cover price.

Samuel French (45 West 25th Street—212–206–8990), the world's foremost publisher of plays for over 170 years, has a modest-sized drama bookshop in the foyer of its offices in Chelsea. The books range from film to theater, with lots of acting editions, even those published by their competitors. Pick up a free copy of Samuel French's catalog, which lists all the plays and musicals they publish.

Skyline Books and Records (13 West 18th Street between Fifth and Sixth Avenues—212–759–5463) has a vast assortment of inexpensive used books, covering every genre imaginable from art and architecture to cooking, philosophy, history, religion, literature, children's, poetry, sociology, erotica and even steamy vintage pocketbooks from the 50s and 60s. The theater section here is big and comprehensive, with paperback plays going for between $3 and $6, and hardback versions (remember those "Fireside Theatre" volumes?) for around $8. Also good is Skyline's Shakespeare section, where you will find several editions of the "Complete Works" as well as individual plays, lots of literary criticism, and even a mint-condition "Facsimile" for $60. Sixty dollars sounds expensive, but it isn't bad considering if you bought it new, you would pay twice as much.

BEST USED BOOKS

The **Strand Bookstore** (828 Broadway—212-473-1452) is the city's biggest, best and perhaps cheapest purveyor of used and rare books. They boast "eight miles" of merchandise, and after visiting their three floors, you won't dispute the claim. For me, this store is nirvana; if I haven't made it at least once every couple of weeks, I suffer from withdrawal. Under one roof you will find hardcovers and paperbacks on every subject, a rare-book department, review copies and recent releases (that are always 50 percent off the retail price), an astonishing assortment of art books, overstocks, and publishers' closeouts. On the sidewalk outside, Strand packs several carts with cheaper than cheap volumes of fiction and non. Of special interest to actors is Strand's theater section; it's enormous and all encompassing, with a huge assortment of acting editions, Shakespeareana and works by G. B. Shaw. Have I mentioned service? The staff here, mostly scruffy middle-aged men and young women in glasses and uncombed hair, is passionate about books and extremely helpful. The only negative thing I can say about this store is, its organization is helter-skelter. As a friend says, "I can never find what I am looking for, but I always find what I didn't know I wanted." If you don't mind spending a lot of time browsing for that bargain Kafka, Woolf, Williams or Wharton, you will love this store. Strand has a second location at South Street Seaport (95 Fulton Street—

212–732–6070) that, though it doesn't compare in size and scope with the mother-store, is a great vendor in its own right.

For those out of the loop, **Theatre Circle** (268 West 44th Street near Eighth Avenue—212–391–7075) looks like another of the many tourist-oriented shops scattered throughout the Theater District. It does carry an abundance of "Ragtime" refrigerator magnets, "Kiss Me Kate" key rings, "Mamma Mia" coffee mugs and "I ♥ NY" mouse pads, in an attempt to warm the hearts of visitors from Bummerville, CA, Tarzan, TX, Ben Hur, VA, Truth or Consequences, NM, Frankenstein, MO and Monkeys Eyebrow, KY. Pass the tchotckes quickly, head to the back room and you will find an outstanding assortment of scripts and theater books. I love this place because they always have what I'm looking for. Frequently, after my agents call with an audition, by the time I arrive at Drama Books or Applause to pick up a copy of the play, it is sold out. Not so at Theatre Circle. Since so few actors know about the back room, this store rarely runs out of stock. Prices here on acting editions are exactly what you'd pay at the other drama book vendors.

Although located in a basement, **Twelfth Street Books** (11 East 12th Street between Fifth Avenue and University Place—212–645–4340) is a brightly-lit, well-organized and cheerful shop specializing in used and rare books. There is an enormous variety here, most in very good condition, at affordable prices. Twelfth Street has an excellent selection of scripts and books on theater, music, and film.

My favorite place to buy brand-new books is the ironically named store **Unoppressive Non-Imperialist Bargain Books** (34 Carmine Street near Sixth Avenue—212–229–0079). No vendor of new merchandise in the entire city comes close to the low prices this wonderful shop charges. Unoppressive's inventory is all publisher closeouts and overstocks, so there isn't a broad selection, but there is always something of interest and

BEST NEW BOOKS

the prices are irresistible. Recently, Donald Spoto's *Laurence Olivier—A Biography,* usually listed at $21.95, was only $3, including tax. A Complete Works by Shakespeare was $8, marked down from $24.95; a biography of Oscar Wilde, usually $14.95, was $6; *The Ultimate Scene and Monologue Sourcebook* with a cover price of $18.95 was only $4; Phyllis Hartnoll's *The Theatre—A Concise History,* usually $14.95, was $4; and Leonard Maltin's *2002 Movie and Video Guide* listed at $20, was only $7. There are gift books, biographies, fiction, art volumes, poetry collections, tomes on religion and eastern philosophy, children's titles, calendars, cookbooks and much more.

CDs

ACCORDING TO MANY of those I polled, **Academy Records** (12 West 18th Street between Fifth and Sixth Avenues—212–242–3000) is the best used CD store in New York, and as one friend said, "Anywhere for that matter." I agree wholeheartedly. Academy's prices and selection are unsurpassed anywhere else in the city. Most CDs average $8.99, with walls and walls of classical CDs for $3.99, many of them still in shrink-wrap. There are great jazz, rock, opera, soul, Broadway and country sections too, as well as VHS movies and vinyl albums galore (mostly classical). While you are there, be sure to check out Academy's budget area where all merchandise goes for around 99¢. In the ten years I have been shopping there, I have found innumerable treasures and never paid full price.

Craig Lopez, the owner of **Accidental Records** (131 Avenue A between St. Marks Place and 9th Street—212–995–2224) in the East Village, claims that his is the only music shop "On the planet that is open 24 hours." I haven't verified this, but for this neighborhood that never sleeps, it's a real plus. The overwhelming clutter and junk-store ambience of this place can be off-putting, but don't let it keep you from going inside. Accidental stocks over 10,000 new, still-in-shrink-wrap CDs representing every genre, with an especially large selection of Pop/Alternative, and all for between $10 and $12 for single albums and $15 to $20 for doubles. A large bargain bin holds CDs priced from $1 to $5. Of the many music styles to be found here, a section, unknown to me before now, of "Antifolk" CDs, is explained by Lopez as a collection of works composed and burned by local artists.

Contrary to what you might think, you can occasionally save money on CDs when shopping at many of the major music **chain stores**. Here's how:

Although the international mega-chain **HMV Records** sells their huge inventory of music at top prices, they do offer a few ways to save money: seek out their "Best of the Best" CDs at greatly reduced prices; shop during their many sales throughout the year; and of special note to actors, AEA members can show a valid membership card which entitles them to a 10 percent discount on any non-sale item that is $14.99 or more. Note: This discount is not valid in combination with any other coupon or discount and is not valid at Ticketmaster or for gift certificates. Obtain a frequent buyers "CD Club" card, which gives members a free CD after they have purchased ten items at $16.99 or higher.

> 565 Fifth Avenue at 46th Street—212–681–6700
> 308 West 125th Street—212–932–9619

At **Record Explosion's** five Manhattan locations, $5.99 is the going rate on a glut of new closeout CDs, including many boxed sets. There is a reason why these are closeouts—there isn't much here, to me at least, that is desirable. In the many years that I've ducked into Record Explosion looking for the titles I want at discount prices, my search has been futile. You may have better luck. This chain also sells new releases of pop, rock and Latin at list price, and has some discounts as low as $1.99.

> 142 West 34th Street—212–714–0450
> 2 Broadway near Stone Street—212–509–6444
> 176 Broadway near Maiden Place—212–693–1510

Tower Records, which charges top retail prices on their outstanding selection of CDs, does have periodic sales and discounts in which select labels or genres are greatly reduced. On my last visit to Tower, hundreds of titles were on sale, with some like Simon and Garfunkel's "Bridge Over Troubled Water," "The Freewheelin' Bob Dylan" and "The Best of Eric Clapton" for only $5.99. Check for sales circulars in *The New York Times* Sunday edition and ads in *The Village Voice*.

692 Broadway at 4ᵗʰ Street—212–505–1500
1961 Broadway at 66ᵗʰ Street—212–799–2500
721–725 Fifth Avenue near 56ᵗʰ Street—212–838–8110

Tower Records Clearance Outlet (20 East 4ᵗʰ Street—212–505–1166) has an amazing stock of used, closeout and clearance CDs at cut-rate prices (starting as low as $2.99). Although the lion's share of the inventory here is classical music and opera, other genres like pop, rock, soul, jazz, Latin, world, blues, gospel, reggae, country, folk and soundtracks are well represented. For new, quality clearance and closeout CDs, there's nowhere cheaper.

The gargantuan **Virgin Megastore** has frequent sales and clearance blowouts on a host of music from all genres. Their weekly sales ads can be found in *The Village Voice*, or stop in whenever you are in Times Square or Union Square.

52 East 14ᵗʰ Street at Broadway—212–598–4666
1540 Broadway between 45ᵗʰ and 46ᵗʰ Streets—
212–921–1020

Maurice Chevalier once sang, "Thank heaven for little girls . . ." I continually sing, "Thank heaven for **Disc-O-Rama**." This bargain institution has the city's best prices on brand-new CDs. The entire inventory of mostly pop, rock, hip-hop and dance (with some classical and other genres) is just $9.99 per CD. That's right, $9.99! And it's not clearance or closeout crap. Disc-O-Rama's stock is comprised of mainstream, top 40, new releases and popular fare—the stuff that's going for $14.99 and higher at most other stores. Disc-O-Rama carries tons of cheap used CDs.

BEST BARGAIN

At its Classical and Clearance outlet store prices start as low as $2.99. Even better, they have occasional sales. On my last visit, they were offering $2-off coupons on all used and clearance items marked at $5.99 or higher.

> 186 West 4th Street between Sixth and Seventh Avenues—
>   212–206–8417
> 40 Union Square East—212–260–8616
> 146 West 4th Street (Classical and Clearance store)—
>   212–477–9410

Bypass the ground floor sales area (no bargains here) at **Generation Records** (210 Thompson Street between Bleecker and 3rd Streets—212–254–1100) and head straight downstairs to their used CD section. Here you will find lots of music, actually organized (wonder of wonders) alphabetically and by genres, with low prices ranging from $2.99 to $11.99. A small bargain rack contains CDs for just 50¢. Most of Generation Records' inventory is rock, hardcore, industrial, punk, metal and electronica, so don't even think about asking the burly, tattooed and profusely pierced sales staff for either the latest Patti Lupone or show tunes; you're liable to evoke leers, guffaws or worse.

Gryphon Records (233 West 72nd Street—212–874–1588) has a smattering of classical, soundtrack, jazz and Broadway CDs for between $5 and $9. What they do really well here is old, rare and out-of-print vinyl, and there is a heap of it at reasonable prices. I especially love this store for their "Spoken-Word" albums. I've found many of Ruth Draper's monologues, as well as original cast recordings of plays like *The Cocktail Party* and *Who's Afraid of Virginia Woolf,* and versions of classic plays like *A Doll's House* with Claire Bloom and *Saint Joan* with Siobhan McKenna.

Couple the ambience of a St. Marks Place music store with an Upper West Side address and you have **N.Y.C.D.** (426 Amsterdam Avenue between 80th and 81st Street—212–724–4466), where you get deep discounts on a slew of used rock, pop, jazz and soundtrack

CDs. Most sell for between $6.99 and $11.99, but search in the several $1 crates and the table outside where all CDs are $2 or ten for $15. For every four used or sale CDs you purchase, N.Y.C.D. will give you a fifth gratis.

Other Music (15 East 4th Street off Broadway—212–477–8150) isn't really a discount outlet, but this great store warrants a mention for its excellent and eclectic collection of alternative and indie CDs. Much of the inventory here you can't find anywhere else (this is the only store in New York to carry Kiki and Herb's anarchic Christmas album) and prices are competitive. To keep bargain hunters happy, Other Music has frequent sales on selected items, and there is a big section of discounted used merchandise.

If you're looking for brand-new CDs at bargain prices, **Rebel Rebel Records** (319 Bleecker Street near Seventh Avenue—212–989–0770) is not your place. All new merchandise sells at list or even slightly higher than seen at the megastores. What is cheap here are used CDs. Prices on the stock of mostly rock and dance music range between $4.98 and $9.98, with several clearance CDs dropping to $1.98 or six for $10. You'll have to do a lot of digging to find what you are looking for, as none of the used stuff is organized but scattered in several cardboard boxes throughout the tiny store.

Rocks In Your Head (157 Prince Street between Thompson Street and West Broadway—212–475–6729) sells, you guessed it, mostly rock. It has a very small section of used CDs with prices ranging from $2.99 to $7.99. If you're looking for something other than rock, check this store out anyway as they have a handful of discs from other genres, such as blues, country, world, soundtracks, trip hop, Arab, jazz and 60s/70s.

Interspersed between all of the vintage clothing stores, tee-shirt shops, junk jewelry stands, sunglass booths and tattoo parlors on **St. Marks Place** between Third and Fourth Avenues, are several joints selling new and used CDs. Given the neighborhood, most deal in the rock/punk/rap realm. Comb carefully through the collections of each of the shops on the block and you are sure to find what you want (and perhaps what you didn't know you wanted) at prices that are a few to several dollars below retail.

13 Compact Discs (13 St. Marks Place—212-477-4376), which specializes in the music that makes one dance (trance, metal, rap, rock, hip-hop and techno), has a good selection of both new and used CDs at prices that are only about a dollar more than Sounds (see page 223) across the street.

Joe's Compact Discs (11 St. Marks Place—212-673-4606) sells used CDs starting at $4.99 and new CDs starting at $9.99. Like most of the shops on St. Marks, the sections here, which represent most musical styles, are barely or badly organized. Although Joe's has the block's largest selection of 99¢ CDs, you'll have to do a lot of trawling through the bad stuff to get to the good. But then, who am I to call anything "bad"? Once in my callow youth, I actually paid hard-earned money for an album by "Wham!" Sheesh.

Mondo Kim's Video and Music (6 St. Marks Place—212-598-9985), beloved by the city's cinephiles for its extraordinary selection of both mainstream and non-mainstream films (see chapter on "Videos and DVDs"), also carries a great assortment of music at reasonable prices. Kim's appeals to a broad range of tastes, everything from establishment to independent, metal to techno, psychedelia to show tunes. Prices here on new releases are about what you'd pay at the larger music outlets, but used CDs start around $5.99 and don't go much higher. Kim's also has a "Bargain Cove" where all CDs are 99¢.

Norman's #2 New and Used CDs and DVDs (33 St. Marks Place—212-253-6162) is the sorriest store on the block. This place has a lot going against it: it's quarters are cramped, new CDs aren't a bargain, there's no rhyme or reason to how things are shelved and the sales staff, who it seems are paid to watch DVDs all day, register annoyance if asked difficult questions like, "Where's the soul section?" However, prices here on the used stuff are pretty good—anywhere from $3.99 to $9.99 on genres that include pop, rock, electronic, world, reggae, blues, jazz and hip-hop.

For the area's best prices and selection on new and used mainstream music, look no further than the two **Sounds** stores in the middle of the block. Here you'll find a huge assortment of new releases and catalog titles at very low prices. Used CDs run from $3.99 to $10.99, and new average from $9.99 to $13.99 (double CDs are $15.99). Sounds also has a few large bargain bins where all CDs are just 88¢.

16 St. Marks Place—212–677–2727
20 St. Marks Place—212–677–3444

FLOWERS AND PLANTS

ONE OF THE THINGS THAT MOST of the New Yorkers I know have at the top of their "To Do" list but never get around to, is to take a predawn jaunt through the **Chelsea Flower District** (on 28th Street between Sixth and Seventh Avenues). For a few hours each early weekday morning, this nondescript area in midtown pulsates with startling colors and exhilarating aromas as it vends it blooms to the city's flower peddlers. Once you've recovered from sensual overload, you'll want to take advantage of the district's low prices on plants and flowers. Although you won't receive wholesale rates, you will find prices at most shops are lower than city florists and gardening centers. If you're not a morning person, no need to worry—most of these vendors are open until early afternoon; but be advised, most of the good stuff will have been snapped up.

The **Chelsea Wholesale Flower Market** (75 Ninth Avenue at 15th Street—212–620–7500), which promises "Unique variety and quality unsurpassed," isn't really a wholesale place, but the prices on most flowers and indoor and outdoor plants are competitive. You'll find every kind of seasonal blossom, freshly picked and arranged in a user-friendly way so that you may easily coordinate your arrangements. If your particular talents don't include artfully assembling roses and Queen Anne's Lace, the experts at the Chelsea Wholesale Flower Market will do the arranging for you at prices that are probably a few dollars less than you'd pay at your neighborhood florist. Balcony gardeners will have a field day here choosing from the market's abundant range of potted vegetables, plants and trees. Those who want to add a dash of the southwest to their Manhattan abodes can choose from a large selection of exotic cacti, which start at just $7. The Chelsea Wholesale Flower Market stocks plenty of inexpensive gardening and plant supplies including pots, soil, baskets, liquid fertilizer, fungicides and insecticides.

If you, or the person you are buying flowers for, aren't fussy about freshness or quality, the city's many **corner grocers and ethnic delis** provide alternatives to expensive florists. Most of these merchants carry a varied selection of decent to beautiful, durable blooms at low prices. In my neighborhood, the three shops where I do most of my flower buying are **Giebrell Deli & Grocery**—681 Ninth Avenue at 47th Street, **7 Brothers Famous Deli** at Ninth Avenue and 49th Street, and **Green Emporium**—791 Eighth Avenue. Each has almost the exact same array of quality flowers for about the same price: a bouquet of carnations sells for $3, or two for $5; a vibrant bouquet of mixed flowers is $10; alstroemeria are $3 a bunch; irises sell for $3 a bunch, or two for $5; colored roses are two dozen for $8 to $10 (except on Valentine's Day or Mother's Day). These same bargains and more can be found at many of your neighborhood corner grocers as well.

New York Flower and Plant Shed (209 West 96th Street at Broadway—212–662–4400) hails itself as "New York's Houseplant Supermarket." With over 16,000 square feet of greenery, flowers and plant and gardening supplies (including a rooftop greenhouse) and a staff of 35 "artisans," botanists and clerks, this claim isn't just bravado. The plants here are all fresh, lush, and well cared for by the expert staff. Prices aren't exactly budget: corn plants (some as tall as six feet) are $39.99; snake plants are $19.99; spathiphyllum are $29.99; rubber trees are $14.99. Because of the quality they are worth the money. The New York Flower and Plant Shed sells a stunning assortment of flowers and offers a full range of florist services, all at competitive prices.

Roses and Blooms (599 Lexington Avenue at 52nd Street—212–758–7673) in the Citicorp Building is, at best, a moderately priced retailer of a huge offering of imported flowers. They do, however, offer one generous bargain (which qualifies them for inclusion in this book): they will assemble and deliver a boxed bouquet of a dozen beautiful 24-inch stem roses, complete with ferns and baby's breath, for just $35. At this price, you can say "Thanks," "Happy Whatever," "I love you," even "Fuck you, I have enough friends," without breaking the bank!

One of the unbelievably inexpensive **Stiles Farmer's Markets** (472 Ninth Avenue at 41st Street—212–967–4918) has recently begun selling fresh-picked flowers and some plants at low prices. Here you can buy baby roses for $10 a dozen and multihued long-stem roses at $10 for two dozen. Irises or orchids are $4.99 per bunch, hothouse tulips are $6 a bunch or two for $10, and miniature carnations are $3 a bunch or two for $5. Large, colorful arrangements of mixed flowers can be had for just $9.99. (For more information about the Stiles Farmers Market, see the "Provisions" chapter.)

New York's biggest, best and oldest farmer's market is the **Union Square Greenmarket** (north end of Union Square at 17th Street between Broadway and Park Avenue South—212–477–3220). Colorful displays of food and produce are upstaged by the many vibrant and aromatic stands heaving with newly harvested, locally grown flowers, potted plants and herbs. Most of these seasonal beauties, picked or potted earlier that same morning, are sold at moderate prices. Better yet, at the end of each market day, many vendors discount their goods as much as 50 percent so they won't have to cart them home. Market hours are Mondays, Wednesdays, Fridays, and Saturdays from 7 A.M. to 6 P.M.

ART SUPPLIES

WITH AN ENORMOUS SELECTION of goods spread over five floors, the giant retailer **Pearl Paint** (308 Canal Street at Mercer Street—212–431–7932) is the city's best resource for art supplies. Not only do they carry just about anything an artist would need or want, but everything here is sold at discount prices. Better yet, Pearl features monthly sales (look for their circular at the store entrance) and offers a 10 percent student discount on all merchandise. Not a student? No problem—just tell them you are—they never ask for ID. Pearl also promises to match any competitor's advertised price (with proof of ad). Recent Pearl deals included a 9 by 12-inch stretched canvas for $2.59; 4 ounce tubes of acrylic paint (assorted colors) for $2.59 each; 37 ml. tubes of oil colors for $2.19; Rembrandt brand oil color set (6 tubes) for $17.99; set of four bristle brushes for oil and acrylics for $9.99; Reeves set of 12 watercolors or gouache colors for $2.99; Loew Cornell pottery tool kit for $5.99; 19 by 25-inch pastel and charcoal papers for 98¢ each; 12-inch wood manikins (male or female) for $7.49 each; 24 by 27-inch soft portfolios in assorted colors for $19.99; and 11 by 14-inch Bristol pads (smooth or vellum) for $5.49. The staff at Pearl Paint, which is mostly comprised of artists, is knowledgeable, friendly and attentive.

General Merchandise Stores

WITH MANHATTAN REAL ESTATE PRICES soaring to astronomical heights, it is harder and harder for the large-to-warehouse-size general merchandise stores to make a go of it. Gone are the Woolworth's and the Bradlees of my early days in New York. However, there are still several places in Manhattan where you can buy essentials (and nonessentials) inexpensively:

Canal Street in Chinatown, known affectionately as "Avenue of the Counterfeits," is a bargain shopper's paradise. On it you will find row upon row of shops, storefronts, cubicles and jerrybuilt booths crammed with everything you'd ever need to stock your pantry, medicine cabinet, closet, desk, cutlery drawer, breakfront, kitchen cupboard, jewelry box and CD rack. The disparate arrayed items here might be plumbing supplies, stereo equipment, kimonos, dishes, 14k gold chains, scarves, slippers, handbags and sunglasses to name a few.

A good deal of the commerce on Canal Street involves the sale of designer knockoffs, or what the police would less subtly classify as "contraband merchandise." Here for about $5 to $15, you can buy ersatz everything: pirated CDs and videotapes, "Kate Spade" and "Prada" handbags, sunglasses, athletic shoes, and "Rolex" and "Philippe Patek" watches. Most of these are shabby items that wouldn't fool even the least discerning from 20 paces. Between the born-every-minute suckers and those who want a "Cartier" watch without paying for a Cartier watch, counterfeit "merch" is big business. A warning: occasionally there are raids on these places because of their questionable goods. If a proprietor of a shop suspects a raid is about to take place, he will suddenly slam his metal gates shut, and the rest of the stores on the block follow his lead. It's not unheard of for shoppers to be locked in while the proprietors scramble to hide the fake goods. A friend of mine actually experienced this and said it was the most fun he'd had in a long time, especially trying to comfort a woman tourist from Ohio who panicked and screamed over and over, "We're going to die. We're going to die. We're going to . . . ."

The **Conway Store** has a handful of locations throughout Manhattan and the boroughs with its biggest concentration of outlets around Macy's on Seventh Avenue and 34ᵗʰ Street. Here you can find mostly low-end items at very low prices. Conway is a favorite place for truly cheap cotton shirts and summer clothing, as well as toothpaste, laundry and dish detergent, cleaning supplies, some brand-name items and a good selection of linens. Check your local listings for the nearest Conway location.

A rung (or two) below Kmart and Target in the quality and ambience department are the many **discount and 99 cents stores** scattered throughout the city. Most are concentrated around Herald and Union Squares, each a sanctuary to a wildly eclectic assortment of items that range from essential to nonessential, and can offer paper towels, canned goods, chocolates, floral-print slippers, "Last Supper" wall clocks, leopard-print toilet seats, American flag beach towels and yellow smiley-face night-lights. Although the quality of the items can be hit or miss, there is literally something for everyone at these stores and they are definitely worth a look. You can find your first set of dishes, glasses and silverware here, as well as cheap bed linens, clocks, phones, bath towels, party supplies and even underwear. Discount stores and locations:

99¢ Creation:
244 West 23rd Street between Seventh and Eighth Avenues

Amazing 99¢ or Less:
122 Chambers Street between West Broadway and Church Street

American Value Centers:
22 West 14th Street between Fifth and Sixth Avenues—212–627–1555
620 Eighth Avenue at 39th Street—212–382–0808

The Bag Man:
261 West 34th Street at Eighth Avenue—212–502–5452

Broadway Job Lot:
8 West 25th Street between Fifth and Sixth Avenues

Chambers Brothers Closeouts:
100 Chambers Street at Church Street—212–766–9660

Dee & Dee:
22 West 14th Street—212–243–5621
97 Chambers Street at Church Street—212–233–3830

Jack's World has a two-level price system: items for 99 cents or less are sold on the ground floor, and those $1 and over on the second floor. Two locations:

16 East 40th Street off Fifth Avenue—212–696–5767
110 West 32nd Street between Sixth and Seventh Avenues—212–268–9962

M & S Bargain Hunters:
519 Eighth Avenue at 36th Street

New York 99¢:
85 Chambers Street between Broadway and Church Streets

Odd-Job and **Odd Job Trading**:
> 169 East 60th Street between Lexington and Third
>> Avenues—212–893–8447
>
> 601 Eighth Avenue at 38th Street—212–714–0106
>
> 36 East 14th Street at University Place—212–741–9944
>
> 299 Broadway at Duane Street—212–964–6574
>
> 465 Lexington Avenue between 46th and 47th Streets—
>> 212–949–7401
>
> 149 West 32nd Street between Sixth and Seventh
>> Avenues—212–564–7370
>
> 390 Fifth Avenue at 36th Street—212–239–3336

R & R Everything 99¢:
> 207 West 14th Street between Seventh and Eighth Avenues

Ralph's Discount City:
> 80 Nassau Street between Fulton and John Streets—
>> 212–964–9386

Weber's Closeout Centers:
> 116 West 32nd Street between Sixth and Seventh
>> Avenues—212–564–3606
>
> 48 West 48th Street between Sixth and Seventh
>> Avenues—212–764–1615
>
> 2064 Broadway at 72nd Street—212–787–1644

Westside Home Center Cleaning:
778 Ninth Avenue at 52nd Street—212–265–1010

Yes 99¢:
> 92 Delancey Street between Ludlow and Orchard
>> Streets—212–473–9428

When **Kmart** announced a few years ago that they would be opening stores in Manhattan, most New Yorkers, me included, collectively gasped and cried aloud "There goes the neighborhood." We feared that this was the beginning of the end, the "suburbanization" of our cosmopolitan home. If Kmart could open here, would Chuck E. Cheez, Costco and an outpost of Branson, Missouri, be far behind? Well, there is a Costco slated to open in midtown in the next year or so, but no, Kmart's presence here in Gotham has not hurt our status as retail capitol of the world. Instead, it has provided an outlet where we can buy everything from office supplies to toiletries, baby clothes, women's lingerie, gardening tools, wristwatches, prescription drugs, perfume and air conditioners under one roof. Although most New Yorkers won't readily admit to shopping at Kmart, my very unscientific poll shows we do. Even the most vocal and jaded Blue Light Special naysayers—preening Chelsea boys, snooty Upper East Side matrons, "I-only-wear-black-and-sleep-'til-5-P.M." East Village artists and sunglasses-at-midnight TV actors can all be found taking advantage of Kmart's low to moderate prices. (See chapter on "Housewares.") Kmart store locations:

> One Pennsylvania Plaza on 34th Street between Seventh and
>   Eighth Avenues—212–760–1188
> 770 Broadway at Astor Place—212–673–1540

BEST BARGAIN

Recently voted "Best Discount Shopping" by the editors of *New York Magazine's* "The Best of New York" issue, **National Wholesale Liquidators** (632 Broadway between Bleecker and Houston Streets—212–979–2400) is by far the city's superior discount merchandise store. Here you can find great deals on food, toiletries, housewares, electronics, toys and hardware. Everything from cotton balls to cookies, clocks, cleanser and Clearasil is marked down 20 to 40 percent off retail (as are all non-alliterative items as well). Best yet, unlike most of the other discount stores, everything on National Wholesale Liquidators' three floors of manufacturers' overstocks and seconds are in pristine condition and don't have dubious expiration dates.

The best and largest of all the discount stores on Canal Street is **Pearl River Mart**. When I sent out my initial e-mail query to friends asking for their suggestions for this book, several wrote back about Pearl River. I was intrigued because I had never heard of the store. So, down I went to Canal Street to check it out. I'm glad I did. This 2-level emporium is a marvel of very cheap, mostly Asian-made products. The aisles teem with both basic necessities and some luxury items, and include everything from imported foods to clothing, cooking supplies, silk handbags, Chinese herbs, loose tea, wallets, stationery, Japanese paper lanterns, bamboo shades, wind chimes and lots of decorative objects at unbelievable prices. Two locations:

277 Canal Street at Broadway—212-431-4770
200 Grand Street between Mott and Mulberry Streets—212-966-1010

In my opinion, of all the general discount merchandise stores out there, **Target** is Valhalla, the big Kahuna. This community-conscious store carries EVERYTHING, and at good prices. The Target housewares section is unparalleled by any other store of its kind. I especially love their Michael Graves designed blenders, coffee pots, flatware, cooking utensils, toasters, alarm clocks, teakettles, picture frames, and knife sets. These ultra-hip domestic items are practical, stylish and designed with a sense of humor. Target features some easy-to-assemble furniture, and carries a large selection of items for the bedroom and bathroom. Penny-pinching fashionistas will have a field day poring through the racks of inexpensive and trendy gear by youthful designer Mossimo. Unfortunately, there are only two Target stores in the New York boroughs (although there are two fairly close to New York in New Jersey, but you need a car to reach them), and they are a pain in the ass to get to. Make the trek however, and a wondrous world awaits you. Look for Target's sales and specials circular inside Sunday editions of the *New York Times*. You may not know this but Target is a huge supporter of Broadway Cares/Equity Fights AIDS. Over the years, they have contributed millions to this worthy organization. So even if Target did not have great discount prices, they would still deserve our patronage. Target locations:

13505 20th Avenue, Flushing, Queens—718–661–4346 (take the 7 train to the end of the line at Flushing/Main Street; from there, you have to take a bus. I recommend you call the store for details

Queens Place, Queens Boulevard and 55th Avenue, Elmhurst, Queens—718–760–5656 (take the E train to Woodhaven, or the G Train to Grand Avenue/Newton)

SAMPLE SALES

ONE OF THE BENEFITS of living in New York is to take advantage of the sample sales that dozens of New York's leading designers and manufacturers hold almost every week. Originally, the term "sample sale" meant exactly that—a sale of designer's samples. Samples are what designers use to entice buyers to purchase their clothing line; at the end of a season when these samples are no longer needed, they are sold to the public at wholesale prices. Today the term is more all encompassing: it includes the sale of any leftover inventory after orders have been filled for retail stores. As you can imagine, these clearance blowouts offer amazing discounts on top-of-the-line clothing, shoes, furniture, linens and housewares and attract hordes of bargain seekers hoping to save megabucks on high-ticket items for their wardrobe and home. To make your sample sale-ing an easy and rewarding experience, I recommend the following:

→ Arrive an hour or more before the sale opens; hardcore sample salers (and there are a lot of them) get there before dawn and almost immediately snap up the best bargains.

→ If you see something you like, buy it—chances are, if you put it down, it won't be there when you return.

→ If you are in the market for something for your home, bring a tape measure as well as pictures and dimensions of the area where you want the item to go. Doing this will help insure that the item fits and goes with your décor as purchases from sample sales are usually not refundable or exchangeable.

→ Most of these sales don't have dressing rooms, so go prepared to try things on in the aisles. That means wearing slim, stretchy clothes that you can slip things over or under. A lady friend who frequents sample sales always wears a sports bra and Lycra tights. She gets a few strange looks, but, as she says, "Who cares, I'm not there to impress people. I'm there to save a fortune."

How can you find out about these weekly wonders? Both the **"Sales and Bargains" section of *New York Magazine*** and the **"Shoptalk" section of *Time Out New York*** provide detailed listings of the dates and locations of sample sales throughout the city. The website www.nysale.com constantly updates its comprehensive list of sales. Also, on any given weekday, saunter through the Garment District and you are sure to see signs or be handed flyers advertising present or future sales. The Garment District is bounded roughly by Sixth and Eighth Avenues and 35th and 41st Streets.

SSS Sample Sale (261 West 36th Street, 2nd Floor—212–947–8748) in the Garment District holds weekly overstock and sample sales of goods by designers and manufacturers at wholesale and below wholesale prices. These sales feature both single and multiple designers, with names like Tahari, Theory, Diesel, and Diane von Furstenberg among many others. The savings here are tremendous—from 50 to 80 percent below retail prices. Advantages of shopping at SSS Sample Sale are that they do have dressing rooms and they do allow you to exchange any item (with the exception of underwear, bodysuits and swimwear, of course) from the same manufacturer as long as the exchange is done within the duration of that manufacturer's sale. For information about present and future sales or to be put on their snail-mail or e-mail lists for upcoming events, call SSS Sample Sale or visit their website at www.clothingline.com.

"BORROWING" APPAREL FROM THE LEADING RETAILERS

NEED SOME NICE CLOTHES for a special occasion or work-related event like an audition, interview, new head shot, party or award ceremony but don't have the cash? An industry secret, told to me long ago, allows you to get around this. Out of the necessity for full disclosure, please don't construe my inclusion of the following as in any way sanctioning such behavior—I'm just the messenger. I feel, though, that it is my duty to pass this secret on to you. Shop at any of the major department or apparel stores that have a *liberal return policy*. Select the items you want, price being no object, and purchase them with a credit card (unless of course you are maxed out—if so, you're out of luck). Do not remove any of the garment care labels or price tags and wear your purchases very carefully. The next day, return the items to the store with a fully rehearsed excuse as to why you no longer want them ("my husband's dot-com tanked," "my fiancée left me for her secretary Fritz, and I bought these things to wear on our honeymoon," "we should have unloaded that Enron stock a long time ago") and have the store credit your charge card. You must return these things looking and smelling brand-new, so when wearing them, make sure to use a generous amount of unscented deodorant, refrain from colognes, stay out of smoky environments, use armpit guards and don't have them dry-cleaned—the lingering smell of dry-cleaning fluid is a dead giveaway. Also, make sure that the items fit right off the rack—once they are tailored, they become yours forever.

FLEA MARKETS

THE FAMOUS AND POPULAR **Annex Antique Fair and Flea Market** (Sixth Avenue between 25th and 26th Streets) is not, I repeat, not a place for the bargain-hungry. There are all kinds of beautiful vintage and antique treasures to be found here—furniture, clothing, china, watches, clocks, decorative pieces, books, collectibles, purses, pens, lamps, jewelry, art work and eyeglass frames—all at prices that you'd expect in this expensive and style-conscious city. Don't let the prices deter you however: View your time at this flea market as a visit to an outdoor museum and enjoy the eye candy. And, the people watching isn't bad either—you'll see all kinds of characters from celebrities and politicians to designers, fashion models, buff Chelsea boys, East Village punks and regular Joes fingering the wares and bargaining with dealers. Perseverance here can pay off: a little diligence and a stomach for haggling can reap gems whose prices will be acceptable to you. I've also found that at the end of the day the dealers are happy to unload their goods at lower prices instead of hauling them home, so don't hesitate to negotiate. The Annex, which averages around 600 dealers and attracts close to 10,000 people per weekend is open on Saturdays and Sundays from sunrise to sunset year-round. Admission is $1.

If the $1 admission price to the Annex offends you, check out the side streets surrounding the Sixth Avenue market and the nearby **Garage Antique Show** (112 West 25th Street between Sixth and Seventh Avenues—212–647–0707). This poor cousin to the Annex is a huge, two-level heated (barely) flea market that specializes in kitsch, the unusual and a lot of junk. As the saying goes, though, "one man's junk is another's gem," and there are a lot of gems to be had here at prices that are much more reasonable than those on Sixth Avenue. If old photos, art by unknowns, reams of nondescript fabric, glass marbles, drawings of plants and insects torn out of ancient encyclopedias, vintage undergarments, antique spectacles, seventies decorative pieces or old magazines, prints and books hold sway over your life, you will hit the jackpot here. Open weekends 7 A.M. to 5 P.M.

The indoor/outdoor **Greenflea Market at I.S. 44** (Columbus Avenue at 76th Street—212–721–0900) has something for everyone and in regard to price and selection is New York's best flea market. This huge "flea" has an abundance of everything you could possibly desire or need in the usual flea market line, such as antique, vintage and new furniture, clothing, jewelry, books, decorative items, prints and records. But it also carries foodstuffs like fresh canned jellies, cider, produce and plants. This market also has lots of stalls that sell necessities like underwear (all new of course), socks, sunglasses and bedding. The prices here are low and the vendors will haggle. Besides these, there are all kinds of beautiful, handmade, collectible, and one-of-a-kind things to grace your home and body that can be bought for a song. The Greenflea at I.S. 44 hours are Sundays from 10 A.M. to 6 P.M. year-round.

The small **Greenflea Market at P.S. 183** (419 East 66th Street at First Avenue—212–721–0900) is ideal for those who want to combine a little antiquing with some grocery shopping. Here you will find produce, prepared foods, fish, eggs and plants as well as items that would not be out of place in Miss Havisham's bedroom. There is more lace, jewelry (costume and real) and silver crammed in here than you'd ever hope to see, unless of course those things are your passion. Open Saturdays year-round from 6 A.M. to 6 P.M.

The **Soho Antiques Fair and Collectibles Market** (Grand Street and Broadway) isn't huge but has a pretty eclectic selection of goods similar to those found at the Annex and the Greenflea at I.S. 44 and for less money. Don't be fooled by this market's "An-

BEST FLEA MARKET

tiques" name; only about half of the dealers sell antique or vintage items. The other fifty percent deal in clothing, accessories and handmade jewelry as well as not-old-enough-to-be-antique furniture, decorative pieces and books, most at prices that won't break the bank. Open every Saturday and Sunday from 9 A.M. to 5 P.M.

THRIFT SHOPS

NEW YORK IS THRIFT SHOP "CENTRAL." There are dozens of these outlets of low-priced, mostly used donated goods, whose proceeds benefit numerous charitable organizations throughout the city. Ostensibly you could furnish your apartment and fill out your wardrobe from any one of these, especially if your fashion sense is shabby-not-so-chic. Still, many of these stores have rendered treasures (I've found a few myself) and are definitely worth a look.

Besides price, the other great thing about thrift shops is that anything you donate to them is tax deductible, which will save you a little money at tax time (and isn't that what this book is all about?) Note: To insure against disputes with the I.R.S. over this deduction, make sure to get a receipt from the charitable organization where you have made your donation; the government requires a photocopy of receipts for any donations whose value exceeds $500. Most places will pick up furniture as well as donations of exceptional quality and value. Call the thrift shop of your choice for drop-off locations, pick-up appointments or further information.

If the city's thrift shops had a flagship store, the **City Opera Thrift Store** (222 East 23rd Street between Second and Third Avenues—212–684–5344) would be the place. The design and layout of this two-story emporium makes you feel—if you don't look too closely at the "merch"—as if you are in a trendy boutique. The condition of most everything here is very good and includes lots of never-used items. The women's section is full of designer dresses, suits, skirts, blouses, sweaters and shoes from a season or two ago with labels like Manolo Blahnik, Dior, St. Laurent, Calvin Klein, Nina Ricci, Adolpho and Jacqueline de Ribes. Upstairs you can locate a good selection of mostly antique and vintage furniture although there are a few modern pieces (a chaise longue upholstered in a sand-colored wool fabric and in impeccable shape was selling for $400). There are pictures and frames galore, housewares, dishes, cups, glasses, books (50¢ for paperbacks, $1 to $3 for hard covers), records ($1 each) and CDs ($4). On a recent visit, the store's window displayed dozens of gold and cream colored Mary McFadden "mother-of-the-bride" (or so they seemed to me) shoes for $35. Women's designer suits were marked around $65 and evening gowns from $10 to $80. In the men's section, there were an inordinate number of pairs of tuxedo pants and black patent leather shoes (did these appear in a recent City Opera production?) for $10 each; designer sport coats and suits between $15 and $25; and men's shirts were $5. The City Opera Thrift Store has occasional sales and all items with a red dot are half-price.

Smack in the middle of the charity shop district on Third Avenue on the Upper East Side, the **Godmother's League Thrift Store** (1459 Third Avenue between 82nd and 83rd Streets—212–988–2858) is more like the thrifts you'd find downtown. There is a lot of clutter, a lot of junk and a lot of dust. Since you're not here for the decor, you're here for deals, if you're willing to dig through shelves and racks of stuff (which for me is the fun part of thrifting) you will find some. Books and records start at $1; women's blouses, skirts, shoes and pants are as low as $10. Men's shirts, shoes and pants also start at $10. There's plenty of luggage, jewelry, furniture (tons of melamine tables and ugly chairs in the basement), old skis, roller blades, china, glassware, toys and shelves of stuff whose purpose is murky to me. On my last foray to Godmother's, all clothing was 50 percent off. Profits benefit the West End Children's Day School, which assists children with special needs.

Goodwill Industries of Greater New York is a not-for-profit organization serving people with mental and physical disabilities, the unemployed, people who are economically disadvantaged, mature workers and disadvantaged youth. Goodwill stores provide a service to the community by offering new and gently used clothing, toys, household items and furniture at low costs. The stores also provide a training ground in retail for persons with disabilities and other barriers to employment, and your purchases help finance Goodwill's rehabilitative programs. The quality and type of goods at these stores is what you'd expect (as are the prices—very low with daily half-price sales on designated items), but unlike many of the city's other thrift shops, there is a surprising paucity of furniture. Goodwill has eight locations in the New York area; check your phone book for the nearest store.

The **Help Line Thrift Shop** (382 Third Avenue between 27th and 28th Streets—212-532-5136), whose sales benefit a 24-hour counseling hotline, is a mini version of the Salvation Army/Goodwill stores; it carries the same dusty merchandise, has the same musty smell and is in disarray. I've been told that there are real finds here, but that has not been my fortune. I saw clothing that was more than "gently worn" on a recent visit, incomplete dish sets, battered TVs that I can't imagine really work and a few pieces of drag queen quality costume jewelry. The Help Line's appeal is its prices . . . the stuff here is dirt-cheap. You can have CDs for $2 each, winter overcoats for $15, "designer" items for both men and women for between $10 and $20. The shop holds periodic sales where all furniture and clothing is half off the marked prices, and they offer free gift certificates so that for a purchase of $50, you receive a $5 certificate; $75 yields $10; and $100 gets you another $15 worth of items.

Housing Works has five stores that help fund its programs to provide housing, support services, job training and advocacy for homeless men, women and children living with HIV and AIDS. You can find some great items at these hip and stylish thrifts at very low prices. Good-quality furniture, eclectic decorative items, books, CDs, housewares and clothes are, for the most part, fash-

BEST THRIFT SHOP

ionable and in good condition. Some of the best stuff is held for
display in each of the store's provocative windows and sold by
silent auction. Housing Works has a high turnover on its goods so
that you can shop at any one of the stores several times a week
and never see the same items twice. Locations:

202 East 77th Street between Second and Third Avenues—
212–772–8461

157 East 23rd Street between Third and Lexington Avenues—212–529–5955

306 Columbus Avenue between 74th & 75th Streets—
212–579–7566

143 West 17th Street between Sixth and Seventh Avenues—212–366–0820

126 Crosby Street south of Houston (Used Book Café)—
212–334–3324

The popular **Memorial Sloane-Kettering Center Thrift
Shop** (1440 Third Avenue near 82nd Street—212–535–1250) supports this charity's hospital and patient-care programs and is
considered the city's premiere thrift shop. Frankly, I don't get all
the hoopla. Yeah, sure, this store carries top-drawer (say that
with a locked jaw) merchandise like antique furniture and china,
chandeliers, sterling silver, designer clothing and estate jewelry.
And yeah, sure, the condition of most everything is pretty near
perfect. But puhleeze, this is a thrift shop, not Saks Fifth Avenue
. . . the prices are just too damn high. For instance: a women's
Chanel suit for $850, a man's sportscoat from Orbachs Depart-
ment Store for $300, a 24-piece set of Tiffany silver goblets and
sherbet dishes for $3600. If you come for the bargains here, you'll
have to work hard to find them. I found some men's pants as low
as $10; a few women's suits and dresses at $35; a couple of men's
suits priced at $45; and a man's three-quarter-length shearling
coat at only $125. This shop also has a $10 "As Is" rack, but with
just a cursory glance, you'll know why. The Memorial Sloane-Kettering store also carries books and housewares, but their prices
are higher than the other thrift shops in the area.

The proceeds of the **Parish of Calvary/St. George's Vintage Furniture Shop** support the church's outreach programs for shelters, AIDS patients and alcohol and drug programs. These stores carry exquisite pre-50s vintage furniture as well as paintings, Oriental rugs, lighting fixtures, mirrors, chandeliers and decorative bric-a-brac. Most of their items are in antique store condition at moderate prices. They have an especially good selection of both dining room sets (some art deco) and bedroom sets. The church also runs a clothing thrift shop in the basement consisting of far from vintage—really of the moment (okay, last year's moment)—items at very affordable prices. The Parish's shops are at:

> 277 Park Avenue South between 21st and 22nd Streets—212–475–6645
> 61 Gramercy Park North—212–475–2674

The very cramped **Out of the Closet Thrift Shop** (220 East 81st Street between Second and Third Avenues—212–472–3573) feels like it is really two stores—a thrift shop and an antique emporium. The antiques here are mostly the kind of stuff you'd see in your grandmother's home, with an abundance of porcelain figurines and dainty lamps, at prices that are on par with local antique dealers. The shop's real bargains are on books and records (starting as low as $1) and men's and women's clothing. Dresses and blouses can be as little as $10; men's suits can be had for $45 and lots of trousers and shirts at $10. One hundred percent of Out of the Closet's proceeds from sales of items that also include silver, crystal, china, framed artwork, collectibles, furniture, crafts, linens, rugs and appliances, supports over 55 organizations and institutions fighting AIDS.

After the **Salvation Army's** 2002 mischief during which they secretly lobbied the Bush White House to gain exemption from the nondiscrimination order that all organizations receiving federal funds are bound to, I can't enthusiastically recommend patronizing their thrift shops. The Army wanted to create a loophole in the law that would allow it to continue receiving taxpayer dollars, but *legally* exempt it from hiring gays and lesbians. Fortunately, the gay press uncovered the imbroglio, and the White House, in an attempt to save face, withdrew its support for the effort.

Worse yet, the Salvation Army rescinded its earlier decision to allow its West Coast division to offer health care benefits to the domestic partners of its employees, after Salvation Army officials received a barrage of criticism from fundamentalist Christian and anti-gay groups, who complained that the popular charitable organization was bowing to pressure by "militant homosexuals." Under this reversal of policy, the Salvation Army will withdraw from or decline to enter into contracts with any city or municipality that requires a domestic partner benefits program as a condition for providing social services programs. Too bad that this organization which does so much good, has done so much bad. Having said that, I will now hop off my soapbox. . . .

The Salvation Army uses the proceeds from its many thrift stores to fund its residential facility for substance abusers. The goods at these stores, which include furniture, housewares, clothing, knickknacks, toys and more (all used of course), are real hit or miss; when they are hits, however they can be home-runs. Women should note that the Salvation Army has no dressing rooms, so if you'd like to try things on, do as a friend of mine does—go wearing running shorts and a sports bra.

I have had two great Salvation Army successes: I paid $700 for a huge, vintage (it was built in the '30s) Empire-style breakfront that I use as a bookcase/storage cabinet/room divider and that always elicits oohs and ahhs from first-time visitors to my home. It is my favorite piece of furniture and the one thing I'm sure I will hang onto until I have shuffled off this mortal coil. For $17.85, I picked up a pair of blond wood Alvar Aalto stools that I've been told are worth $1,000 a piece.

There's gold in them thar stores! There are eight Salvation Army locations in the greater New York area; consult your local listings for the nearest store.

The boutique-like **Spence-Chapin Thrift Shops**, which fund this nonprofit organization's commitment to finding homes for infants and children, carry a variety of items at very low prices. At both Upper East Side stores, there is new and gently used "better" clothing, accessories, shoes, jewelry and handbags, with separate sections selling designer fashions and furs. Other items for sale include books, records, tapes, CDs, furniture (some antique and vintage), art, china, silverware, glassware, linens, housewares, computers, software and video games. The prices in the stores' clearance areas are so low, they're practically giving the stuff away. Recently, I found racks of women's overcoats and dresses for $20, a case of $5 jewelry, a basket of slightly used purses for $10, new purses for just $15, and a box of items like china and glassware for $1 each. Furs and furniture were all 50 percent off marked prices. Hardcover books are always $1 each; paperbacks are 50¢ each or three for $1. These shops are definitely a step above the Salvation Army and Goodwill stores, with most merchandise in good condition.

> 1473 Third Avenue between 83rd and 84th Streets—
> 212–737–8448
> 1850 Second Avenue between 95th and 96th Streets—
> 212–426–7643

The Center for Urban Community Services (CUCS) provides services for homeless and formerly homeless people, especially those with mental illness, HIV/AIDS and chemical dependency. CUCS' programs include street outreach, a drop-in center, transitional and permanent housing and vocational and employment programs. To underwrite some of these programs and to provide training and jobs for tenants of its supportive housing, CUCS runs the **Sugar Hill Thrift Shop** (409 West 145th Street between St. Nicholas and Convent Avenues—

212–281–2396). This charming and popular shop carries inexpensive vintage clothing, gently used household goods, toys, and antiques. You can also find newer merchandise here along with the same stuff you'd expect to see at any other thrift shop, all at very low prices.

OTHER NEW YORK CITY THRIFT SHOPS:

→ **Angel Street Thrift Shop:** 118 West 17th Street between Sixth and Seventh Avenues—212–229–0546

→ **Arthritis Foundation Thrift Shop:** 121 E. 77th Street between Park and Lexington Avenues—212–772–8816

→ **Cabrini Thrift Store:** 520 Main Street, Roosevelt Island—212–486–8958

→ **Cancer Care Thrift Shop:** 1480 Third Avenue at 84th Street—212–879–9868

→ **Care Partners Thrift Shop:** 475 Atlantic Avenue, Brooklyn—718–852–2437

→ **Council Thrift Shop:** 246 East 84th Street between Second and Third Avenues—212–439–8373

→ **Good Old Lower East Side Thrift Shop:** 17 Avenue B at 2nd Street—212–358–1041

→ **Monk Thrift Shop:** 165 Avenue A at 9th Street—917–534–0511

→ **St. Luke's Thrift Shop:** 487 Hudson Street between Christopher and Barrow Streets—212–924–9364

→ **St. Margaret's House Thrift Shop:** 49 Fulton Street near Gold Street—212–766–8122

→ **Sirovich Thrift Shop:** 331 East 12th Street between First and Second Avenues—212–228–7836

→ **Vintage Thrift Shop:** 286 Third Avenue between 22nd and 23rd Streets—212–871–0777

STREET FAIRS

HARDLY A WEEKEND GOES BY from late spring through the summer to early fall that a street fair is not going on in some part of the city. Although they take place in the city's many diverse neighborhoods, every one of them is mostly composed of the same kinds of stuff—lots of funnel cake vendors, Italian sausage sandwich makers and "Pina Colada" stands. So much for diversity! However, the street fairs also attract several entrepreneurs who are selling all kinds of things you might want for prices that are less than you'd pay at a retail store. Visit the street fairs for deals on everything from plants and 100 percent cotton sheet sets to jewelry, art, men's/women's/children's clothing, sunglasses, pottery, Japanese crockery and tea sets, toys, internet service providers and long distance phone companies, CDs, videos, towels, candles, home furnishings, hats, makeup, temporary tattoos, leather handbags and wallets, and even cheap ten-minute massages. For a complete listing of street fairs, consult either the "Weekend Fine Arts/Leisure" section of the Friday edition of *The New York Times,* the "Around Town" section of *Time Out New York, The New York Press* or *The Village Voice.*

OUTLET STORES

BECAUSE OF REAL-ESTATE PRICES, there are no Outlet Malls in Manhattan. But a handful are reasonably accessible by bus, car or train. These upscale malls feature the best and brightest designers, manufacturers and retailers of clothing, housewares, handbags, accessories, perfumes, linens, china, stemware, and luggage. They are oases for designer-addicted bargain shoppers, who find most merchandise discounted between 25 percent and 70 percent off their original prices.

Although these malls host stores that are trendsetters of taste and the fashionable, their settings have a distinctly "camp" quality. Most are designed to look like faux Colonial, country or fishing villages, complete with artificial shingled cottages, fake cobblestone streets, weathervane adorned roofs and bell-clanging trolleys. I don't know why this is; perhaps Outlet Mall mucky-mucks test-marketed and found that most Americans like shopping in sterile, counterfeit environments. The urban-edged New Yorker in me can only take so much of this squeaky-clean kitsch before I start breaking out in hives; fortunately, the savings these Outlet Malls provide is a perfect salve:

Considered the oldest Outlet Mall in the nation, **Liberty Village** (Flemington, New Jersey—908–782–8550—www.premiumoutlets.com) is the area's most intimate outlet center. Liberty Village has only sixty stores including Calvin Klein, Donna Karan, Tommy Hilfiger, Perry Ellis, Nautica, Jones New York, Izod, Bass, Nine West, Etienne Aigner, Fossil, Sunglass World, and Villeroy & Boch. Because of its size, Liberty Village draws smaller crowds than the other area malls, which is a blessing for mob-phobic, long-line-loathing shoppers. From Manhattan, take the Trans-Bridge bus from the Port Authority Bus Terminal (800–962–9135); buses depart every couple of hours between 7:30 A.M. and 8:15 P.M. Round-trip is $23.30, $10.80 for seniors, and $11.60 for children under 12.

Tanger Outlet Center, (Riverhead, New York—800–407–4894—www.tangeroutlet.com), located on Long Island, is a short, pleasant journey from the city. This discount shopping center is really two separate malls linked by a trolley and has over 160 stores featuring a "Who's Who" roster of designers, manufacturers and retailers. Brands include Aldo, Anne Klein, Barney's New York, Bath and Body Works, Benetton, Bombay, Books Warehouse, Children's Place, Christmas Market, Club Monaco, Dana Buchman, Danskin, Disney, Eddie Bauer, Harry and David, Hugo Boss, Hoover, Joe Boxer, Lillian Vernon, Lindt Chocolate, Mikasa, Noritake, Pepperidge Farm, Pottery Barn, Skechers, Samsonite, The Wiz, Zales. There are two ways to get to the Tanger Center: by bus, take Sunrise Coach Lines, which departs several times a day from Port Authority (800–527–7709)—round-trip is $29, free for children under 5. By train, take the Long Island Rail Road from Penn Station (718–330–1234, www.lirr.org) to Riverhead; round trip is $30.50 peak, $20.50 off-peak; $15 for seniors anytime; for children - $15 peak, $10.50 off-peak.

Woodbury Commons, (Central Valley, New York—845–928–4000—www.chelseagca.com) the mother of all area Outlet stores, offers everyday savings of 25 percent to 65 percent on the world's greatest designers. Here you'll find Armani, BCBG Max Azria, Dolce & Gabbana, Christian Dior, Frette, Gucci, Kenneth Cole, Malo, Max Mara, Judith Leiber, Neiman Marcus, Saks Fifth Avenue, Polo Ralph Lauren, Salvatore Ferragamo, TSE, Versace, Waterford, Wedgwood, Le Creuset, and more. In addition, outlet mall regulars like Banana Republic, Nike, Patagonia, Gap, Guess, Brooks Brothers and Cole Haan are here. To get to Woodbury Commons, take

BEST OUTLET MALL

the Short Line Bus from Port Authority (800–631–8405—www.shortlinebus.com). Round-trip is $22.45, $12.45 for children; seven buses leave throughout the day, the first at 7:15 A.M., the last at 6:15 P.M.

HAGGLING

IN MERRIAM-WEBSTER'S Collegiate Dictionary, *haggle* is defined as both "to cut roughly or clumsily" and "to annoy or exhaust with wrangling." According to the Random House Dictionary, to *haggle* is "to bargain in a petty, quibbling manner." Until recently, haggling was regarded by many (shopkeepers, the shy, cowards) with the same negative connotations and considered the bailiwick of people termed ballsy, aggressive and terminally cheap. In New York, haggling was solely the province of specific neighborhoods (the Lower East Side and Canal Street) and restricted to particular products such as antiques, leather goods, jewelry and electronics. Suddenly, however, the practice has become *de rigueur* throughout the five boroughs and at a number of retailers. Even department stores are getting into the act: a 2002 *New York Times* article about haggling cited a Bloomingdale's customer who negotiated down the cost of two sofas and got them at half their marked price.

Chalk this change up to the sagging economy and the aftermath of September 11, as more and more consumers are using haggling as a way to get the best for less and hold on to a little more of their hard-earned cash. Retailers are encouraging negotiation as a way to finalize a sale they might not make otherwise.

How does one haggle? Easy. If there is a product or service you desire but don't want to pay the list price, ask for a discount. There are a lot of ways to do this: "How much will you come down?" "Can you do any better on the price?" "Would you accept X amount?" "I saw this at such-and-such a place for less. Can you match it or do better?" The worst that can happen is that you will be told no.

Fancying myself an expert at haggling (I've gotten everything from furniture to books, clothing, paint and appliances as well as services like gym memberships, yoga classes and medical care by doing this), the following are my sure-fire suggestions to become a savvy negotiator:

1) Don't reserve negotiating only to stores that honor or better a competitor's advertised price. Many more retailers than you'd imagine will haggle. You won't know which ones unless you try.

2) Bargain with confidence. If you act at all timid or embarrassed, the merchant will see it and will barely deal, if at all.

3) Start with a number lower than you're willing to pay, as the retailer may accept this figure. If not, wrangle up to the amount you deem satisfactory while acting as if you're being forced to go higher than you wanted.

4) Cash speaks louder than credit; retailers are more likely to haggle for the paper stuff than the plastic.

5) Be prepared to walk away from a sale if the negotiation breaks down. More often than not, if you start to leave, the retailer will agree to your proposal or, at the very least, make a counteroffer. For a lot of merchants, a lesser sale is better than none at all.

Now, screw up your courage and go out there and haggle!

"CRAIGSLIST"

THE WONDERFUL COMMUNITY-BASED website **Craigslist** (http://newyork.craigslist.org) is an ideal place to find almost anything you're looking for at rock-bottom prices. This free site, which is part classifieds, part forums, and part civic outreach, was established to "provide a trustworthy, efficient means for folks to get the word out regarding everyday stuff, and connect with others locally to find jobs, housing, companionship, community." Craigslist makes good on this by offering copious "help wanted" listings as well as those for community needs and events (covering everything from childcare to classes, ridesharing, activity partners, pets, artists, musicians and more), personals and housing (see chapter on "Finding a Home"). Its Forums section offers discussion groups on hot topics like politics, restaurants, housing, the job market, nightlife and romance.

Craigslist's huge "Stuff for Sale" section gives New Yorkers the opportunity to list whatever it is they want to unload. Here you'll find a multitude of offerings from bicycles, motorcycles, cars, trucks, computers, technical equipment, electronics, to tickets to arts and sporting events, furniture, general merchandise and much more. Also listed are moving and apartment sales, "items wanted," and members of the community looking to swap or barter goods and services. Craigslist is totally free to browse, provides an easy and accessible way to search for the items you are looking for, allows no ads and has prices that are far below what you'd pay at most retailers.

WEEKLY SALES LISTINGS AND DISCOUNT COUPONS

EACH WEEK READ *New York Magazine* and *Time Out New York* to locate all kinds of sales that are happening throughout the city. The categories vary widely, from clothing and accessories stores to food purveyors, gyms and health clubs, beauty spas, housewares and home emporiums, hair salons, opticians and even service businesses like dog-walkers, dry-cleaners, personal shoppers and organizers, and house cleaning services. *New York Magazine Shops* published twice a year by *New York Magazine,* not only lists the best stores in Manhattan, but also includes articles on sample sales, bargains and discounts.

Do you receive those annoying packets of **"Val-Pac Coupons"** or **"Super Coups"** in the mail that you immediately throw away without opening? Most New Yorkers do. Next time, actually open the envelope and look at what is offered. You'll be surprised at the specials and savings. Coupons are mostly for car services and rug-and-fabric cleaning companies, but occasionally offer discounts to restaurants, health clubs, parking garages, moving and storage companies, pharmacies, and other retailers, and these can save you a lot of money. If for no other reason, use them for the discount car services to take you to New York area airports; you can save anywhere from $5 to $15 over what you'd pay to take a cab

The Village Voice a free, left-leaning newspaper, hits the newsstands every Tuesday evening. Besides its comprehensive articles on everything from New York City politics to music, art, theater, concert listings, it is a veritable guide to everything cheap in New

York. It is packed with ads for inexpensive stores and services, including futons, furniture, gyms, travel agents, electronics, cameras, mobile phones, music stores, opticians, clothing, restaurants, kung fu classes, even inexpensive doctors, dentists, liposuction and laser eye surgery. The Voice's Classifieds section is considered one of the best sources for finding an apartment (see chapter on "Apartment Hunting") in the city—not to mention a job, a "massage" or even a potential life partner!

The **website www.nysale.com** is a great tool for the sales savvy New York shopper. This one website lets you search for current and future sales by specific products, date, category or store. Each day, NYSale.com lists sample sales, going-out-of-business sales and clearances from department stores like Bloomingdale's and Barney's to small boutiques and designer showrooms. Store categories on the site include women's, men's and children's apparel, accessories, jewelry, furnishings, eyewear, maternity and much more. NYSale.com provides links to leading designers and manufacturers and free information on the most current sales via e-mail. Membership at NYSale.com is free, but you must register if you want to surf the site or receive their daily e-mail messages about current sales.

Bargain Retail Areas

Why not combine shopping with a walk? Even in this very expensive city there are whole corridors of bargain retail areas where you'll find incredible deals while becoming acquainted with several distinctive neighborhoods:

The **Bowery below Houston** has many discount lighting and restaurant supply stores.

The side streets near **City Hall** from Broadway to Church Street swarm with discount retailers. Particularly noteworthy are Chambers, Duane and Reade Streets where you can find a glut of cut-rate linens, toiletries, books, paper goods, party supplies and clothing.

Canal Street, of course, which I have already discussed in my chapter on "General Merchandise Discount Stores," has innumerable electronics and surplus stores as well as other shops carrying a surfeit of cheap counterfeit everything.

14th Street between Union Square South and Eighth Avenue has several stores that carry a multitude of cheap items. Here you'll find lots of toys, sheet sets, umbrellas, towels, paper goods, party supplies, CDs and clothing you probably won't buy (unless you are costuming a play about people with no taste).

Many of the streets between Sixth and Eighth Avenues in the **Garment District** (41st Street to 34th Street) have discount fabric, notions, trim, button, ribbon and lace shops as well as "Wholesale to the Public" clothing stores.

The entire **Lower East Side** has been designated New York's "Historic Bargain District" (for more information call 212–226–9010) and the title is apt. This area, which has been the bargain center of the city for the last hundred years, is a mecca for inexpensive goods like CDs, sunglasses, designer apparel, fabric, luggage, retro furniture, lighting fixtures and much more. Also, some of the city's best cheap restaurants, bars and cafes are in this neighborhood.

The **Madison Square Garden/Penn Station area**, especially the **north side of 34th Street between Seventh and Eighth Avenues** (the anchor on this block is the Conway Department Store; see chapter on "General Merchandise Stores") houses several low-price clothing, shoe and gift stores. I do not know the quality of the merchandise these stores carry, but a quick march through each showed me incredibly low prices.

St. Marks Place, home to New York's punkers, club kids and other colorful characters, has tons of inexpensive CD stores lining both sides of the streets. You'll find a lot of tattoo parlors, jewelry stores, booksellers and street vendors hawking everything from obscene tee-shirts to sunglasses and hats. Even if you don't buy anything here, you'll definitely have a good time gawking at the passersby.

Sixth Avenue between 24th and 32nd Streets is lined with all kinds of discount specialty stores selling shoes, hats, clothing, plants, fabric and notions, gifts, watches, Army/Navy surplus items and much more.

PART VI

All Work and No Play...

ICONS OF NEW YORK

A WHILE AGO, I was going through a dry spell when I couldn't get work to save my life. I had lots of auditions and was called back for almost everything, but couldn't book a single job. I was unhappy and frustrated. I shared my frustration with my agent Nancy who said, "Craig Wroe" (she always calls me by my full name), "don't worry about it. The more you sweat it, the worse you'll do in future auditions. Know that you'll work again and in the meantime, do fun things around the city, play on the weekends and enjoy your life."

This was one of the best bits of advice I've ever received. It helped me change my attitude and reminded me not only that I am more than just an actor, but also that I should be taking advantage of all the pleasures this amazing city has to offer. Now, my daily mantra is "enjoy your life."

There's a world of wonders for us to explore in this great big city of ours, and most are free or incredibly cheap. Now that you've taken care of the nuts and bolts of living in New York—gotten settled, found a home and furnished it, opened a bank account, discovered the cheap places to buy groceries, laid claim to your favorite inexpensive restaurants, scoped out the stores that carry the affordable clothes you like, learned how to get around town, gotten a haircut and massage, found a doctor, and shared all your frustrations with a shrink—it's time to enjoy your life. Hopefully the following will help you do that.

With more than 6,000 animals spread over 265 acres, the **Bronx Zoo/Wildlife Conservation Society** (Bronx River Parkway at Fordham Road, Bronx—718–367–1010) is the nation's largest urban zoo. The Bronx Zoo was one of the first in the world to showcase its animals in habitats that recreate the environment and terrain of their natural homes. Of special note is the zoo's newest attraction, Congo Gorilla Forest, a habitat for several primates including two troops of gorillas, and other animals that are indigenous to the African rainforest. Although this is primarily a walking zoo, there is a train, an aerial tramway and a monorail to whisk you from one area to another. *Free on Wednesday*.

Whether by foot, bike or skate, the trek across the **Brooklyn Bridge** provides the most awesome view of New York. Looking south you can see the Statue of Liberty, New York Harbor and the Verrazano Narrows Bridge; looking north you can see some of the network of bridges (all of which were built after the Brooklyn Bridge) that connect Manhattan to Brooklyn and Queens; to the west are the shimmering buildings of the Financial District; and to the east, the rooftops and trees of Brooklyn spread to the horizon. The bridge itself is a thing of beauty. Sixteen years in the making and completed in 1883, the bridge's graceful gothic towers have been immortalized in paintings, film, poetry and even an ad campaign (a popular ad shows the arches altered to look like Absolut bottles). As you stroll along the pedestrian walkway, be sure to read the plaques detailing the bridge's history and commemorating its architects and twenty workers who died during construction.

The **Brooklyn Heights Promenade**, which runs along the East River between Cranberry and Remsen Streets in Brooklyn Heights, provides romantic views of the sceptered isle of Manhattan, the Statue of Liberty and Ellis Island. Ever since the events of September 11, 2001, the view, sans the World Trade Center, is heartbreaking; what was once a favorite spot to ogle the Manhattan skyline has become a quiet place for mourning and catharsis. To get to the Promenade, take the N, R, 2, 3, 4, or 5 subway to Court Street/Borough Hall.

The **Cathedral of St. John the Divine** (Amsterdam Avenue and 110th Street—212–316–7540), home to the Episcopal Diocese of New York and already the world's largest cathedral, is (and will be for the unforeseeable future) still under construction. This very progressive church is not only a place of worship, but is also a monument and memorial to famous writers, immigrants, firefighters who have lost their lives in the line of duty, victims of genocide, and those who have died from AIDS. Throughout the year, St. John offers concerts, art exhibitions, poetry readings, lectures and dance performances. *Admission to the Cathedral is always free,* (although donations are encouraged) and guided tours are $3.

When you're in the mood to splurge, and it's well worth the money, take a **Circle Line** boat ride around Manhattan. It's a fun, relaxing way to see our famous skyline in all its glory and to get a feel for the size of the island. It's also a great thing to do with out-of-towners, and, on a 90-degree day, a breath of air for apartment dwellers. Circle Line's two- and three- hour cruises depart from Pier 83 (West 42nd Street at Hudson River). The two-hour trip travels around lower Manhattan, while the three-hour cruise circles the island; both excursions include a close up view of the Statue of Liberty. Prices for the two-hour cruise: adults (13 and over) $20, seniors (65 and over) $17, children (3–12 years old) $10; for the three-hour cruise: adults $25, seniors $20, children $12. Operating hours vary throughout the year; call 212–563–3200 for a schedule or visit their website at www.circleline.com.

The **Columbia University Observatory** (Pupin Hall, 2960 Broadway at 116th Street) *is free and open to the public two Fridays per month from September through May.* Show up an hour after sunset and follow the signs to the roof, where you can spend two hours stargazing under the guidance of an astronomy grad or professor.

Coney Island (1000 Surf Avenue at West 10th Street, Brooklyn—718–372–0275), one of the first and most flamboyant amusement parks in the country, is now a shell of its former self. Most of the rides have been abandoned or ravaged by time and fire, and the feeling of lost opulence is palpable. Still though, there is a lot to do and see here. There are several moderately priced rides, attractions and sideshows you can catch including the 75-year-old Cyclone wooden roller coaster that continues to induce near heart attacks. For me, Coney Island's major draw is its people watching along the three-mile boardwalk. You think you've seen colorful characters in the East Village? Nothing tops some of the folks you'll see here. Make sure to check out, at least once, the Coney Island Mermaid Parade. Held on the last Saturday in June, this very campy parade marches from Surf Avenue and 10th Street to Steeplechase Park, and features some of the zaniest mermaid-inspired floats and costumes that you have ever seen.

Ever since the devastating events of September 11, 2001, the **Empire State Building** (350 Fifth Avenue at 34th Street—212–736–3100) has once again become the tallest skyscraper in New York. This Art-Deco gem, completed in 1931, is without a doubt, one of the most famous structures in the world. Not only is it a landmark, an office building, and a one-time perch for King Kong, it also offers visitors spectacular aerial views of the city. From the observatories on the 86th and 102nd floors, you can see as far as eighty miles away in all directions. This is the best place to go to understand the city's layout, to bring out-of-towners for some oohing and ahhing or to have a romantic interlude. *Admission to the observation decks is an affordable $9, $7 for seniors, $4 for children between 5 and 12 and free for those under 5.* Due to tightened security, prepare to wait on line an hour or more, especially in peak summer months.

The enormous and intimidating **Federal Reserve Bank of New York** (33 Liberty Street between Nassau and William

Streets—212–720–6130), modeled after a Florentine Renaissance palace (and just as impenetrable), processes approximately $400 million dollars a day and holds about a quarter of the world's gold bullion in vaults five stories below street level. *Free* one-hour tours of the gold vault, cash area and money-related exhibits are held weekdays on the half-hour between 9:30 A.M. and 2:30 P.M. To book one of these popular tours, contact the Bank by mail or phone at least two weeks in advance.

Grand Central Terminal (East 42nd Street between Madison and Lexington Avenues) has just completed a years-long cleaning/restoration/renovation, which has returned this transportation hub to its former sparkling beaux-arts glory. Be sure to take in the constellations of the zodiac that grace the ceiling on the Main Concourse as well as the famous clock atop the information kiosk in the center of the hall. Although Grand Central is a fully operational train station, it is a destination in its own right with frequent art exhibits, upscale restaurants and bars, European-style food purveyors, a food court, trendy retail shops and occasional classical music performances. Two groups offer *free* organized tours of the terminal—Grand Central Partnership leads tours every Friday at 12:30 P.M. (meet across the street at the Philip Morris Building, 120 Park Avenue at 42nd Street—212–883–2468), and the Municipal Art Society conducts tours every Wednesday at 12:30 P.M. (meet at the central information booth on the Main Concourse—212–439–1049).

Reputed to have been built on the spot where the film *West Side Story* was shot, **Lincoln Center** (65th Street at Columbus Avenue—212–546–2656) is one of the world's largest and most famous arts complexes (see chapters on "Viewing Theater," "Viewing Dance," "Viewing Opera" and "Listening to Music"). Lincoln Center's main performing halls include Alice Tully, Avery Fisher, Metropolitan Opera House, New York State Theater, Vivian Beaumont Theater and the Mitzi E. Newhouse Theater and can accommodate over 13,000 audience members on any given night. Lincoln Center is also home to the newly renovated New York Library of the Performing Arts (see chapter on "Books, Plays and Scripts"), the Juilliard School of Music, the Fiorello La Guardia High School of the Performing Arts and the Walter Reade Movie Theater. The Center's Italianate plaza, large water fountain, reflecting pool and Damrosch Park (home to the Big Apple Circus in winter and various performances during the Lincoln Center Out-of-Doors Festival in the summer) are peaceful havens for spectators as well as anyone seeking a respite from the city.

For a "behind-the-scenes" look at the Center, you may take a backstage tour of the Met, Avery Fisher Hall and New York State Theater costing $9.50 for adults, $8 for students with ID and $4.75 for children. Tours, lasting about an hour, depart from the desk at the downstairs concourse level at 10:30 A.M., 12:30 P.M., 2:30 P.M. and 4:30 P.M. For more information regarding tours or to make reservations, call 212–875–5350.

The **Metropolitan Museum of Art** (Fifth Avenue and 82nd Street), which is always *"Pay-As-You-Wish,"* welcomes more than 5 million visitors annually, and its unrivalled collections span 5,000 years of art, culture and history from every part of the world. (See chapter on "Museums" for a more in-depth description.)

Famous the world over for the stone lions posted in front of its gorgeous beaux-arts façade, the **New York Public Library— Humanities and Social Sciences Library** (455 Fifth Avenue at 42nd Street—212–869–8089) is the main branch of the library system and one of the city's architectural gems. Be sure to check out the Rose reading room—about as ostentatious and awe-inspiring a main reading room as anything I've ever seen. If you find yourself at the library on a warm sunny day, sit on the steps out front for some of the best people watching in New York. *Free guided tours are conducted at 11 A.M. and 2 P.M. Monday to Saturday.*

Located in Flushing Meadows Park, the **Queens Wildlife Center** (111th Street and 53rd Avenue, Queens—718–271–1500) features mostly animals found in North America, a walk-through aviary and a children's petting zoo. *Adult admission is $2.50, $1.25 for seniors, 50¢ for children under 12.*

Riverside Church (490 Riverside Drive at 120th Street—212–870–6700), built by the Rockefeller family, is home to the world's largest carillon. The 400-foot tower, which holds 74 huge bells, also offers dramatic views of the city and across the Hudson. *Admission is always free.*

Give yourself a free, self-guided tour of the Art-Deco master-piece **Rockefeller Center** (Fifth Avenue between 49th and 51st Streets—212–632–3975). In 19 buildings occupying 22 acres of some of the most expensive real estate in the world, Rockefeller Center has a vast array of public art. There are murals, mosaics, sculpture, metalwork and enamels as well as the famed Prometheus statue that soars above the ice rink, and the majestic Atlas who balances the world on his shoulders in front of the International Building. Rockefeller Center is also home to Radio City Music Hall and the NBC studios. During the Christmas holidays, be sure to take in the colossal Christmas tree, which is decorated with thousands of colorful lights.

The four-minute ride on the **Roosevelt Island Tramway**, for the same price as the bus and subway, gives you expansive views of Manhattan and Queens from 250 feet above the East River. Once you've arrived on Roosevelt Island, stroll along the promenade that faces the city or take the minibus tour of the island for only a quarter. For a bit of romance, board the tramway at night with your companion and a bottle of wine (be discreet).

St. Patrick's Cathedral (Fifth Avenue and 50th Street—212–753–2261), the seat of the Catholic Diocese in New York and a supporting player in the film *Easter Parade,* is a Gothic Revival masterpiece inside and out. *Admission for worshippers and visitors alike is always free* and there are religious services daily.

The round-trip ride on the **Staten Island Ferry** (718–815–BOAT), which takes a half hour each way, *is always free* and has breathtaking views of the city, the harbor, the Brooklyn Heights Promenade, Governor's Island, Ellis Island and the Statue of Liberty. Taking the ferry on a balmy summer night is without a doubt the most romantic (not to mention cheapest) way to woo a potential life partner. For some people, it's better than foreplay! You can catch the ferry at Manhattan's southernmost tip at Battery Park.

The **Staten Island Zoo** (614 Broadway, Staten Island— 718–442–3100), which is tiny in size but enormous in ambition, is home to a large and varied menagerie of creatures including animals found in the tropical rainforest and the African savannah. The zoo houses aquarium displays, a definitive collection of reptiles and a farmlike setting where children may feed and pet animals and ride ponies. *Entrance is a very affordable $3 for ages 12 and up, $2 for children between 3 and 11, and free for those under 3; Wednesdays between 2 P.M. and 4:45 P.M. are always "Pay-As-You-Wish."*

The **Statue of Liberty** is both New York City's and the nation's greatest landmark and most enduring symbol of freedom. Designed by French sculptor Frederic-Auguste Bartholdi and built soon after the Civil War, the Statue of Liberty was originally a gift to commemorate the Franco-American alliance. By the end of the 19th century, however, its significance changed: seen by sea-borne immigrants making their way into the harbor toward Ellis Island (see chapter on "Museums"), the statue came to be synonymous with immigration and the freedom these people would experience in their new homeland.

BEST CHEAP DATE

Today, you can get a close-up view of Lady Liberty for $7 ($6 for seniors, $3 for ages 3 to 17, free to tots under 3) that includes a walk around the grounds, tour of the museum located in the pedestal which details the statue's history, a glimpse of the internal framework designed by Gustave Eiffel (of the Tower fame), and even climb to the crown. Purchase tickets for the Statue of Liberty at Castle Clinton or across Battery Park from the South Ferry terminal. Ferries run every 30 minutes between 9:30 A.M. and 3:45 P.M. on weekdays and every 20 minutes between 8:30 A.M. and 4:10 P.M. on weekends.

TAKE A HIKE

THE BEST AND LEAST EXPENSIVE WAY to see New York's many diverse and interesting neighborhoods is to walk. From Inwood to Battery Park, Harlem, the Lower East Side, the Upper West Side, Times Square and the Theater District, Flower District, West Village, Soho, Tribeca, Little Italy, Chinatown, Washington Heights, Financial District, Murray Hill, Turtle Bay, Upper East Side and Morningside Heights on Manhattan to the Bronx, Brooklyn, Staten Island, and Queens, there is an abundance of places to discover. Whether you wander haphazardly, meander with a guidebook in hand or take a walking tour, there is no better way for you to become familiar with this place you now call home.

Of the infinite number of New York City guidebooks out there, my favorite is **Frommer's Memorable Walks in New York** (4th Edition), by Reid Bramblett. This inexpensive guide (list price: $12.99, Amazon.com price: $10.39) offers ten great walking tours through the city's most colorful neighborhoods that are entertaining and educational. I especially recommend doing these walks with a friend, taking turns reading to each other as you ramble around.

If you'd like some expert guidance while navigating through Gotham, there are several outfits that offer a variety of low-priced **walking tours** covering almost every inch of the city. Although many of these excursions attract tourists, the majority are devised for New Yorkers, natives and transplants, who wish to have a more penetrating sense of the city's history and culture. Enthusiastic professionals who have an encyclopedic knowledge and obsessive love of the neighborhoods they cover usually conduct these enlightening tours, and they take joy in imparting that love and knowledge to their listeners.For a complete listing of the current week's walking tours, be sure to check out either the "Weekend Fine Arts/Leisure" section of the Friday edition of *The New York Times* or the "Around Town" section of *Time Out New York*.

BEST BARGAINS

Adventure on a Shoe String (300 West 53rd Street—212–265–2663), at just $5 per person, is the least expensive walking tour in the city. This outfit has a large and always changing selection of tours, which are led by fun, informative Manhattanphiles.

Big Onion Walking Tours (212–439–1090), founded and guided by Columbia grad students, offers informative visits into many of New York's historic areas and ethnic neighborhoods. Most tours are around $12. Call for more information and a complete schedule of tours.

Brooklyn Center for the Urban Environment (Tennis House, Prospect Park, Brooklyn—718–788–8500) offers several inexpensive tours throughout the year concentrating on the architecture and neighborhoods of Brooklyn.

Joyce Gold History Tours of New York (141 West 17th Street—212–242–5762) feature two- to three-hour weekend walking excursions covering the history, culture, architecture and evolution of New York's most lively neighborhoods. Joyce Gold, a history professor at NYU, conducts these jaunts with themes ranging from Diplomatic New York to Rockefeller New York, Religious Manhattan, Colonial New York, Broadway Theatrical, Ethnic New York, A Day in Brooklyn and Noshing Manhattan. Tours are $12 each. Call or check the website (www.nyctours.com) for more information.

I'll Take Manhattan Tours (732–270–5277) conducts weekend trips through many of the city's most interesting and historic neighborhoods including Tribeca, Greenwich Village, Soho, Millionaire's Mile, Chinatown, Gramercy Park, Lower East Side and the Metropolitan Museum of Art Historic District. All tours are $10 and depart at 1 P.M. Call or visit their website (www.newyorkcitywalks.com) for more information and a tour schedule.

The Lower East Side Business Improvement District (261 Broome Street—212–226–9010) will send you a free guide to the Historic Orchard Street Shopping District, which not only contains an extensive listing of the area's merchants, but also has a map and walking tour detailing the Lower East Side's historic immigrant past. Every Sunday at 11 A.M. from April through December, an escort from the Lower East Side Business Improvement District conducts a free walking tour of the area (meet at Katz's Deli, corner of East Houston and Ludlow Streets). Call for your free guide or more information regarding the Sunday walking tours.

Mainly Manhattan Tours (212–755–6199) gives three different weekend tours that cover Greenwich Village, the Upper West Side and the area between Grand Central Station and the United Nations. Tours are $10. Call for more information.

Radical Walking Tours of New York (539 53rd Street, Brooklyn—718–492–0069) offers 15 different excursions, all led by political activist Bruce Kayton, to many of the sites of the city's revolutionary and political movements. Tours are all about 3 hours and cost $10. Call for a complete schedule of tours.

Street Smarts N.Y. (212–969–8262) leads entertaining themed weekend hikes to some of New York's most tony neighborhoods as well as areas of ill repute. All tours are $10. Call for schedule.

SOMEWHERE THAT'S GREEN

CONTRARY TO THE CLICHÉ that New York is nothing but a series of glass and concrete canyons, there are several extraordinarily beautiful parks, gardens and serene swaths of green scattered throughout the five boroughs. Each is a refuge from the hassle of city life. With beauty aplenty and myriad athletic and cultural activities, the city's parks and gardens contribute much to the mental and physical health of all New Yorkers.

The following is only a sampling of the city's many wonderful green spaces. For more information and a complete directory of city parks, call the New York Parks Department or visit their website at www.nyc.gov/parks.

Located at the southern tip of Manhattan on the Hudson River, **Battery Park** is a favorite destination for many New Yorkers. Besides the exquisite views of the Statue of Liberty, Ellis Island and New York Harbor, city folk come to picnic, roller blade, bicycle, jog, play sports, attend any one of the many music and dance performances, gawk at the yachts, visit the Museum of Jewish Heritage and watch the sunset. Although set among office and apartment buildings, Battery Park is one of the most tranquil places in Manhattan.

Open March to October, the **Brooklyn Botanic Garden** (900 Washington Avenue between Eastern Parkway and Empire Boulevard, Prospect Heights, Brooklyn—718–623–7200) features over 50 acres of plants and flowers in specialized gardens. The Cranford Rose Garden is home to over a hundred varieties of roses and the Japanese Garden has several cherry trees, weeping willows and one of the world's largest collections of bonsai trees. Of special interest to actors is the Shakespeare Garden, which grows eighty plus plants that the Bard names in his works. Free all day on Tuesday and on Saturday from 10 A.M. to noon.

Bryant Park (Sixth Avenue at 42nd Street), located behind the main branch of the New York Public Library and built right above some of the library's stacks, is a sanctuary. On warm days, the park is an ideal place to kick off your shoes, sit on the grass and watch the world go by. In the summer, you can catch a free concert or classic movie on the Great Lawn (see chapters on "Viewing Film" and "Listening To Music").

Created in 1858 by Frederick Law Olmstead and Calvert Vaux, **Central Park** (from 59th Street to 110th Street between Fifth Avenue and Central Park West) encompasses over 840 graceful acres in the very center of Manhattan. It was built over a desolate area of marshy swamps, garbage dumps and shantytowns inhabited by the city's poorest residents, and today provides a "green" escape from the hustle and bustle of this hectic city. The park's carnival-like atmosphere on weekends in the spring, summer and fall makes it the favorite retreat of most New Yorkers. There are innumerable free and inexpensive things to do here. You can . . . run, skate or cycle around the park's 6.5 mile loop; hear free concerts at the Central Park Summerstage, Bandshell or on the Great Lawn; play softball, football, tennis, soccer or basketball at fields or courts located throughout the park; see free Shakespeare performances at the outdoor Delacorte Theatre; Zen out at the tranquil Strawberry Fields; run or power-walk around the reservoir; commandeer mini-sailboats at the Conservatory Water; fish in the Harlem Meer; take a carousel ride; ice skate at the Wollman or Lasker rinks in winter; rent a rowboat at the Loeb Boathouse; dine at Tavern on the Green; soak up some rays in the Sheep Meadow; walk the dog or commune with nature just about anywhere. If you'd like to know more about the park's history, flora, fauna or the stories behind its many statues, there are several free walking tours year-round (call 212–360–2726).

Flushing Meadows-Corona Park in Queens, home to the 1939 and 1964 World's Fairs, has sculpted gardens, lots of rambling lawn, an 18-hole pitch 'n' putt golf course and a lake where you may rent paddle- and row-boats. The park houses a few remnants of the '64 World's Fair, like the Unisphere, the New York Hall of Science and the New York State Pavilion. After Shea Stadium, the park's second most popular attraction is the Queens Museum of Art; here you may view a scale model of the city that is constantly added to and altered to reflect New York's ever-changing cityscape (see chapter on "Museums").

Presently under construction, **Hudson River Park** will eventually stretch almost the entire West Side, connecting the existing Battery and Riverside Parks. When completed, a lawn together with flower and plant beds will parallel the expanse of the West Side Highway incorporating most of the abandoned piers into its design. Also planned, believe it or not, are sand beaches. Pedestrian and bike/skate paths are already finished, allowing you to go from the Staten Island Ferry to the George Washington Bridge without ever leaving these paths.

Several ghosts of "Old New York" seem to haunt **Madison Square Park** (23rd Street to 26th Street between Madison and Fifth Avenues), which is more famous for what it was than what it is. Originally a public cemetery, it was in Madison Square Park that a game called "New York Ball," the precursor to baseball, was played. The torch held aloft by the Statue of Liberty was displayed here while funds were being raised to construct her pedestal. P.T. Barnum's Hippodrome stood here, as did the original Madison Square Garden. And it was here that Harry Thaw, the enraged husband of Evelyn ("the girl on the velvet swing") Nesbitt, murdered Stanford White, the father of New York's beaux-arts architecture.

Today, the atmosphere of the park is more low-key and serene than in its historic past. The lush green lawn and towering trees provide a perfect setting for reading, meditating, or "taking a load off." After a long reconstruction and the addition of some fanciful new public art, Madison Square Park is more appealing than ever.

The **New York Botanical Garden** (200th Street at Kazimiroff Boulevard, Bronx—718–817–8700) across the street from the Bronx Zoo, is considered one of the world's best horticultural preserves. Set in 250 vibrantly colorful acres, the New York Botanical Gardens features 28 specialty gardens and plant collections including the Peggy Rockefeller Rose Garden, a 40-acre uncut hemlock forest, the T.H. Everett rock garden and waterfall, the Enid A. Haupt Conservatory (a glass greenhouse reminiscent of London's Crystal Palace), and the "Please Touch" Everett Children's Adventure Garden. The Garden offers several money saving passes with free grounds admissions all day Wednesday and Saturdays from 10 A.M. to 12 P.M. Metro-North trains depart from Grand Central Terminal and stop at the Botanical Gardens throughout the day. By subway, take the B or D train to Bedford Park and then walk east eight blocks.

Designed by Frederick Law Olmsted and Calvert Vaux (the architects who created Central Park), **Prospect Park** (718–965–8951) is a 526 acre green retreat in the middle of Brooklyn. Although covering less real estate than Central Park, Prospect Park is no less ambitious in its offerings. Here you may rent paddle boats, ride the Carousel (built in 1912 and accompanied by a Wurlitzer calliope) for just 50¢, picnic, bird watch, jog, cycle, ride horses that may be rented at the Kensington Stables, and in-line skate. Season-specific park activities include ice-skating at Wollman rink in winter and musical concerts, children's theater and storytelling at the Prospect Park Bandshell in the summer (see chapters "Listening to Music" and "Viewing Dance"). You may also take a free tour of the Park's two historic homes, Litchfield Villa (built in the 1800s) and Lefferts Homestead, a preserved Dutch farmhouse built in the 1700s, which serves as the Park's headquarters and is home to the Children's Historic House Museum.

Smaller but no less dramatic than its cousin in the Bronx, the **Queens Botanical Garden** (Flushing Meadows-Corona Park—718–886–3800) is a feast for the visual and olfactory senses. The Botanical Garden features a 5,000-bush rose garden, an arboretum, several specialty gardens and for those New Yorkers who have a backyard (or a balcony), a home compost demonstration. The Queens Garden is open April to October and is always free.

Riverside Park, which extends from 72nd to 125th Streets along the Hudson River, is a huge playground for young and old alike. Everywhere you look, there are sunbathers, cyclists, rollerbladers, joggers, strollers, chess players, children romping on swing sets, al fresco diners, park bench jockeys and frazzled mothers (or are they nannies?) pushing prams. If you'd like to play an organized sport, there are tennis/basketball/handball courts and baseball fields aplenty. For those with a yen for some aesthetic stimulus, there are lots of sculptures to gaze on, flowers to adore and views across the Hudson to glory in.

Once considered unsavory and unsafe, **Union Square Park** (between Broadway and Park Avenue South and 14th and 17th Streets) had a facelift about a decade or so ago and has become a favorite gathering spot for local residents and workers. The park, now pulses with activity with hot-dogging rollerbladers and skateboarders dominating the south end of the park and the north end featuring a wonderful year-round farmer's market (see chapter on "Provisions"). In between, stall-holders sell books, CDs and art prints at reasonable prices, one or two people strum guitars and croon to no one in particular, and bench-perchers watch the passing parade. In summer, a large outdoor bar, that resembles a German beer garden, caters to a crowd of mostly models, trendoids and model/trendoid-wannabes.

Before becoming a park, **Washington Square** (between 4th Street and Waverly Place and Fifth Avenue and MacDougal Street) had many incarnations . . . originally home to Native Americans, by the mid-1600s it had become an enclave for freed slaves. By the late 1700s, it became an anonymous burial ground for the area's poor (it is believed there are 15,000 bodies buried here) and during the Revolutionary War, a place for public executions. It was not until the early 19th century that it became a park and the center of life in Greenwich Village. Today, Washington Square Park still hums with activity: musicians and street performers vie for loose change, NYU students catch a few rays between classes, not-so-discreet hemp entrepreneurs mutter "smoke, smoke" to passersby, hard-core chess hustlers focus intently on their games, locals trade gossip as they walk their dogs, and children scamper everywhere.

The Bronx estate **Wave Hill** (675 West 252nd Street, Riverdale—718–549–3200), once home to such luminaries as Teddy Roosevelt, Mark Twain, Arturo Toscanini and William Thackeray, has one of the city's most beautiful European gardens. Overlooking the Hudson River and Bronx Palisades, Wave Hill's internationally acclaimed gardens and horticultural collection (over 3200 seasonal plants and flowers in formal settings and greenhouses) provide a serene and idyllic landscape in which to commune with nature. Besides the bountiful flora, Wave Hill has educational programs, such as garden basics with tours, talks and workshops as well as cooking demonstrations and lectures. Other programs include poetry readings, art exhibitions and music and dance concerts (see chapters on "Listening to Music" and "Viewing Dance"). Open year-round, Wave Hill is free November 25 to March 14 as well as every Tuesday and Saturday morning until noon. (Call for directions).

MUSEUMS

MUSEUMS ARE ESPECIALLY IMPORTANT for us as actors. Not only do they fulfill our intrinsic need for art and beauty, but they can also assist in our creative process. By closely examining drawings, paintings, sculpture, jewelry, artifacts, furniture, fashion and weaponry from any given era, we can learn much about the history, culture and social life of the people of that period. Scrutinizing how a Bronzino nobleman rests his hand on the hilt of his sword, how a Restoration-era countess fingers her fan, or how a Bruegel peasant dances in drunken abandon, tells us volumes about these people, their comportment, their social status, their characters. Whenever I am cast in a period play, I run to a museum to study the paintings of that era. How do the people in those paintings stand? How do they sit? What is their social mask? How are they dressed? What can I infer about their states of mind? This is a tremendously beneficial tool for me as I go through the process of creating someone from another era.

New York is undoubtedly the greatest museum city in the world. The diversity and magnitude of the collections is unrivalled anywhere and enriches the cultural and social lives of all New Yorkers. The best part about our museums is that we have free or inexpensive access to almost all of them. Although most of the major museums do charge an admission fee, they each suspend their usual fees at some point during the week. The following is a list of New York museums that have Free or "Pay-As-You-Wish" admissions:

American Museum of Natural History/Hayden Planetarium (79th Street and Central Park West—212–769–5000). *Free Sunday to Thursday, 4:45 to 5:45 P.M., Friday and Saturday, 7:45 to 8:45 P.M.* I can't help but think of Holden

Caulfield's field trip to the Museum of Natural History in J.D. Salinger's *The Catcher in the Rye* every time I visit this museum. So much of the museum is still exactly as Salinger described it in his 1951 novel. The old-fashioned dioramas of the Akeley Hall of African Mammals and the giant whale room with its quaint aquatic life exhibits make me feel as though I've suddenly been transported back to the museum of the 1950s. However, other parts of the museum (the newly renovated Hayden Planetarium, the Rose Center for Earth and Space and the dinosaur halls on the top floor) are so new and modern that they seem to have opened only yesterday. Be sure not to miss the Hall of Human Biology and Evolution which displays the mysteries of human development and includes bones and fragments of "Lucy," who is believed to be the oldest early human, as well provides interactive computers. Other must-sees are the Morgan Hall of Gems, which glitters with diamonds, emeralds and rubies and contains the Star of India Sapphire, the world's largest; and the Wallace Wing, which contains the world's largest assembly of fossilized mammals. The museum also houses an Imax movie theater and a stunning light and sound show but both are an additional charge.

The Asia Society (725 Park Avenue at 70th Street—212-288-6400). *Free daily noon-2 P.M.* The Asia Society presents exhibitions of Asian art including Asian-American works. Free or inexpensive symposia, musical performances, film screenings and a "Meet the Author" series are also scheduled here throughout the year

Audubon Terrace Museum Group (613 West 155th Street between Broadway and Riverside Drive). *Always free.* Once part of the Audubon estate and game preserve, it now houses three museums and societies:

The **Hispanic Society of America** is dedicated to the arts and culture of Spain and Portugal and includes works by El Greco, Velazquez and Goya. The Society also contains ceramics, mosaics, an ornate Spanish Renaissance court, religious artifacts and a 100,000-volume research library. (212–926–2234)

The **American Numismatic Society** houses a collection of coins and paper money from the last 26 centuries. (212–234–3130)

The **American Academy of Arts and Letters** honors American writers, composers, painters, sculptors and architects. Although it is not actually a museum, the Academy occasionally sponsors free public exhibitions of works drawn from its permanent collection. (212–368–5900)

Bronx Museum of the Arts (1040 Grand Concourse at 165th Street—718–681–6000). *"Pay-As-You-Wish" and free all day Wednesday.* This small museum of contemporary art, located in the Bronx Courthouse, showcases its permanent collection of established artists as well as exhibitions by emerging Bronx artists.

The Brooklyn Historical Society (128 Pierrepont Street, Brooklyn—718–222–4111). *Free Monday.* Set in a National Historic Landmark building, the Society is a museum, library and archives center devoted to Brooklyn's diverse culture, community and heritage. Themed exhibitions and displays culled from the permanent collection are just two of the Society's many offerings.

The Brooklyn Museum of Art (200 Eastern Parkway, Brooklyn—718–638–5000). *Always "Pay-As-You-Wish" and free on the first Saturday of every month from 5–11 P.M.* The museum's free first Saturdays offers "fabulous" free entertainment as well. The Brooklyn Museum's million plus permanent collection contains significant Asian, African, Oceanic and New World works as well as American painting, sculpture and decorative art. Notable are the museum's extensive ancient Egyptian collection and contemporary art galleries, with works by Louise Nevelson, Larry Rivers and Leon Polk Smith among many others.

China Institute in America (125 East 65th Street between Park and Lexington—212–744–8181). *"Pay-As-You-Wish."* The Institute's purpose is to promote understanding and appreciation of traditional and contemporary Chinese culture, civilization, and heritage. Its two galleries present original and traveling exhibitions on topics ranging from traditional Chinese paintings to calligraphy, folk arts, textiles and architecture.

The Cloisters (Fort Tryon Park, Washington Heights—212–923–3700). *Everyday except Mondays is "Pay-As-You-Wish."* This museum, which is a branch of the Metropolitan Museum of Art, is a tranquil oasis in Washington Heights. Pieced together from parts of 12th and 13th century European monasteries, it houses the Met's vast medieval art and architecture collection. Not to be missed are the world-famous Unicorn Tapestries and the Treasury, which contains incredibly delicate illuminated manuscripts and miniature carvings. The Cloisters offers spectacular views of the Hudson River, making it one of New York's favorite retreats on hot summer days, and an ideal place to bring a date or loved one on a cool, clear spring evening.

Coney Island Museum (Astroland Amusement Park, 1208 Surf Avenue at West 12th Street, Brooklyn—718–372–5159). *99¢.* This museum exhibits remnants of old rides along with pictures, antiques and memorabilia chronicling Coney Island's happier, more carefree days. The view out of the Museum's windows is also a lot of fun, as they look directly onto Coney Island's landmark rides like the Cyclone roller coaster, the WonderWheel and the Parachute Jump.

Cooper-Hewitt National Museum of Design (2 East 91st Street at Fifth Avenue—212–849–8300). *Free Tuesdays 5* *to 9 P.M.* Housed in the Carnegie Mansion, the Cooper-Hewitt, part of the Smithsonian Institution, is the only museum in the U.S. dedicated exclusively to historical and contemporary design. It exhibits objects of daily life—textiles, prints, drawings, wall coverings and the decorative arts.

Dahesh Museum of Art (601 Fifth Avenue at 48th Street—212–759–0606). *Always free.* This is the only museum in the U.S. dedicated to the collection, preservation, exhibition and interpretation of European academic art of the 19th and 20th centuries. The collection includes Orientalism, landscapes, and pastoral scenes by artists whose work you rarely, if ever, see in any other collections.

Ellis Island Immigration Museum (Ellis Island—212–363–3200). *Free.* This museum pays tribute to the 12 million immigrants who passed through the island on their way to resettling in America. The artifacts, photos and memorabilia on exhibit here are a moving reminder of the struggles our forebears endured to create a new, more prosperous life for themselves in this then new nation. Note: Although admission is free, there is a fee for the boat that transports you to the island.

El Museo del Barrio (1230 Fifth Avenue at 104th Street—212–831–7272). *"Pay-As-You-Wish."* El Museo del Barrio features the art and culture of Puerto Rico, the Caribbean and Latin America through its extensive collections and varied exhibitions of video, painting, sculpture, photography, theater and film.

Fire Museum (278 Spring Street at Varick—212–691–1303). *Always free.* This tiny museum, set in a former firehouse, displays vintage fire engines and other fire-fighting paraphernalia from the last century. This is a great place to bring your kids—hopefully it will inspire them to become firemen/women, instead of actors like their parents.

Forbes Magazine Galleries (62 Fifth Avenue at 12th Street—212–206–5548). *Always free Tuesday to Saturday 10 A.M. to 4 P.M.* The Forbes Galleries collection contains the largest number of Fabergé Imperial Easter Eggs in the world, as well as jewelry, fully decorated miniature rooms, an array of antique toy boats and toy soldiers, and important American historical papers.

Freakatorium (57 Clinton Street between Rivington and Stanton Streets—212–375–0475). *Always free.* Set in a store-front on the Lower East Side, this museum is filled with sideshow memorabilia. Collected and curated by sideshow performer Johnny Fox, the items here are, well . . . freaky! This place is a definite change of pace from the Met and Natural History.

Garibaldi-Meucci Museum (420 Tompkins Avenue, Staten Island—718–442–1608). *"Pay-As-You-Wish."* This 1840's Gothic Revival home is a memorial to the lives and works of inventor Antonio Meucci and Italian patriot Giuseppe Garibaldi, both of whom lived here. The Museum also collects, preserves and interprets artifacts and ephemera detailing the history of the Italian community in New York.

Grant's Tomb National Monument (Located at 122nd Street and Riverside Drive—212–666–1640). *Always free.* At this landmark in Riverside Park on the Upper West Side, you can actually find out who is buried in the tomb! There is an exhibit focusing on Ulysses S. Grant's very interesting life and a history of the Civil War.

Solomon R. Guggenheim Museum Uptown (1071 Fifth Avenue at 89th Street—212–423–3500). *"Pay-As-You-Wish" on Fridays, 6 to 8 P.M.* Designed by Frank Lloyd Wright and completed in 1959, the Guggenheim Museum houses a permanent collection of modern art, which ranges from Impressionism to

286 • AN ACTOR PREPARES.... TO LIVE IN NEW YORK CITY

contemporary art, including installations and photography. Throughout the year, The Guggenheim also sponsors several exhibits of modern and contemporary artists.

Guggenheim Museum Soho (575 Broadway at Prince Street—646–613–7250). *Free Saturday 6 to 8 P.M.* The Guggenheim Soho, filling two floors of a historic 19th-century building, mounts changing exhibitions drawn from their permanent collection or coordinated with the uptown museum.

Hall of Fame for Great Americans (City University of New York, 181st Street and Martin Luther King, Jr. Boulevard, Bronx—718–289–5100). *Free.* Designed by Stanford White to pay homage to the Pantheon in Rome, this neglected, open-air limestone terrace is situated on the highest natural point in the Bronx. The Hall features over 100 bronze busts of exceptional American scientists, writers, scholars, educators, military personnel and politicians, which the National Sculpture Society once called the finest collection of its kind in America.

Harbor Defense Museum of Fort Hamilton (Fort Hamilton Military Community, Building 230, Brooklyn—718–630–4349). *Always free.* The Harbor Defense Museum's raison d'être is to showcase the importance of the U.S. Army to the New York area. On exhibit, weapons, uniforms, models, dioramas and much more trace the history of the Army's presence here in New York.

International Center of Photography (1133 Avenue of the Americas at 43rd Street—212–860–1777). *Free Friday 5 to 8 P.M.* The ICP is the city's only museum devoted exclusively to photography and is home to several exhibitions throughout the year.

Japan Society (333 East 47th Street at First Avenue—212–832–1155). *"Pay-As-You-Wish."* A work of art in its own right, the Japan Society sponsors exhibitions of traditional and contemporary Japanese art two or three times a year. The Society also presents lectures, performances and a Japanese film series.

The Jewish Museum (1109 Fifth Avenue at 92ⁿᵈ Street— 212–423–3200. *Free Tuesday 5 to 8 P.M.* Centuries of art from the biblical days to the present illuminate the scope and diversity of Jewish culture and history at the Jewish Museum. Unique interactive displays offer varied perspectives on the Jewish experience: in the Audio Café, visitors can sit in a pre war-era European café and listen to recorded voices speaking about the issues of the day; elsewhere, modern rabbis offer differing views on Talmudic questions via computer touch screens.

Library for the Performing Arts (Lincoln Center, 111 Amsterdam Avenue at 66ᵗʰ Street—212–870–1630). *Always free.* Besides being a phenomenal research facility, the Performing Arts Library also hosts frequent and free exhibits on the life and work of distinguished actors, choreographers, directors, composers, designers, playwrights, singers, dancers and musicians. (See "Personal and Professional Resources").

Metropolitan Museum of Art (Fifth Avenue and 82ⁿᵈ Street). *Everyday except Mondays is "Pay-As-You-Wish"*—and they really mean it. The "Met" welcomes more than 5 million visitors annually and its unrivalled collections span 5,000 years of art, culture and history from every part of the world. The American Wing of the Museum contains the most comprehensive collection of American paintings, sculpture and decorative arts in the world, and the Egyptian and Islamic collections are considered to be among the finest outside their homelands. The Florence and Herbert Irving Galleries for the Arts of South and Southeast Asia contain 1,300 works from India to Indonesia created between the third millennium B.C. and the early 19ᵗʰ century. My favorite part of the museum, the 19ᵗʰ Century European Paintings and Sculpture Galleries, houses the Met's superlative collection of Impressionist paintings. Be

BEST BARGAIN

sure to check out the mummies and sarcophagi in the Egyptian Galleries as well as the Temple of Dendur, an ancient temple that the Met rescued from weather, flooding and neglect and moved intact from its original site in Egypt. Actors will find the Costume Institute, located on the ground floor of the museum, of particular interest. This collection houses tens of thousands of costumes and accessories from the world over from the 17ᵗʰ century to the present and offers rotating exhibits. On summer days, the Gerald and Iris B. Cantor Roof Sculpture Garden is a popular place for museumgoers to sunbathe while taking in the art and the breathtaking views of Central Park and the Manhattan skyline. The Met's extensive free concert and lecture series (212–570–3949) makes it possible for New Yorkers to "hear great art" throughout the year.

Municipal Art Society (457 Madison Avenue between 50ᵗʰ and 51ˢᵗ Street—212–935–3960). *Always Free.* Housed in a gorgeous historic building behind St. Patrick's Cathedral, the Society presents exhibitions on urban design, architecture and public art.

Museum for African Art (36–01 43ʳᵈ Avenue at 36ᵗʰ Street, Long Island City, Queens—718–784–7700). *Free all day Sunday and the third Thursday of every month from 5:30–8:30 P.M.* Dedicated to the presentation of African art and culture, the Museum for African Art sponsors two major exhibitions yearly as well as several smaller shows, each based on a unifying theme. The Museum's collections span many centuries, from ancient to contemporary, and include works by both African and African-American artists.

Museum of American Financial History (28 Broadway at Exchange Place—212–908–4110). *Free except Sunday and Monday.* An affiliate of the Smithsonian Institution, the Museum of American Financial History was established to extol American entrepreneurial spirit and the democratic free market. Through its exhibitions, the Museum presents the history of Wall Street and the achievements of American businessmen and women from Alexander Hamilton and J.P. Morgan to present-day dot com capitalists.

Museum of American Folk Art (Columbus Avenue at 65th Street—212–977–7170). *Free on Fridays from 6 to 8 P.M.* This museum exhibits a wide range of American folk art from pottery to quilts, carved wood and toys. Periodically, the museum hosts free lectures, demonstrations and performances. Be sure to browse through the museum shop, which carries some unique, American hand-crafted items that are ideal as gifts for those hard-to-shop-for agents and casting directors.

Museum of American Illustration (128 East 63rd Street between Park and Lexington Avenues—212–838–2560). *Always free.* This museum presents shows that focus on the evolution of American illustration from past to present.

Museum of Arts and Design (40 West 53rd Street— 212–956–3535). *"Pay-As-You-Wish" Thursday 6 to 8 P.M.* This is the leading art museum for 20th-century crafts in glass, metal, fiber, wood and clay. There are large temporary exhibitions that change every three months and smaller shows exhibiting works from the permanent collection.

Museum of Chinese in the Americas (70 Mulberry Street at Bayard Street, 2nd Floor—212–619–4785). *"Pay-As-You-Wish."* Set in the heart of Chinatown, MoCA traces the complex and diverse history and culture of Chinese in the Western Hemisphere. MoCA's extensive collection of primary resource material on the Chinese American experience includes oral histories, photographs, documents, personal and organizational records, sound recordings, textiles, artifacts, and a library with over 2,000 volumes. The Museum also offers walking tours, lectures, book readings, performances and arts workshops.

Museum of the City of New York (1220 Fifth Avenue at 103rd Street—212-534-1672). *Everyday except Mondays is "Pay-As-You-Wish."* All of the objects housed in the Museum of the City of New York relate to the history and traditions of New York City. A toy gallery populated with antique dolls and dollhouses, period rooms from the late 17th to early 20th centuries, and a display of antique fire engines are always on display. Of special interest to actors is the ongoing show "Broadway! 125 Years of Musical Theatre" which surveys the Great White Way's history through costumes, set models and designs, posters, programs and photographs.

Museum at F.I.T. (Fashion Institute of Technology Campus, Seventh Avenue at 27th Street—212-217-5800). *Always free.* This museum presents fun, eclectic exhibits on clothing, costumes and textiles. At the end of each academic year, the Museum showcases the work of its recent graduates.

Museum of Modern Art (11 West 53rd Street between Fifth and Sixth Avenues—212-708-9400). *Free Friday 4:30 to 8:30 P.M.* The Museum of Modern Art contains more than 100,000 paintings, drawings, sculptures, works on paper, photographs, films, videos and other objects and houses an unrivalled permanent collection of 20th-century art. Monet's "Water Lilies" and the Abby Aldrich Rockefeller Sculpture Garden (a great place to bring a sack lunch and dine al fresco in the spring, summer and fall) are two of MOMA's many highlights. Note: Due to major renovations and an expansion, MOMA has moved to temporary quarters in the old Swingline staple factory in Queens until summer 2005. This huge space is a fresh alternative to the 53rd Street location and an ideal staging area for large exhibits like "Autobodies: Speed, Sport, Transport," which presents the Museum's collection of cars for the first time. (MOMA Queens—33rd Street at Queens Boulevard, can be reached on the #7 train).

Museum of Television and Radio (25 West 52nd Street between Fifth and Sixth Avenues—212–621–6800). This Museum is not free, however, they do offer *10 percent discounts to SAG and AFTRA members* with valid union cards on day visits (which is usually $6) and yearly memberships (usually $50). The yearly membership is one of the best deals in town: it gives unlimited access to the museum's database; and we actors can write it off on our tax returns as "Research." Membership also includes invitations to members-only receptions, seminars and special events; 10 percent discounts on videos, cassettes, publications and all purchases in the museum shops; as well as discounts on seminar tickets and express check-in for daily screenings. This is one of my favorite museums and a great resource for actors. The museum's collection contains more than 95,000 TV and radio programs made over the past 70 years. The public can use a computerized catalogue system with an enormous database to access the museum's collection of programs ranging from news to commercials to comedies to dramas to variety shows. I find it especially helpful as a research tool when I am preparing an audition or role, and have used its vast database to view everything from TV documentaries about Nazi Germany to portions of "Your Show of Shows" and BBC productions of Shakespeare plays. Throughout the year, the museum also hosts several film series that focus on topics of social, historical, popular or artistic interest; ask for a schedule at the front counter.

National Academy of Design Museum (1083 Fifth Avenue between 89th and 90th Streets—212–369–4880). *Free Fridays 5 to 6 P.M.* In 1825, the National Academy of Design was founded to "promote the fine arts through exhibition and instruction." To fulfill its charter, the Academy maintains a permanent collection of some of America's most distinguished design artists, and hosts major exhibitions throughout the year.

National Lighthouse Museum (1 Lighthouse Plaza, St. George, Staten Island—718–556–1681). *"Pay-As-You-Wish" —Reservations required.* The 19th-century building that houses this museum was originally the United States Lighthouse Depot, the country's main center for the technological development and manufacture of lighthouses. The Museum explores the science and lore of lighthouses.

National Museum and Archive of Lesbian and Gay History (The Lesbian and Gay Community Services Center, 208 West 13ᵗʰ Street between Seventh and Eighth Avenues—212–620–7310). *Free daily 6 to 9 P.M.* This museum presents works by lesbian, gay, bisexual and transgendered artists throughout the year. Call for exhibit dates.

National Museum of the American Indian (1 Bowling Green—212–668–6624). *Free daily 10 A.M. to 5 P.M.,* Thursday until 8 P.M. Housed in the beautiful beaux-arts-style 1907 Customs House, the Museum exhibits the finest pieces of the Smithsonian Institution's immense collection of Native American artifacts.

Newhouse Center for Contemporary Art (Snug Harbor Cultural Center, 1000 Richmond Terrace at Snug Harbor Road, Staten Island—718–448–2500, ext. 260). *"Pay-As-You-Wish."* The Newhouse Center is the main exhibition space at Staten Island's best-known art and performance site, the 83-acre Snug Harbor Cultural Center. The Center features exhibitions of contemporary artists and occasionally shows works owned by the Staten Island Institute of Arts and Sciences.

New Museum of Contemporary Art (583 Broadway between Houston and Prince Streets—212–219–1222). *Free Thursday 6 to 8 P.M.* Located on the same block as the Museum for African Art and the Guggenheim Soho, the New Museum exhibits the very latest in contemporary art. Not one to shrink from controversy, the Museum presents shows that are often gritty, cutting-edge and can sometimes even "frighten the horses." In spite of protests and Cardinal O'Connor's condemnation, it was the New Museum that exhibited André Serano's photographs of bodies in a morgue, and a crucifix in a vial of urine. If you want to know what is happening in contemporary art *right now,* this is the place to go.

New York Hall of Science (47–01 111th Street at 46th Avenue, Flushing Meadows, Queens—718–699–0005). *Free Thursday and Friday 2 to 5 P.M.* Originally opening during the 1964/65 World's Fair, the Hall of Science has more than 225 hands-on and easy-to-understand exhibits covering everything from the science of light and sound to biochemistry and physics.

New York Historical Society (2 West 77th Street at Central Park West—212-873-3400). *"Pay-As-You-Wish."* The oldest continuously operating museum in New York, the Historical Society presents periodic exhibits culled from its vast treasury of New York historical objects and artifacts such as the neon signs of Times Square. I love this museum and learn something new about the city every time I go. It makes me proud I'm a New Yorker.

New York Police Museum (100 Old Slip—212-480-3100). *Always free.* The exhibits here detail the history of the NYPD, and feature displays of the hardware and vehicles used in keeping the peace since the Department's inception.

New York Public Library—Humanities and Social Sciences Library (455 Fifth Avenue at 42nd Street—212-869-8089). *Always free.* Not only is this the main branch of New York's library system, it is one of the city's architectural gems. Famous the world over for the stone lions Patience and Fortitude posted in front of its gorgeous beaux-arts façade, this research-only library presents frequent and well-curated exhibitions. Two of my favorite shows in recent years were a retrospective of the life and works of cartoonist Charles Addams (Creator of the "Addams Family" cartoon), and *Becoming Visible*, which chronicled the pre- and post-Stonewall history of the gay and lesbian movement. Be sure to check out the Rose reading room—about as ostentatious and awe-inspiring as anything I've ever seen. *Free guided tours are conducted at 11 A.M. and 2 P.M. daily.*

New York Transit Museum—Grand Central Terminal Gallery (Shuttle Passage-way, Grand Central Train Station, 42nd Street and Lexington Avenue). *Always free.* This museum contains art, models, transit maps, architectural drawings and exhibits detailing the history of the New York transit system.

Noble Maritime Museum (Snug Harbor Cultural Center, 1000 Richmond Terrace at Snug Harbor Road, Staten Island—718-447-6490). *"Pay-As-You-Wish."* The Noble Maritime Museum focuses on the writings, photographs, works of art and artifacts of the sailor and artist John Noble. The Museum also presents temporary exhibitions of art and works related to the sea, sailing vessels and to Noble himself.

Isamu Noguchi Garden Museum (36–01 43rd Avenue at 36th Street, Queens—718-721-1932). *"Pay-As-You-Wish."* The Garden Museum, which was once the site of sculptor Isamu Noguchi's studio, is now home to many of his stunning pieces. The Museum is a whimsical escape from the hustle and bustle of Manhattan and a great place to bring a date. On the weekends, there is a $5 shuttle bus that leaves from the Asia Society (70th Street and Park Avenue in Manhattan) every 30 minutes from 10 A.M. to 5 P.M.

Pierpont Morgan Library (29 East 36th Street at Madison Avenue—212-685-0610). *Everyday except Monday is "Pay-As-You-Wish."* This Renaissance-style former home of financier J. Pierpont Morgan houses a distinguished collection of manuscripts, rare books and drawings detailing the art, history and culture of civilization between the Middle Ages and the 20th century. Treasures from the collection include musical scores, Thoreau's *Journal,* Dickens's *A Christmas Carol* and the only surviving fragment of Milton's *Paradise Lost.*

Queens Museum of Art (Flushing Meadows Corona Park, Queens—718-592-9700). *"Pay-As-You-Wish."* Located on the site of the 1964/65 World's Fair (you know, the place with the giant metal globe that you pass on the way to Shea Stadium and LaGuardia Airport), The Queens Museum presents contemporary art exhibitions and is home to a scale model of the entire city of New York. The Museum claims that the model changes and grows as quickly as the city does; I pity the poor fools who are in charge of the Times Square section—they must be losing their minds trying to keep up!

Nicholas Roerich Museum (319 West 107th Street at Riverside Drive—212-864-7752). *"Pay-As-You-Wish."* The Russian-born Nicholas Roerich is world famous as an architect, explorer, artist and philosopher. Through his writings and art, Roerich was a passionate promoter of an appreciation of the value of the cultural heritage of all nations and how that appreciation can help achieve world peace. The Museum, home to several hundred of Roerich's paintings, is an homage to his life's work, pacifism and spirituality. Especially noteworthy are his paintings from travels in Tibet. This little-known museum is a definite must-see for both the art it houses and the philosophy it espouses.

Rose Museum at Carnegie Hall (Seventh Avenue and 57th Street—212-903-9600). *Free.* This museum houses some of the world-famous concert hall's most cherished memorabilia in its collections and archives, including photographs, letters, autographs, programs, and other items, all chronicling the Hall's rich history.

Scandinavia House: The Nordic Center in America (58 Park Avenue between 37th and 38th Streets—212-779-3587). *"Pay-As-You-Wish."* Scandinavia House presents a wide variety of exhibitions covering the life, culture and traditions of the five Nordic countries—Denmark, Finland, Iceland, Norway and Sweden. The exquisite ultra-modern building in which Scandinavia House is located is itself a showcase of Scandinavian design, material and culture. On long-term loan from the National Museums of the five Nordic countries is a selection of modern and contemporary paintings by famous Scandinavian artists.

Skyscraper Museum (39 Battery Place—212–968–1961). *Always free.* This museum provides a detailed history of tall buildings the world over through photos, drawings and other artifacts.

Staten Island Institute of Arts and Sciences (75 Stuyvesant Place, St. George, Staten Island—718–727–1135). *"Pay-As-You-Wish."* The Institute has a treasure trove of possessions, from bugs and botanicals to decorative works and paintings by native New York artists as well as great masters like Chagall, Lautrec and Dürer.

Studio Museum in Harlem (144 West 125th Street between Malcolm X and Adam Clayton Powell Boulevards—212–864–4500). *First Saturday of each month is free.* Established as the first black fine-arts museum in the U.S. during the height of the civil-rights movement, the Studio Museum draws from its permanent collection of photographs, paintings and sculpture by African, African-American and Caribbean artists to present two outstanding exhibitions a year.

Waterfront Museum (Barge #79, 290 Conover Street at Pier 45, Red Hook, Brooklyn—718–624–4719). *Always free,* but only open for special events—call for schedule. Set in the middle of New York Harbor on a wooden 1914 railroad barge, this unique museum documents New York's history as a port city. The exhibits, however, are upstaged by the spectacular views of Manhattan and the harbor. The Waterfront's free activities include a summer concert series on Saturdays, July through August.

Whitney Museum of American Art (945 Madison Avenue at 75th Street—212-570-3676). *Free Thursday 6 to 8 P.M.* The Whitney contains more than 10,000 works of 20th-century American art and actively promotes the work of living artists. Not to be missed is the Whitney's often-controversial Biennial Exhibition, which displays a very diverse collection of contemporary artists.

Whitney Museum at Philip Morris (120 Park Avenue at 42nd Street—917-663-2453). *Always free.* This 6,300-square-foot sculpture court and gallery space occupies part of the ground floor of the Philip Morris corporate headquarters and exhibits the work of contemporary American artists in coordination with the Whitney's uptown branch.

There are several other great museums throughout the five boroughs that I have omitted because they don't meet my free or almost-free criterion.

ART GALLERIES

I ONCE SAW A TEE-SHIRT that said "So Many Men, So Little Time." That's how I feel about New York's art galleries. There are so damn many of them. Not that that's a bad thing; it's just hard to keep pace. Just when I think I have visited them all, another thirty sprout up. And, they are appearing in different neighborhoods. Once upon a time, Soho, the upper reaches of Madison Avenue and 57th Street were the art gallery centers of Manhattan. Now, galleries can be found all over the city, in former warehouses in Chelsea, the meatpacking district in Greenwich Village, on the Lower East Side, in Tribeca, even Williamsburg and DUMBO (Down Under the Manhattan Bridge Overpass) in Brooklyn.

New York's surfeit of galleries has been a windfall for art lovers. They offer an up-to-the-minute education on the most current trends in the art world. They exhibit something for every taste, from the archaic to the arcane; from the obtuse to the obscene; from the eclectic to the existential; from the insipid to the inspired. They represent all mediums you can think of (and a lot you can't). They provide a reason to explore the interesting and diverse neighborhoods where they are located. Best of all, they are free.

A stimulating way to spend the day without spending any money is to do a gallery crawl. Pick a neighborhood where galleries congregate and walk. You'll be amazed, awed, sometimes bored, often moved, and perhaps even shocked. And it won't cost you a penny.

For a complete listing of galleries, shows, hours, addresses and phone numbers, pick up a copy of *The Gallery Guide*, free at any gallery or museum. Extensive gallery information may also be found in the **"Choices" section of *The Village Voice,*** the **"Art" sections of *Time Out New York,*** and ***New York Magazine,***

The New Yorker's **"Goings On About Town"** and the **Friday "Weekend" section** of *The New York Times.*

Also, there is a shuttle that will transport gallery visitors between Soho, Chelsea and elsewhere on Saturdays. For more information, call the Art Shuttle at 212–769–8100.

Viewing Theater

BESIDES BRINGING US A LOT OF JOY (hopefully), attending the theater regularly is beneficial for our craft and our careers. It is vital for us to know what's happening in the theater. We must be familiar with the work of playwrights, directors, actors and designers, many of whom we will no doubt collaborate with at some stage in our careers. The plays that are being done in New York today will be done elsewhere next season and we will very likely be auditioning for those productions.

Going to the theater, moreover, is a great way to network. Theater professionals, whom you should know and work with, go to the theater all the time. This is a way to meet those people.

Most important, there is much we can learn by watching others work. Viewing good *and* bad acting is always a learning experience and can both enhance our growth and influence our work. Great acting can be an epiphany, an inspiration, and a standard by which we try to measure our own work. Lazy, mediocre and just plain bad acting can serve to shed light on our own shortcomings, expose the traps of our craft and remind us of how fragile this thing is we do for our livelihoods.

As critical as it is for us to go to the theater, it is not always easy. Theater is expensive. Every season, ticket prices go up, shutting out modestly paid actors from attending. Luckily for us, there are several ways to beat the system. With a little bit of planning, ingenuity, networking and cunning, you will never have to pay full price for the theater again. You could conceivably attend most theater for free. When I'm not in a play, it's not unusual for me to go to the theater 3–4 times a week, and I have not paid full price for a ticket more than twice in the last several years. Indeed, most of the theater I have seen has been totally gratis.

The following are several ways you can beat the high price of theater-going without having to resort to seeing only deconstructed Wedekind plays performed in taxidermists' lofts on the Lower East Side. I have done and do each of these, and save hundreds of dollars on theater tickets yearly:

Actors Equity occasionally is given complimentary Broadway, off-Broadway and showcase tickets to distribute to its members. There is no rhyme or reason as to when these freebies are disbursed. Since it is at the producer's discretion and needs that they are given to Equity, weeks can go by with no comps at all. Whenever you are in midtown, it won't hurt to run up to the second floor members' lounge to check on availability. Actors' Equity Association, 165 West 46th Street at Seventh Avenue, 2nd floor Members' Lounge.

Use your Equity card to gain entrance into any **AEA Approved Showcase** in the city. These plays, usually produced on a minuscule budget and in some of New York's funkier theater spaces, are meant to showcase the talents of theater artists to the people who will be hiring them or finding them work. Finding an agent in the city is as hard as finding an apartment, and every actor has heard that abominable phrase "Let me know when you're in something." A showcase often can be the "something." Because struggling individuals or companies with next-to-no money produce these, Equity allows actors to work for no pay. In return, AEA members may view these shows at no cost. You can find a list of these off-off-Broadway shows in the "Cue" section of *New York Magazine,* in *Time Out New York,* or the "Sunday Arts and Leisure" section of the *New York Times.*

The **Broadway in Bryant Park** (Sixth Avenue between 40th and 42nd Streets—212–768–4242) series, which plays on several Thursdays in midsummer, presents Broadway and off-Broadway stars performing numbers from their shows. These free lunchtime outdoor concerts begin at 12:30 P.M. and last about an hour and a half. Call for a schedule.

Although you won't be able to see an entire show at **Broadway on Broadway** (43rd Street and Broadway—212–768–1560), you will have the privilege of getting a sneak peak of scenes from the season's new productions. This free event, which takes place every year on the first Sunday after Labor Day, happens right in the middle of Broadway and Times Square and draws a huge crowd of theaterphiles, stargazers, Broadway pundits quick to offer their verdicts on the viability of each show, and the merely curious.

Another great way to see a show for free is to attend a **final dress rehearsal**. The night before a play's first preview, there is almost always a final dress—this is the culmination of weeks of rehearsal and the only opportunity to test a show before it plays in front of a paying audience. There are a couple of ways to get in. If you know people involved in the show, let them know you want to be put on the list. If you don't know anyone, go anyway. Since it is not an official performance, most theaters are not real strict about who gets in. They want butts in the seats to learn from the audience what works and what doesn't. Check the "Guide to the Lively Arts" in the *New York Times* everyday to see what is about to begin previews. Then show up at the theater around curtain time the night before that first performance, act like you belong there, walk in confidently and take a seat.

I've seen a lot of theater by going to the final dress. I even saw the final dress of the gonzo hit *The Producers* this way—a friend was given two passes and invited me to be her date. Now that the show has opened to "second-coming" reviews and has received every award known to man, people are clamoring for tickets, the show will probably run for the next millennium, and scalpers are asking for, *and getting,* $500 a ticket. Lucky me.

Every summer, **The New York Shakespeare Festival at the Delacorte Theatre** in Central Park presents 2 or 3 free productions of plays by Shakespeare and others under the stars. These productions usually have theater, film and TV names in the leading roles and are often brisk, brazen and fresh interpretations of the classics. Line up on the grass the day of the performance you wish to see. What time you get there should be determined by how popular the show is and who is starring. To insure that you secure a ticket, get there early, and bring a blanket, a book and plenty of water and food. (Meryl Streep and Kevin Kline recently appeared in *The Cherry Orchard* in 2001 and hopeful audience members camped out all night.) Tickets are dispersed at 1 P.M.—two per person. You can hold a place in line for your friends, but they must be there when the tickets are given out. Check listings for performance dates. (Entrance at 79th and Central Park West or 81st and Fifth Avenue). Note: A limited number Delacorte Theatre tickets are given out on the day of performance from 1 to 3 P.M. at the Public Theatre (425 Lafayette Street between 8th and 9th Streets). On selected dates, tickets are distributed in the other four boroughs; call 212–539–8750 for information.

The best way to see theater is to network with your friends and colleagues. You're an actor, right? You know actors and theater professionals, right? You probably know actors and theater professionals who are doing shows right now, right? Tell any actor, director, designer, producer, usher, house-manager, dresser, stage-manager, crew person and ticket booth employee you know who is doing a show that if the theater is **"papering"** any of the previews, to count you in. "Papering" a house is a practice most producers use in which free tickets are disbursed so that the actors and creative team can determine how the show plays in front of a full audience. At the same time, producers don't want audience members who paid full price to see a lot of empty seats and worry that they have spent their money on a turkey.

BEST BET

A little-known way to see free theater off-Broadway is to become a **volunteer Usher**. Most off-Broadway companies need ushers for every performance, and for about an hour of your time (stuffing *Playbills*, learning your assigned seating area and escorting audience members to their seats), you are rewarded with a free place to watch the performance. Besides the free ticket, the other advantage of ushering is, even if the show is a big hit or sold out, you are still guaranteed a seat.

The following theaters have a Volunteer Usher program:

Atlantic Theatre Company

336 West 20th Street between Eighth and Ninth
  Avenues—212–645–8015
Call and ask to speak to the Audiences Services
  Manager.

Bouwerie Lane Theatre/Jean Cocteau Repertory Company

330 Bowery at Bond Street—212–677–0060
Call and tell them you would like to be a Volunteer
  Usher.

Cherry Lane Theatre

38 Commerce Street at Grove Street—212–989–2020
Call and ask to speak to person in charge of Volunteer
  Ushers.

Classic Stage Company

136 East 13th Street between Third and Fourth
  Avenues—212–677–4210
Call two weeks prior to when you want to see the
  show and ask for the House Manager.

Irish Repertory Theatre

132 West 22nd Street between Sixth and Seventh
  Avenues—212–727–2737
Call and ask to speak to the Box Office Manager.

Manhattan Theatre Club

City Center, 130 West 55th Street between Sixth and
Seventh Avenues—212–399–3000
Call and ask to speak to the person in charge of
Volunteer Ushers.

New Group

St. Clement's Church—423 West 46th Street—
212–691–6730
Call and ask to speak to the Administrative Manager.

New York Theatre Workshop

79 East 4th Street between Bowery and Second
Avenue—212–460–5475
Call and speak to someone in the Box Office
after 2 P.M.

Pearl Theatre Company

80 St. Mark's Place between First and Second
Avenues—212–598–9802
Call and ask to speak to the Audience Services
Manager.

Performance Space 122

150 First Avenue at 9th Street—212–477–5829
Call and ask for ext. 306.

Performing Garage

33 Wooster Street between Broome and Grand
Streets—212–966–3651
Call and ask to speak to the House Manager.

Playwrights Horizons

416 West 42nd Street between Ninth and Tenth
Avenues—212–564–1235
Call and ask to speak to the person in charge of
Volunteer Ushers.

Primary Stages

354 West 45th Street—212–333–4052

Call and ask to speak to someone regarding Volunteer Ushering.

Roundabout Theatre Company

The American Airlines Theatre—227 West 42nd Street—212–819–9800

Go by the theater Box Office between 10 A.M. and 6 P.M. and sign up for the date you'd like to work.

Second Stage Theatre

307 West 43rd Street at Eighth Avenue—212–787–8302

Call and ask for the House Manager.

Signature Theatre Company

555 West 42nd Street between Tenth and Eleventh Avenues—212–244–7529

Call the Box Office and tell them you'd like to sign up as a Volunteer Usher.

Soho Repertory Theatre

46 Walker Street—212–941–8632

Call and ask to speak to the person in charge of Volunteer Ushers.

Theatre for the New City

155 First Avenue at 9th Street—212–254–1109

Call and ask to speak to person responsible for Volunteer Ushers.

Union Square Theatre

100 East 17th Street at Union Square—212–505–0700

Call and ask to speak to the person in charge of Volunteer Ushers.

Vineyard Theatre
108 East 15th Street at Union Square East—
212–353–3366
Call and ask for the Usher Hotline, then leave your
name and phone number and the House Manager
will call you back.

Okay, so you don't know anyone working on a play; you're too scrupled to sneak into a dress rehearsal; you have an aversion to escorting hordes of people to their seats; you are allergic to the lounge at Equity; your dog ate your Equity card; you refuse to see any theater that is presented in a former meat locker; and you hate the great outdoors. Well, you probably won't be seeing much *free* theater. Never mind—there are still several ways you can attend at greatly reduced rates:

Audience Extras (212–989–9550) handles leftover tickets, often for coveted house seats, to plays, musicals, concerts and dance performances. Membership is a one-time fee of $30, but after that, each ticket will cost you only $3. Most tickets are sold on the day of performance. Call for further information and details on membership.

There is always someone standing in front of a theater **hawking tickets**. You've seen them—the little lady with blue hair at the matinee whose friend Selma suddenly got sick; the pinstriped stock broker whose date stood him up; the sad-sack suburban housewife whose husband just remembered there was a playoff game on TV. In hope of getting their money back on these nonrefundable tickets, they halfheartedly wave them in the air, looking for a taker. This is where your charm, acting ability and a little of the "lean and hungry look" will come in handy.

Approach the person and ask them how much they are asking for the ticket. They will tell you the full price. In as sweet a way as you can muster, say that you cannot afford to pay that

308 • AN ACTOR PREPARES.... TO LIVE IN NEW YORK CITY

much; that you came to the theater with the intention of buying a $15 Standing Room ticket and that is all you've got. Suggest to the seller that *if they do not sell the ticket by curtain time,* you would buy it from them for the price you would have paid for S.R.O. They will almost immediately say, "No, I need to get full price for the ticket." State that you understand completely, but just in case they cannot sell it, you will wait. Inevitably, they will give you a condescending smile (they always do), as if to say "Of course I'll sell this ticket." Smile back, walk away, but stand in a place where they can see you.

The closer it gets to curtain time, the more desperate they will become and the less successful. At a minute or so before curtain, approach them again and say something to the effect that $15 is better than nothing. At this point, they will perform the transaction, grateful to have made anything on the ticket.

This is a trick an actor friend taught me in my early days in New York and as far as I can remember, it has never failed me. It is very hard to sell a single ticket at the last minute, even for a Broadway blockbuster. And, human nature being what it is, the seller will ultimately always want to make something on the ticket instead of swallowing the full amount. For your part, it takes a total lack of modesty as well as some tenacity and courage to pull this off successfully. Don't forget, you're going to be sitting next to the seller who will be stewing over his/her inability to get more than a fifth of the ticket's value. Note: Do yourself a favor and don't go to the theater with $100 bills and ask the seller to make change; this is a sure way to guarantee the transaction will founder.

The **Hit Show Club** service distributes free coupons redeemable at participating box offices for anywhere from a third to a half off regular ticket prices of the large, long-running Broadway blockbusters. Hit Show Club coupons can be found at libraries, bookstores, visitor centers, at the club office (630 Ninth Avenue between 44th and 45th Streets—212–581–4211) or via mail. Each coupon may be exchanged for up to 4 reserved seats at least one hour before the performance or can be mailed to the theater, giving a date and alternate date with payment. The coupon is usually not valid for the first 11 rows of the orchestra and availability is subject to prior sale. No refunds, no exchanges.

The **International Fringe Festival** (212–429–8877), which takes place in several locations on the Lower East Side over two weeks in August, presents a myriad of theater companies and performers from around the world. As the name of the festival implies, most of the companies featured are of an experimental or avant-garde bent. Tickets for all events are a reasonable $12, or you may purchase a pass for five performances for $55. Call for schedule.

New York Theatre Workshop (79 East 4th Street between Second and Third Avenues—212–460–5475), who I feel does some of the most interesting and cutting-edge work in town, has a terrific general rush ticket policy—two hours before curtain, all leftover tickets are sold for a very reasonable $10.

The **Joseph Papp Public Theatre** (425 Lafayette Street between 8th and 9th Streets—212–260–2400) offers tickets for $15 cash if there are any left 30 minutes before show time.

When producers need to "paper" a house for certain performances (such as opening nights, when critics are in the house, special events and benefits) with discreet, courteous and well-groomed individuals, they donate tickets to **Play by Play.** Play by Play then offers them to its members. You think you're discerning, friendly, and can clean up on occasion? If so, you're an ideal candidate for Play by Play membership. To join, you pay a yearly fee of $99 and a service charge of $3 per ticket (you are entitled to two tickets per each available event). A couple of shows and your membership has practically paid for itself. Occasionally producers will want to gauge audience response to their show and will ask Play by Play members to complete a survey and score sheet. You're thinking "some nerve," they make you be nice, dress up and pretend like you paid a fortune for these tickets, and now you have to fill out a damn survey? Don't worry, they are easy to complete, consisting primarily of multiple choice and numerical scoring. Trust me, it's worth it . . . the seats the producers provide are very good and the events that they are "papering" are almost always special performances. Tickets to events are listed through a telephone hotline and can be ordered Monday through Friday 2 P.M. to 5 P.M. Tickets are offered for performances anytime from the day of the listing up to 72 hours in advance. To become a member or for more information, call or write Play by Play at 165 West 46th Street, Suite 412, New York, NY 10036—212–868–7502.

For about $20 and a valid student ID, you can purchase a **Student Rush** ticket. Many, but not all, of the theaters offer Rush seats although no two theaters have the same distribution policy; some disburse them in the morning, others only make them available 30 minutes before show time. Go by the theater and inquire if they have Student Rush and what time those tickets are given out. Line up early as Rush tickets are limited and popular.

Standing Room Only tickets, which range from $15 to $20, are sold on the day of performance and usually only if the show is sold out. Since not all theaters can accommodate standing room, go by the theater and inquire if they have S.R.O. The wonderful thing about "Standing Room" is that you are above the heads of the audience. Although your feet and legs may get a little tired, you have a great view of the stage . . . and every seat in the orchestra section. During the first act, scope out where the empty seats are, there are always a few, even for the biggest hits. As soon as the lights come up at the intermission, walk quickly to that seat and sit. It is now yours. I've done this numerous times and have seen some of Broadway's greatest plays this way—Lily Tomlin's *The Search for Signs of Intelligent Life in the Universe, Dreamgirls, The Beauty Queen of Leenane, The*

King and I, Les Liaisons Dangereuses (ten times . . . I liked the play). Not once was I hassled or asked to leave the seat.

Something I've never done but comes highly recommended, is to **surf the websites of the city's theater companies** (i.e. Roundabout, Manhattan Theatre Club, New York Theatre Workshop, et al.) and get on their e-mail lists. If these companies need to fill empty seats at the last minute, they will contact everyone on their list and offer tickets at a huge savings. The friends who have done this say they have never paid more than $20 and almost always have been placed in house seats.

Committed to building audiences and supporting the performing arts in New York City, the **Theatre Development Fund (TDF)** oversees three different discount ticket programs. The most famous of these is the **TKTS Booth**, located in the center of the theater district in Duffy Square. TKTS sells tickets at a 25 to 50 percent savings (with a $2.50 service charge per ticket) for most Broadway and off-Broadway offerings. The lines form a couple of hours before the booth opens and can look intimidating. Don't fret though, they move quickly. A secret I learned years ago is to go much later, after 6:30 or 7 P.M. when the lines have subsided; it is later in the day that the booth actually offers a better selection of shows and seats. Why? Hoping to sell them at full price, most theaters hold on to their best seats until the last minute and transfer them to TKTS close to curtain time if they haven't been sold. (*TKTS Duffy Square—47th Street at Broadway—212-221-0013. For evening performances open Monday–Saturday 3 to 8 P.M.; Sunday 11 A.M. to 7 P.M.; for matinee tickets open Wednesday and Saturday 10 A.M. to 2 P.M.; and Sunday 11 A.M. to 2 P.M. Cash or traveler's checks only.*) Until September 11, 2001, there was also a TKTS booth at 2 World Trade Center. The new booth is located at the South Street Seaport (199 Water Street between Front and John Streets, at the southeast corner of the Resnick-Prudential Building). This outpost is not nearly as busy as the

BEST BARGAIN

Duffy Square facility, meaning shorter lines and wait. Other conveniences of this facility include earlier opening hours, and matinee tickets may be purchased here the day before a show. (*Open Monday to Friday 11* A.M. *to 5:30* P.M.; *Saturday 11* A.M. *to 3:30* P.M.)

TDF's second major program involves its mailing list of over 80,000 members to whom it offers discounted tickets via snail- and/or e-mail on a rotating basis. The discounts under this program are tremendous—as much as 75 percent or more for both Broadway and off-Broadway shows. The caveat . . . to be eligible for membership, you must be one of the following: student, teacher, union member, retired person, performing arts professional, clergy, or member of the armed forces. Eligible applicants may write to TDF (enclosing a self-addressed stamped envelope) for an application form at 1501 Broadway, New York, NY 10036 (212–221–0013). You may also download and fill out the form online (www.tdf.org). Either way, you must provide proof of eligibility and pay a $20 processing fee (which is waived for members of the acting unions during their first year on the mailing list).

Thirdly, TDF offers a **Voucher Program**, which is a book of four passes for $28 to cutting-edge, off-off-Broadway theater as well as to unconventional music and dance events. Each voucher is good for one admission within a year from the date of purchase. Vouchers are only available to those on the TDF mailing list.

Along with its great services, TDF sends quarterly newsletters and periodic e-mail updates of available shows, also maintains a website where you can find everything you need to know about its programs, and provides information by phone on all theater, dance and music events in the city (212–768–1818). Join the mailing list, take advantage of the TKTS booth, and enjoy the savings TDF extends to you.

Twofers are free vouchers that work much the same way as the Hit Show Club coupons. These vouchers may be found in hotels, libraries, bookstores, visitor centers, etc., and allow you to buy two tickets for slightly more than the price of one. Like the Hit Show Club coupons, Twofers are mostly for the large, long-running Broadway standards.

At the **Vineyard Theatre** (108 East 15th Street— 212–353–0303), professional performing artists who show a paid-up union card may purchase a membership for only $15 and then pay just $10 per show for the entire season. Call for more details.

The theater-related **websites www.Playbill.com** and **www.TheatreMania.com** periodically offer substantially discounted tickets (up to 50 percent off) to a number of Broadway, off-Broadway and off-off-Broadway shows. Check these sites often as ticket availability changes daily. For just $99 (and a $4.50 processing fee per ticket), you can join TheatreMania's **"Gold Club,"** a theater club that provides members with a full year's access of complimentary tickets for two to participating shows. Offerings include Broadway, off-Broadway, off-off-Broadway, Long Island shows, comedy, dance and music. "Gold Club" members also receive a free subscription to the bi-weekly "TM Insider" newsletter, which contains the latest information on what's happening in the theater as well as exclusive discount offers. Once a member, you may access the Gold Club's complimentary show database (check often as it is updated throughout the day) and make reservations on a first-come/first-reserved basis.

Viewing Film

I LOVE BRINGING OUT-OF-TOWNERS to the movies in Manhattan. I love seeing their dumbstruck reactions when they learn that it costs $10 to see a movie.

I remember years ago when ticket prices edged up to $7.50. Then Mayor Ed Koch was indignant and suggested in an interview that all New Yorkers boycott the movies. Koch rallied the troops . . . we were all filled with ire and high dudgeon and ready to sacrifice our film watching needs on principle. Come the following weekend, however, the withdrawal was too much and we headed in droves to the multiplexes where we begrudgingly plunked down $7.50 for our film fixes.

Today it is no different. Although resentful, we shell out $10 for the visual, aural and emotional thrill we get there in the dark. We'd probably do the same tomorrow if tickets jumped to $20. Going to the movies is just too important and desirable an activity for us. We love movies. We discuss them like they are current events (and sometimes they are). We analyze plot, we scrutinize acting. We especially love to opine about a particular film's merits, or lack thereof. We scan film reviews as if they were sure-bet stock tips. Movies are what New Yorkers do. I am happy to report that there are several ways that we lemmings can beat the high cost of film-going—some that are available to all New Yorkers, and some only to actors.

The **AMC Chain of Theaters** (42nd Street just east of Eighth Avenue and 34th Street west of Eighth) offers filmgoers its **Movie Watcher's Frequent User Card**. Each time you purchase a movie ticket at AMC, present your Movie Watcher's Card at the Box Office. Once you've bought ten tickets, AMC will give you one free pass to view a film of your choice in any of their theaters. Your Movie Watcher Card, also accrues points toward free concessions items and entitles you to free popcorn on Wednesdays. Ask for a Movie Watcher Card application at the AMC Box Office.

The **Brooklyn Bridge Park Summer Film Series** (718–802–0603), sponsored by the Brooklyn Bridge Park Coalition, shows free movies in Empire-Fulton Ferry State Park on the waterfront between the Brooklyn and Manhattan Bridges. The series is held on Thursdays in July and August and begins promptly at 8:45 P.M. If you're not into the film, the dramatic views of the bridges and the lower Manhattan skyline will more than capture your attention. Call for a schedule and directions.

At the **Brooklyn Heights Cinema** (70 Henry Street, Brooklyn—718–596–7070), the first show of the day costs only $4. In addition, a "Bargain Day" special on Mondays and Tuesdays makes all screenings $4.

One of the things that I think makes this city great is the **Bryant Park Film Festival**. Running on Monday nights (rain date on Tuesday) from June to August, this free festival features film classics such as *Sorry, Wrong Number, Mildred Pierce, Auntie Mame, Breakfast at Tiffany's* and *War of the Worlds*. There is nothing quite like the sight of thousands of New Yorkers of all ages, races, persuasions and sizes merrily cavorting on the lawn before and during the show. Everywhere you look, you can see people talking, laughing, sharing food. The roar of excitement that the crowd lets loose at the beginning of the prefilm cartoon can be heard down to the Battery, and the happiness continues throughout the evening. It is a decidedly festive atmosphere and makes you almost forget you live in the most jaded city in the world. Disney has nothing over this place. Bryant Park on a

BEST FREE MOVIES

Monday night in summer is the happiest place on earth. Note: Screenings begin at sunset, but arrive early to secure a place on the lawn.

In the summer months, **Celebrate Brooklyn** sponsors a free film festival under the stars every Thursday evening at dusk at the Prospect Park Bandshell. The films are usually classics like *Rebel Without a Cause* and *Around the World in 80 Days* and are preceded by live music or storytellers. Call Brooklyn Information and Culture (718–855–7882) for a full schedule of screenings or check their website—www.celebratebrooklyn.org.

Cinema Classics Screening Room (332 East 11th Street between First and Second Avenues—212–677–5368), deep in the heart of the East Village, is hands down, the least glamorous place to view film in the city. Badly framed movie posters hang haphazardly on graceless brick walls and the screen is of the pull-down variety, like the ones your parents used to show home movies on. This theater's appeal, besides the low ticket price (just $5.50), is its eclectic programming; the films screened here are drawn from art-house, classic and foreign genres and are almost always engaging. Call for a schedule.

The **Cobble Hill Cinema** (265 Court Street, Brooklyn—718–596–9113) is a "first-run," five-screen movieplex that has bargain showings throughout the week. Monday through Friday, all shows before 5 P.M. are only $5; tickets all-day Tuesday are only $5; and Saturday and Sunday matinees before 2 P.M. are $5.

The Media Center at the **Donnell Library** (20 West 53rd Street between Fifth and Sixth Avenues—212–621–0618) has an extensive library of film and videotapes. You may view any of these at the library for free if you make an appointment 24 to 48 hours in advance. The library's immense catalog of titles will amaze you. The Media Center also sponsors film screenings every Wednesday and Thursday in the fall, winter and spring and Wednesdays in the summer. Call the Media Center or consult the NYPL website (www.nypl.org) for a complete schedule.

Most of the other **New York City Libraries** (see chapter on "Books") show free films and documentaries sporadically throughout the year. For more information and a schedule of screenings, contact your local library, pick up the monthly "events" booklet or go to the New York Public Library website at www.nypl.org and click on "Events," then search by borough or library.

If you can't bear all that happiness in Bryant Park, or all those people, but still want to see a movie in the great outdoors, head to the Hudson River—Piers 25 and 54 to be exact. In the summer, the Hudson River Park Trust presents **Riverflicks**, a series of free movies that play a couple of times each week. Unlike Bryant Park, they throw in free popcorn as well. All films at Pier 25 are rated G or PG. Call 212–533–PARK for a weekly schedule of screenings and locations.

Paid-up members of **Screen Actors Guild** in good standing have three ways they can get into a movie for little or no money. The "no money" way first:

→ The Screen Actors Guild Awards, which are considered one of the industry's most prized honors, presents 13 awards for acting in film and television. The awards acknowledge the greatness of both individual performers as well as the work of the ensemble of a drama and comedy series and the cast of a motion picture. The SAG Awards are unique in the composition of its voters. Two randomly selected panels of 2100 SAG members choose the nominees for television and motion pictures. The final ballot of nominees is then sent out to the entire active SAG membership (over 98,000 members), who vote their choice for the outstanding performances of the year. From November through January of each year, those SAG members who are fortunate enough to be chosen for the SAG nominating committee, together with a guest, may view for free just about any movie at just about any theater. All you need to do is show your SAG Nominating Committee card and a picture ID at the Box Office. Keep your fingers crossed that you are lucky enough to be chosen for the nominating committee. Even if you don't have that privilege (I haven't yet—ugh!), there is still a window of about six weeks after the nominations are announced when you and a guest can see any of the nominated films for free. To view the nominated films, show your valid SAG card and a picture ID at the Box Office. For a list of Award nominated films, check the ballot that is sent to you in February or the SAG website (www.sag.com). During February and early March, check any New York newspapers' ads to see if SAG members are given free entry.

→ About twice a year, the three major film chains—AMC, UA and Sony/Loews/Magic Johnson—each offer a limited number of discount coupons to all Screen Actors Guild members. These coupons, which are $5 each, may only be purchased at the SAG offices (1515 Broadway, 44th Floor) from 9:30 A.M. to 4:30 P.M. They are valid for a year from the date of purchase, may be used at any participating theater nationwide and are good for any show time except during "special engagements," generally within the first ten days of a new release. Pay for coupons by cash, money order or cashiers check only. Although there is no official distribution date for the coupons, they are usually released in April and September. This offer is on a first-come/first-served basis—SAG is allotted a finite number of tickets; once those are sold out, there are no more until the following distribution period. The Guild's monthly newsletter informs members of the coupon sale; you may also call the Business Office (212–944–1030) and ask the date of the next distribution. You are allowed to purchase a maximum of 50 coupons per person per day; you must show your paid-up SAG card at the time of purchase. Note: AMC and Sony/Loews/Magic Johnson cinemas charge a $1 surcharge. Even with the surcharge, $6 (which is approximately what the rest of the country is paying) is a hell of a lot better than $10 to see a movie.

→ For $75, the Screen Actors Guild Film Society of New York offers its members and a guest the opportunity to see 20 "first-run" films. The Film Society, which functions as a showcase for "contemporary products of the film industry," presents these films through the courtesy of the distributors at no cost to the Society. Your nominal membership is used to defray operating costs. To become a member of the Society, either walk in and pick up or call and request an application from the SAG Committee Office (1515 Broadway, 44th Floor— 212–944–1030). You must correctly fill out and sign the application and return it with your signed check. Your Film Society membership card will be sent the last week in August; the screenings begin in September. All Film Society screenings are held at the Directors Guild of America (110 West 57th Street between Sixth and Seventh Avenues) on Mondays and Tuesdays at 1 P.M., 3:30 P.M., 6 P.M., and 8:30 P.M. You may request the day and time you would like, but if you want an evening screening act fast as they fill up quickly.

BEST BARGAIN

Each Wednesday evening in July and August, the **Socrates Sculpture Park** (Broadway at Vernon Boulevard, Long Island City, Queens—718–956–1819) in collaboration with the Museum of the Moving Image and the Partnership for Parks presents an outdoor festival of international film. Admission is free and all films begin at sunset. Festival sponsored prescreening music and dance performances begin at 7 P.M.

Sony's Wonder and Technology Lab (550 Madison Avenue between 55th and 56th Streets—212–833–7620) offers free summer movie screenings at 6 P.M. on Thursday evenings. Ostensibly, the films they show are kid's flicks, but who died and made *Dr. Strangelove* and *Labyrinth* children's films? Yet, they were both on the Sony Wonder roster in 2001. For a complete schedule of screenings, check their website at www.sonywondertech-lab.com. Although the films are free, you must call to make reservations in the week of the screening that you would like to attend.

Probably due to the glut of new state-of-the-art, stadium-seating film palaces just blocks away, the multiscreen **State Theatre** (1540 Broadway between 45th and 46th Streets) inside the Virgin Record Store has recently become a discount movie house. For just $4.95, you can see either "first-run" films that have exhausted their stay at other venues or Indian "Bollywood" features.

Every Wednesday night at 8 P.M., the downtown lounge **Void** (16 Mercer Street between Grand and Canal Streets—212–941–6492) has free movie screenings of classic and contemporary films. Instead of the usual popcorn and soda, at Void you can sidle up to the bar and order a moderately priced adult beverage. Arrive early for a decent seat.

VIEWING LIVE TELEVISION

SEVERAL TELEVISION TALK AND VARIETY SHOWS are shot right here in the Big Apple daily, and every one of these needs a live studio audience. It's free to see any of these tapings, however, the waiting period for many of the more popular shows like *Late Show with David Letterman* and *Saturday Night Live* can be as long as a year. For tickets, send a postcard with your name, address, dates you would like to attend, and day and evening phone numbers.

Ananda Lewis Show—Send your request for tickets a month in advance of when you would like to attend.

The Ananda Lewis Show
P.O. Box 1326
Radio City Station
New York, NY 10019

The Daily Show tapes every Monday through Thursday at the show's studios, located at 513 West 54th Street near Tenth Avenue. Doors open at 5:45 P.M. You must be 18 or over to attend. Write a month in advance of when you would like to see a taping.

Daily Show Tickets
1775 Broadway, 9th Floor
New York, NY 10019

It's Showtime at the Apollo tapes Thursday through Sunday during January and August only, but you may write for tickets year-round. Send your request no less than a month in advance of when you would like to go.

It's Showtime at the Apollo Tickets
3 Park Avenue, 40th Floor
New York, NY 10016

Late Night with Conan O'Brien—Call or write a month in advance of the tape date you desire. You may reserve up to five tickets. Standby tickets are also available on tape days, Tuesday through Friday, at 9 A.M. at the 49th Street entrance of 30 Rockefeller Plaza, but you have to return at 4:15 P.M. to see if there is indeed room.

NBC Tickets
30 Rockefeller Plaza
New York, NY 10012
212–664–3056 ext. 1

Late Show with David Letterman—Write or call to order tickets well in advance of when you want to see the taping (as much as a year in advance!). For standby tickets *on the day* of the show, call 212–247–6497 at 11 A.M. The Late Show tapes Monday through Thursday.

Late Show Tickets
Ed Sullivan Theatre
1697 Broadway
New York, NY 10019
212–975–1003

Live with Regis and Kelly—Send a postcard at least a year in advance of when you want to see a taping. You are allowed up to four tickets. For standby tickets, line up at the corner of 67th Street and Columbus no later than 7 A.M. on weekdays.

Live with Regis and Kelly Tickets
Ansonia Station
P.O. Box 230–777
New York, NY 10023
212–456–3537

Maury Povich Show tapes Tuesday through Thursday at 10:30 A.M. and 1 P.M. at the USA Studios. On average, the show is booked about three weeks ahead of taping. When sending your request, make sure to include the number of tickets you would like.

Maury Tickets
Studios USA
15 Penn Plaza/Grand Ballroom
New York, NY 10001

Montel Williams Show—Request tickets two weeks ahead of taping. Tape dates are Tuesday through Thursday at 10 A.M., 1 P.M. and 4 P.M. You are allowed up to four tickets.

Montel Tickets
433 W 53rd Street
New York, NY 10019

The People's Court—Call or write several weeks in advance of when you would like to see a taping. The show tapes Tuesdays and Wednesdays in the morning and in the afternoon. Taping times will be confirmed with your ticket request.

The People's Court Tickets
401 Fifth Avenue
New York, NY 10016
888–780–8587

Caroline Rhea—Call or e-mail for future dates. Standby tickets are available at 7:30 A.M. on tape days (Monday through Wednesday at 10 A.M. and Thursday 10 A.M. and 2 P.M.).

NBC Tickets
30 Rockefeller Plaza
New York, NY 10012
212–664–3056 ext.3

Ricki Lake Show—Tapings for this show are on Wednesdays and Thursdays at 3 and 5 P.M. and Fridays at 1 and 3 P.M. Write or call for tickets or go in person at least an hour before taping.

Ricki Lake
401 Fifth Avenue
New York, NY 10016
212–352–8600

Sally Jessy Raphael—Send your request a month ahead of taping. Tape days are Monday through Wednesday at noon and 3 P.M. Arrive at least an hour prior to taping.

Sally Jessy Raphael Show
Studios USA
15 Penn Plaza/OF2
New York, NY 10001

Saturday Night Live—Only accepts requests for tickets in August, and you may not ask for a particular date or quantity of tickets. There are standby tickets, but are nearly impossible to score. To try your luck, get on the standby line on the mezzanine level of Rockefeller Center (at 49th Street) by 9 A.M. the morning of the taping.

NBC Tickets
30 Rockefeller Plaza
New York, NY 10012
212–664–3056 ext.4

Total Request Live—For tickets, call 212–398–8549 a month before you would like to attend. TRL airs live Monday through Friday at 4 P.M. There is a slim chance that you can secure a standby ticket; arrive at least two hours before the show begins. You must be between 16 and 24 to gain admittance.

MTV Studios
1515 Broadway at 45th Street
New York, NY 10019

The View—Send your request two to three months prior to when you would like to see a taping. Standby tickets are available on tape days; arrive by 9 A.M.

Ticket Coordinator
The View
320 West 66th Street
New York, NY 10023

Who Wants to be a Millionaire tapes Monday, Tuesday and Thursday at 4 P.M., and Wednesday at 12:30 P.M. and 4 P.M. Write with your request for tickets (only four per household) two months prior to your desired tape date.

Who Wants to be a Millionaire
Columbia University Station
P.O. Box 250225
New York, NY 10025

The website www.nytix.com offers a constantly updated listing of all the television shows shot in New York as well as information on obtaining tickets. It also offers a $1.99 a minute phone service you can call to find out about the availability of standby tickets for each show.

LISTENING TO MUSIC

BESIDES BEING THE ART, dance, theater, business, fashion, retail and museum capital of the world (not that I am at all jingoistic), New York is also the greatest city in the world for music. On any given day or night, live music is everywhere throughout Gotham—concert halls, Broadway and off-Broadway theaters, bars, clubs, restaurants, parks, museums, street corners; even the subway platforms serve as impromptu stages for a variety of musical offerings.

There is something in New York for every musical taste. When it comes to classical music, we have one of the best and oldest American symphony orchestras, the New York Philharmonic, and the most famous concert venue, Carnegie Hall, which plays host to the world's great orchestras and singers. Two of the most famous opera companies, the Metropolitan and the New York City Opera, reside here. And the city has more outlets that present chamber music, soloists and orchestras than do some entire countries.

Nowhere in the world, except perhaps New Orleans and Newport during their festivals, has more jazz offerings. As for rock, blues, punk, world, experimental and progressive, the best way to gauge just how much of it is out there is to open *The Village Voice* music section each week. The number of pages (32 in the *Voice* as I write), ads and listings devoted to these musical categories is astounding. For we budget-conscious ones, several places in New York offer music at little or no cost:

FREE MUSIC

For some real get-down, hand-clapping, foot-stomping gospel, there's no better place on the planet than **Abyssinian Baptist Church** (132 West 138th Street—212–862–7474) on a Sunday morning. Abyssinian's raucous, spine-tingling gospel choir performs during the 9 A.M. and 11 A.M. services; a large area of the church has been designated for tourists and aficionados. Arrive early as the line to get in goes around the block; more than once I've been turned away. The cost for this uplifting experience is just a dollar. Of course, if the spirit moves you, you may always give more.

The **Bronx Symphony Orchestra** (2141 Muliner Avenue, Bronx—718-601-9151), composed of professional and serious nonprofessional musicians, presents free symphonic concerts throughout the year. Call for schedule.

The **Brooklyn Academy of Music** sponsors three different free concert series during the summer months. The **BAM Free Concerts in Brooklyn Parks** (212-360-8290) series offers over a dozen evening concerts in parks throughout the borough, featuring R&B, jazz, funk, blues, reggae and salsa. **BAM Outside** (718-636-4100) presents free noonday concerts of popular music at nearby MetroTech Center (Flatbush Avenue and Myrtle Avenues). **BAM Rhythm and Blues Festival at MetroTech** presents free R&B concerts at noon on Thursdays in July and August. Call for schedule and location.

Bryant Park (Sixth Avenue at 42nd Street—212-768-4242) presents free classical music and jazz in the open air throughout the summer months. Performers and times vary, so call for schedule.

Castle Clinton (Battery Place at State Street—212-835-2789) presents free Thursday evening concerts in July and early August. The roster of performers varies from rock, blues, jazz and gospel and has featured such groups as The Crash Test Dummies, The Blind Boys of Alabama and jazz legend John Scofield. Seating is very limited and on a

328 • AN ACTOR PREPARES.... TO LIVE IN NEW YORK CITY

first-come/first-served basis; concerts are at 7 P.M. with access to the venue beginning at 5 P.M. Call for schedule.

During the summer months, **Celebrate Brooklyn** (Prospect Park Bandshell, 9ᵗʰ Street and Prospect Park West, Brooklyn—718–855–7882) stages free world-class music concerts al fresco at the beautiful Prospect Park Bandshell. The music is performed by some of the world's leading groups and individuals, in anything from reggae to classical, world, pop, hip-hop, Latin, Celtic, ethno-techno, salsa, funk, rock, jazz, blues, bossa nova, electronica, dub, Sufi-rock, avant-garde, rap, Afro-Caribbean and Rai. Call for a complete schedule.

From mid-June to late August, **Central Park Summerstage** (F Playfield 72ⁿᵈ Street near Fifth Avenue in Central Park—212–360–2777) hosts an astounding line-up of world famous and almost-famous groups. The musical offerings span all genres with something for everyone; all, except a couple of special concerts, are free. Call for schedule.

Through its **Concerts in the Parks** series (212–875–5709), the **New York Philharmonic** presents free outdoor summer concerts in city parks in all five boroughs. Concerts begin at 8 P.M. and finish with a flourish of fireworks. Call for schedule.

The **Continental Center** (180 Maiden Lane at Front Street—212–799–5000) in the Financial District presents the free Juilliard Artists in Concert series every Tuesday afternoon at lunchtime. Call for schedule.

Every Tuesday evening from late June through July, the **Cooper-Hewitt Museum** (2 East 91ˢᵗ Street at Fifth Avenue—212–849–8400) hosts its free Cross-Currents concert series, which presents a wide spectrum of musical genres appealing to most every taste. Call for schedule.

There is never a cover or drink minimums to hear jazz at **Detour** (349 East 13th Street between First and Second Avenues—212–533–6212), which showcases New York's new and rising combos nightly. Besides the free admission, drinks at this venue are inexpensively priced, with Happy Hour (Monday through Friday from 4 to 7 P.M.) two-for-one drinks.

Call or write in advance for tickets to great free classical music concerts held at **The Frick Collection** (1 East 70th Street at Fifth Avenue—212–288–0700) from September to May each year. You can also show up thirty minutes before a concert and try to secure a "no-show" seat.

Harlem Week (Harlem—212–862–8477), the world's largest black and Latino festival, features art exhibitions, music, film, and dance presentations and a huge festival on Fifth Avenue from 125th to 135th Streets in early to mid-August. Music performances include jazz, gospel and R&B. Call for a schedule of events.

The ten-week **Hudson River Festival** (212–945–0505/212–528–2733), held in the summer months, presents free music, dance, theater and storytelling events as well as art exhibitions. The festival is held at several riverside venues including Battery Park, the Winter Garden of the World Financial Center, Castle Clinton and the Battery Park Esplanade. Call for a complete schedule.

The **Martin Luther King, Jr., Concert Series** (718–469–1912) at Wingate Field on Kingston Avenue across from Kings County Hospital in Brooklyn presents free concerts of jazz, R&B, oldies, gospel and Caribbean music on Mondays in July and August at 7:30 P.M. Call for a schedule.

The **Library for the Performing Arts** at Lincoln Center (111 Amsterdam Avenue at 66th Street—212–870–1630) periodically presents free classical and Broadway music concerts. Call for details and check the monthly NYPL booklet of events.

The **Lincoln Center Out-of-Doors Festival** (Lincoln Center and Damrosch Park, 64th Street at Columbus Avenue—212–875–5108) offers a spectacular roster of free music concerts and dance events (featuring the great and nearly-great) daily for three weeks in August. Call for a complete schedule.

The music, mostly rock, at **Luna Lounge** (171 Ludlow Street between Houston and Stanton Streets—212–260–2323) on the Lower East Side is always free. The performance space in the rear of the bar is comfy and the drinks here are inexpensive. As the music is free, the quality varies widely, with some of it nasty bad. Call for a schedule of performances.

From September to June, the **Metropolitan Museum of Art** (1000 Fifth Avenue at 82nd Street—212–570–3949) hosts a staggering number of free concerts of music from around the world. Moreover, the Met presents chamber music in the bar and piano music in the cafeteria on Friday and Saturday evenings, making it one of the best "cheap date" spots in New York. Phone for the schedule or check the monthly events booklet.

An ideal way to experience great music and hear excellent up-and-coming performers and composers, all at no cost, is to attend a concert at one of New York's exceptional **music schools**. Call any or all for their complete concert schedules:

> **Bloomingdale School of Music**—323 West 108th Street—212–663–6021

> **Juilliard School of Music**—Lincoln Center, 60 Lincoln Center at 66th Street—212–769–7406. Throughout the school year—September to May—Juilliard presents al-

most daily student recitals at its **Paul Recital Hall**, with larger events taking place most Wednesdays at 1 P.M. at **Alice Tully Hall**.

Manhattan School of Music—120 Claremont Avenue at Broadway—212–749–2802

Mannes College of Music—150 West 85th Street between Columbus and Amsterdam Avenues—212–580–0210

St. Paul's Chapel (211 Broadway at Fulton Street— 212–602–0874) offers free lunchtime concerts of mostly classical music every Monday at noon throughout the year. Call for schedule.

The **Seaside Summer Concert Series** (718–469–1912) in Asser Levy Park in Brooklyn offers free concerts of rock, disco, Latin and contemporary music on Thursdays in July and August beginning at 7:30 P.M.. Call for schedule.

In the summer months, **South Street Seaport Concerts** (Pier 17, Fulton Street at South Street on the East River— 212–732–8257) presents several free concerts throughout the week: Latin jazz and salsa concerts on Wednesdays; the "Sam Goody Home Before Midnight" showcase of new bands on Thursdays. During the Christmas holidays, the chorus of St. Cecilia's performs traditional and international carols on choir risers that are configured into the shape of a giant Christmas tree. In the spring and fall, there are free midweek dinnertime jazz concerts, often featuring some of the form's greatest performers. Call for schedule.

Trinity Church (74 Trinity Place—212–602–0747), one of the oldest and most beautiful churches in New York, offers free year-round concerts every Thursday at 1 P.M. Chamber groups, choruses and soloists are among the performers heard here. Call for schedule.

Every Tuesday at 8 P.M. in July, the **Washington Square Music Festival** (Washington Square Park, LaGuardia Place at West 4th Street—212–431–1088) features outdoor concerts of mostly chamber orchestra and big band music. Call for schedule.

At lunchtime or after work catch free concerts in all musical genres at the **World Financial Center Winter Garden** (West Street between Liberty and Vesey Streets—212–945–0505). Call for schedule.

INEXPENSIVE MUSIC:

At the intimate Lower East Side club **Arlene Grocery** (95 Stanton Street between Ludlow and Orchard Streets—212–358–1633), three to eight local bands are featured nightly. The talent here can sometimes be hit or miss, but with the low cover charge and cheap drinks, it is worth the risk—you may go on a night when tomorrow's superstars are performing. Call for schedule.

At **Arthur's Tavern** (57 Grove Street near Bleecker Street—212–675–6879), there is never a cover charge to hear a continuous stream of jazz and blues from 9 P.M. to 3 A.M., although they have a two drink minimum on weekends and one drink on weeknights.

Classic rock, jazz and blues is what you'll hear on the intimate stage at **The Back Fence** (155 Bleecker Street at Thompson Street—212–475–9221). There is a $5 cover on Fridays and Saturdays with a two-drink minimum, no cover on weeknights. Performances begin at 6 P.M. to appease both hardcore music junkies and those who go to bed early.

The **Baggot Inn** (82 West 3rd Street between Thompson and Sullivan Streets—212–477–0622), an Irish pub that features music nightly, charges only $5 most evenings (Mondays and

Wednesdays are free). Music ranges from Celtic to Irish rock, funk and blues as well as open mike nights when the uninhibited have the opportunity to make asses of themselves. Drink prices here are also cheap.

The **Bitter End** (149 Bleecker Street between Thompson Street and LaGuardia Place—212–673–7030) has been the springboard for the careers of countless bands and vocalists since 1961, and still presents talent it believes will be tomorrow's superstars. On any given night, you can hear several up-and-coming groups as well as an occasional headliner, for a reasonable $5 to $10. Call for schedule.

The **Blue Note** (131 West 3rd Street between MacDougal Street and Sixth Avenue—212–475–8592), considered the "Jazz capital of the world," is the city's most famous jazz venue and with a roster of performers that reads like a Who's Who of jazz greats, it is also one of the city's most expensive. But you can hear music here inexpensively. On Fridays and Saturdays from 2 to 4 A.M., you can catch a jam session for a paltry $5. On Sundays, you get music with the Blue Note's reasonably priced jazz brunch of food and drink for $18.50. Call for a complete list of headliners and to make brunch reservations (required).

Bronx Arts Ensemble (Golf House, Van Cortlandt Park, Bronx—718–601–7399) presents a variety of concerts in differing venues throughout the borough. Tickets are usually around $10 although many summer performances are free. Call for schedule and location.

Carnegie Hall (881 Seventh Avenue at 57th Street—212–247–7800) has $8 student rush tickets for certain performances. Call for information.

If loud, unruly music is your thing, then **CBGB** ((315 Bowery at Bleecker Street—212–982–4052) is the place for you. Considered the venue that introduced punk music to the world, CBGB presents a variety of mostly "underground" bands nightly for a modest cover charge of $3 to $10. If, on the other hand, you like your music a little more tame, go next door to **CB's 313 Gallery** (313 Bowery—212-677-0455) for softer, more acoustic offerings at about the same cover price.

The jazz club, **Cleopatra's Needle** (2485 Broadway between 92nd and 93rd Streets—212-769-6969), charges no cover to hear music but stipulates a $10 drink minimum per set at each table.

The punk palace **Continental** (25 Third Avenue between St. Mark's Place and Stuyvesant Street—212-529-6924) features hardcore punk and rock groups nightly, with occasional surprise superstars like Iggy Pop and Deborah Harry dropping in to do a song or two. Call for schedule.

The **Elbow Room** (144 Bleecker Street between Thompson Street and LaGuardia Place—212-979-8434) is a large venue (as the name implies) that features several local rock, jazz and blues bands nightly for a cover of about $7. Call for schedule.

The Knitting Factory's (74 Leonard Street between Broadway and Church Streets—212-219-3006) huge array of music performances vary in price from $5 to $12.

In July, the **Lincoln Center Festival** (Lincoln Center, Columbus Avenue at 65th Street—212-875-5928) holds dance, theater, opera and music events by worldwide artistes. Tickets go for as little as $15 with even cheaper student discounts. Call for more information.

Merkin Concert Hall (129 West 67th Street between Broadway and Amsterdam Avenue—212-501-3330) offers probably the most eclectic program of concerts in the city. Performances scheduled cover the musical spectrum from ethnic to early, classical, jazz and experimental. Tickets start at just $8. Call for schedule.

The **Mostly Mozart** summer festival of concerts at Alice Tully and Avery Fisher Halls at Lincoln Center (212–875–5399) does include a few free performances as well as offering fifty $10 tickets (available on the day of the event) for every concert. Call for schedule.

To hear the great **New York Philharmonic Orchestra** (Avery Fisher Hall, 10 Lincoln Center at Columbus Avenue and 65th Street—212–875–5030) is not a cheap proposition as ticket prices can go as high as $300. To attend a performance at reduced rates look for:

→ Student Rush tickets at $10 available on weeknights. Call 212–875–5030 at 10:30 A.M. on the day of the concert for availability.

→ Friday matinee concert seats for as little as $25.

→ Discount seats for several Saturday matinees; reduced rates vary by performance.

→ $25 orchestra seats are occasionally available for unsold seats. You can only purchase these tickets on the day of the performance.

Call for more information regarding discounts and a full schedule of concerts.

Founded at the turn of the century by a student who wanted to make music accessible to the masses, the **People's Symphony Concerts** (201 West 54th Street—212–586–4680) offers great orchestral music performed by the city's top musicians for as little as $5, and no more than $12. Concerts are held at the Washington Irving High School auditorium (40 Irving

Place at 16th Street) and at Town Hall (123 West 43rd Street at Sixth Avenue). Call for schedule.

On Saturday afternoons at the **Theodore Roosevelt Birthplace** (28 East 20th Street between Broadway and Park Avenue South—212-260-1616), there are quaint piano concerts held in the home's auditorium for a mere $2, which also includes a tour.

Roulette (228 West Broadway between White and North Moore Streets, 2nd Floor—212-219-8242) presents a concert series of adventurous music by internationally famous music "experimentalists." Tickets are usually around $10. Call for schedule.

At **Small's** (183 West 10th Street between Waverly Place and West 4th Street—212-929-7565) a meager cover charge buys you a full night of music from 10 P.M. until 8 A.M. And you don't have to worry about an expensive 2-drink minimum—here you have to bring your own.

Smoke (2751 Broadway between 105th and 106th Streets—212-864-6662) is free Sunday to Wednesday and never has a cover of more than $20 on Thursday to Saturday. Smoke hosts a rotation of great jazz bands, and there is always a jazz headliner dropping in to jam.

Symphony Space (2537 Broadway at 95th Street—212-864-5400) on the Upper West Side programs an always interesting and eclectic array of free and reasonably priced musical performances throughout the year. Tickets start at around $10 and rarely exceed $20. Call for schedule.

Town Hall (123 West 43rd Street at Sixth Avenue—212-840-2824), the original "Tammany Hall," is a great concert venue that hosts a variety of musical performances ranging from classical to jazz, rock, popular, big band and world music. Cheap seats go for as little as $10; Town Hall also offers discount ticket books for even greater savings. Call for schedule and more information on discount tickets.

Alice Tully Hall (Lincoln Center at Broadway and 66th Street—212–875–5050) concerts sometimes have student and senior rush seats available. Call around 11:30 A.M. on the day of the performance.

Wave Hill (675 West 252nd Street, Riverdale—718–549–3200) has a concert series from fall to spring, bringing audiences to its Armor Hall for a variety of classical music and jazz performances. Call for schedule and directions.

Zinc Bar (90 West Houston Street between LaGuardia Place and Thompson Street—212–477 8337) charges only $5 nightly to hear great world music including African, Brazilian, flamenco, jazz, Latin and samba. Call for schedule.

VIEWING OPERA

WHO WOULD HAVE THOUGHT that opera could thrive on the seedy Bowery in the East Village? Anthony and Sally Amato, that's who. In 1948, they founded the **Amato Opera Theatre** (319 Bowery at Bleecker Street—212–228–8200) that in the 53 years since then has presented thousands of performances of over forty of the world's great repertory operas, as well as rarely performed works and world premieres. The Amato Opera productions are all fully realized and the casts are filled by many well-known singers as well as aspiring young artists. You won't need opera glasses at the Amato . . . the auditorium is tiny enough—only 107 seats—that you will have a very clear view of the tenor's tonsils and the spinto's spit. Amato stages six productions throughout the year. Tickets are $28; $23 for seniors and students. One caveat: Because part of the Amato's mission is to provide a testing ground for young singers seeking training and experience in opera performance, the casting can sometimes be weak.

The not-for-profit **American Opera Projects, Inc.** (138 South Oxford Street, Brooklyn 11217—718–398–4024) develops, nurtures and produces new American operas and innovative opera projects and gives performances at several venues around the city. American Opera Projects commissions new works primarily from American librettists and composers and presents them in workshop performances. The musical styles and themes of this company's work are diverse, reflecting the vast range of contemporary American culture. AOP's works are top rate, the opera stories are fascinating (I especially loved their production of *Fireworks*, an opera about a sweet alien who is sent to earth to find out why colored lights are shot into the sky the same time each year), and the singers are culled from pros and up-and-comers. Tickets to most performances are as low as $12, $10 for students and seniors.

Established in 1967 to provide a platform for aspiring singers, the **Bronx Opera** (718–365–4209) presents one known and one rarely performed opera each season. All Bronx Opera productions are sung in English with a full chorus and orchestra, and are performed in the Bronx's Lehman College Lovinger Theatre, in Manhattan's John Jay College Theatre, and Long Island's John Cranford Adams Playhouse of Hofstra University. Ticket prices are $15 for performances in the Bronx and $35 elsewhere. Telephone for schedule and location of performances.

The **Center for Contemporary Opera** (P.O. Box 258, New York, NY 10044—212–758–2757), which is dedicated to the creation and performance of contemporary American opera and opera in English presents four fully mounted productions per season. Many of the works, which are presented in venues throughout the city, are either New York City or world premieres. For most performances tickets are between $20 and $25.

People pay upwards of $250 for a single ticket to see the **Metropolitan Opera**. That's right, $250! You don't have to. Standing-room tickets to the Met (30 Lincoln Center Plaza—212–362–6000) are available for $11 and $15. Then, you can often slide into an unoccupied seat (the ones that go for $250) once the performance begins—just keep an eye out for the overly efficient and often surly ushers who patrol the Standing-room section during the first several minutes of the performance. If you are too timid to steal a seat, you can always purchase one up in the "nosebleed" section (known formally as the Family Circle) for less than $20. Leave the opera glasses at home and bring a telescope. In the summer, the Metropolitan Opera also offers a series of free concerts in the parks throughout the city. For information or a schedule of performances, call the Met Ticket Line at the number above.

BEST BARGAIN

The **New York City Opera** (New York State Theatre, 20 Lincoln Center—212–496–0600), which in the last few years has had a resurgence as one of the city's preeminent cultural institutions, provides audiences three ways to save at the Box Office:

→ **Custom Subscription Plan** lets you create your own series of four to six performances of the productions you want to see when you want to see them. This plan also entitles you to exchange privileges and preferred seating. Ticket prices under this plan start as low as $20 per performance.

→ **Discover Series** lets you create your own flexible and convenient series of three operas with the benefit of exchange privileges and preferred seating. Tickets for each performance in this plan start at around $23.

→ **Individual Tickets**—If you order tickets prior to the season, you can get the best seats available and pay a lower advance-purchase ticket price. If purchased early, Individual Tickets start at around $24.

Note: The ticket prices I quote are for the back rows of the Fourth Ring—the seats furthest from the stage. However, at the New York City Opera, you can always move to better seats after the intermission. The New York City Opera does offer $10 **Rush Seats** for seniors and students that may be purchased on the day of performance, and $12 **Standing Room** tickets. The old trick of standees grabbing seats soon after the performance begins works as well here as it does at the Met.

New York Grand Opera (212–245–8837) offers free, fully mounted opera performances under the stars at the **Central Park Summerstage** (Rumsey Playfield, Central Park at 72nd Street and Fifth Avenue—) every Wednesday night in July. They do not have a roster of international divas and divos (what do you expect for free?) but the singers are very good and don't get in the way of the music. Call for a schedule and more information.

Opera Company of Brooklyn (P.O. Box 21815, Brooklyn, NY 11202—718–986–3294) presents performances at various locations throughout Brooklyn of affordable, high quality opera in intimate and innovative productions. Opera Company of Brooklyn's repertoire is drawn mostly from popular fare like *Madame Butterfly, The Elixir of Love, and Amahl and the Night Visitors,* and features established singers as well as promising young talent. Individual tickets range from $18 to $23 and low-price subscriptions are available.

The **Regina Opera** (1251 Tabor Court, Brooklyn—718–232–3555) has been presenting operatic productions and concerts in Brooklyn since 1970. What is astounding about this company is that they charge so little for so much. Each opera is fully staged, designed and costumed, and is accompanied by a 35-piece orchestra. Casts are a mix of professionals and student singers. You get all this for $12. Amazing. Better still, seniors only pay $8, high- and middle-school students pay $5 and children are free. The Regina presents three operatic productions of four performances each and five operatic and popular music concerts yearly. Admission for the concerts is $6, $5 for students and again, children are free. Call for schedule of performances.

VIEWING DANCE

The **Brooklyn Arts Exchange** (421 Fifth Avenue at 8th Street, Park Slope, Brooklyn—718–832–0018) programs various dance performances by emerging choreographers and dancers. Tickets for these concerts range from $6 to $12

Throughout the summer months, **Celebrate Brooklyn** (Prospect Park Bandshell, 9th Street and Prospect Park West, Brooklyn—718–855–7882) presents free dance performances by some of the metropolitan area's leading companies, like Mark Morris Dance Group, Ben Munisteri Dance Company and RhythMEK.

On Fridays in July and August, **Central Park Summerstage** (Rumsey Playfield, Central Park at 72nd Street and Fifth Avenue—212–360–2777) features free outdoor dance concerts of new works by emerging choreographers and companies. Call for a schedule.

By trekking to the uppermost reaches of the city, you will be rewarded by some very fine dancing at **Dances for Wave Hill** (675 West 252nd Street, Riverdale—718–549–3200). For only $4, (plus the Metro North fare to Riverdale), you can enjoy this dance series in the great outdoors of Wave Hill during the month of July. (Take Metro North from Grand Central terminal to Riverdale, and then walk south five blocks to Wave Hill). Call for schedule.

At one of New York's largest and most reputed dance training centers, **Dance Space Center** (451 Broadway between Grand and Howard Streets—212–625–8369) in Soho, which provides quality dance education through a wide variety of classes, workshops and performance programs, you may attend in the black box theater student performances and concerts by a variety of local dance companies. You can also see a "Works in Progress" series (a bi-monthly showcase of informal performances by new and experienced artists looking for feedback to help facilitate the development of their work) and "Raw Material" showcases that enable emerging artists to affordably perform their work in a professionally produced concert. Prices for these performances are never more than $15 and many of them are free or "Pay-As-You-Wish."

Dance Theatre Workshop (219 West 19th Street between Seventh and Eighth Avenues—212–691–6500) is probably New York's primary presenter of "the next big thing" in dance. Many of the choreographers and dancers seen here today are emerging artists who hope to use their Dance Theatre Workshop performances as a springboard to becoming tomorrow's stars. The Workshop's very full roster of work is always innovative, experimental and provocative and there is something here for every taste and temperament. Tickets are between $15 and $20. Volunteer for their usher program, where for a couple of hours of your time folding programs and seating the audience, you will be given a free seat. Call for information about the usher program and for a full schedule of events.

Danspace Project at St. Mark's Church in the Bowery (Second Avenue at 10th Street—212–674–8194) provides a lofty home for downtown dance. Besides hosting dance concerts throughout the year, Danspace Project's special programs include "Global Exchange," presenting the work of international artists and choreographers and "City/Dans," highlighting the work of homegrown choreographers. Danspace Project tickets cost between $12 and $20.

For twenty years, the **Downtown Dance Festival** (212–219–3910) has held free afternoon dance performances on the Great Lawn in Battery Park during the last week in August. These recitals begin at noon and feature a mix of styles, including modern, ethnic, youth groups and even Morris dancers. Call for schedule.

Harlem Week (Harlem—212–862–8477) includes presentations during its large black and Latino festival that offers art exhibitions, music, film, and a huge festival on Fifth Avenue from 125th to 135th Streets in early to mid-August. Call for a schedule of events.

The ten-week **Hudson River Festival** (212–945–0505/ 212–528–2733), held in the summer months, presents dance as well as free music, theater and storytelling events and art exhibitions. Events take place at several riverside venues including Battery Park, the Winter Garden of the World Financial Center, Castle Clinton and the Battery Park Esplanade. Call for a complete schedule.

Myriad dance companies from around the world perform in the **International Fringe Festival** (212–429–8877), which takes place in several locations on the Lower East Side over two weeks in August. As the name of the festival implies, most of the companies featured are of an experimental or avant-garde bent. Pay a reasonable $12 for all events, or purchase a pass for five performances at $55. Call for schedule.

The **Joyce Theatre** (175 Eighth Avenue, at 19th Street— 212–242–0800), once a movie theater, is now the premier presenter of contemporary dance in the city. Throughout the year, the Joyce hosts several renowned companies like Eliot Feld's Ballet Tech and Pilobolus Dance Theatre. You can purchase standing room tickets if all seats are sold. The Joyce is one of the few theaters featuring dance that still has a volunteer usher program. To become a volunteer usher, call 212–691–9740 after 8:30 A.M. and ask for the House Manager.

In July, the **Lincoln Center Festival** (Lincoln Center, Columbus Avenue at 65th Street—212–875–5928) presents dance, among its theater, opera and music events from the world over. Tickets go for as little as $15 with even cheaper student discounts. Call for more information.

The **Lincoln Center Out-of-Doors Festival** (Lincoln Center, Damrosch Park, 64th Street at Columbus Avenue—212–875–5108) offers a spectacular roster of free dance events and music concerts (featuring the great and nearly-great) daily for three weeks in August. Call for a complete schedule.

The **Merce Cunningham Studio** (55 Bethune Street, 11th Floor, between Washington and West Streets—212–691–9751) in the Westbeth complex is the rehearsal space for Merce Cunningham's company by day, but at night, young choreographers and dancers utilize it to showcase their work. Since anyone who can afford to rent this space has access to it, the work can be real hit-or-miss. A miss is not so bad when you are only paying $10, which is the average cost of tickets at this venue. Call for a schedule.

The **Metropolitan Opera House** (Lincoln Center, Columbus Avenue at 65th Street—212–362–6000), home to the **American Ballet Theatre** in the spring, hosts several international dance companies throughout the year. Tickets here for dance are not as high as they are for opera, but are still pricey, topping at over $150. To save money, do the same thing I suggested for the opera, buy a standing room ticket for $15. As soon as the performance begins, look around for an empty seat and stake your claim to it. Once the ushers who patrol the standing room area leave (about ten minutes into the performance), quietly and unobtrusively, take your seat.

Continuing a tradition that first began in the 1960s, **Movement Research at Judson Church** (55 Washington Square South at Thompson Street—212–477–0351) presents free Monday evening performances from September through June each year. The Judson Church concerts feature the work of both emerging and established choreographers.

Unfortunately the **New Victory Theatre** (209 West 42nd Street between Seventh and Eighth Avenues—646–223–3020) only infrequently hosts dance, but when it does, the work, the companies and the choreographers are always first-rate. In the past, such dance luminaries as Mark Morris, Suzanne Farrell and Mikhail Baryshnikov have performed here. With the cheapest seats costing only $10 for the upper balcony, and because this house is rather intimate, you will have an excellent view of the stage and it won't cost a fortune.

With a company of 90 dancers and an active repertory of over 150 works, the **New York City Ballet** (New York State Theatre, Columbus Avenue and 65th Street—212–870–5660) is one of the foremost ballet companies in the world. Happily, this company makes its repertory available to everyone through its many low-priced ticket programs. These programs include:

→ **Individual Tickets** start at $16 for the back rows of the fourth ring, but you can always move to better seats after the intermission (just make sure they have been vacated).

→ **$10 Student Rush Tickets**—Any high school or university student with valid student ID may purchase one ticket either online through NYCB's website or in person at the New York State Box Office window, although Student Rush is not available for every performance. Availability is posted weekly and can be checked at NYCB's web site or by telephoning the Student Rush Ticket Hotline at 212–870–7766. Student Rush tickets must be purchased on the day of performance. For weekday and evening performances, online ticket orders must be placed by 3 P.M.; for weekend matinees by 11 A.M. These tickets depend on availability, with seating locations assigned by the Box Office.

→ **Fourth Ring Society**—For a $10 fee, you are then entitled to purchase tickets in the Fourth Ring for $25 to $35 (usual prices are $28 to $45). As a member of the Fourth Ring Society, you may go as often as you like, buy your tickets in advance for any performance, attend pre-show lectures, and are given thank-you gifts like free cappuccino at each performance, an NYCB tee-shirt and discount coupons for area restaurants.

→ **Standing Room Tickets** cost $12, then you can use the old trick of sliding into seats soon after the performance begins.

P.S. 122 (150 First Avenue at 9th Street—212–477–5829) presents all kinds of dance performances from the avant-garde to the outrageous. Most of the work here is new and is created and performed by emerging dance professionals. Ticket prices to see dance at P.S. 122 are very inexpensive, between $9 and $15.

NEW YORK CITY
INFORMATION OUTLETS

Alliance for Downtown New York
City Hall Park (at Park Row and Broadway)
212–566–6700

Fashion Center Information Kiosk
Seventh Avenue at 39th Street
212–398–7943

NYC & Company / I ♥ NY
Convention and Visitors Bureau Visitors Information Center
810 Seventh Avenue (between 52nd and 53rd Streets)
212–484–1222

Times Square Visitors Center
1560 Broadway between 46th and 47th Streets
212–869–1890

CULTURAL LISTINGS

There is a plethora of listings available to us actors and nonactors, both in periodicals and on the internet, detailing the events and attractions of any given week in the city. Most contain information on music, dance, theater, museums, parks, film, art galleries, walking tours, events for children, entertainment venues, political meetings, shopping, nightlife, fashion, book signings, lectures, restaurants and much more:

NEWSPAPERS AND MAGAZINES:

The **"Around Town" section of *Time Out New York*** offers a comprehensive list of happenings in and around New York every week. Many if not most of these events are free and range from political debates and rallies to celebrity sports tournaments, music boat cruises, bicycle tours, Revolutionary War reenactments (yeah, the British invaded Staten Island), seminars, book readings, workshops, career fairs, cultural arts festivals, crafts fairs, as well as the expected concert, walking tours, museum, gallery, performing arts, film, and street fair listings.

In the **"Weekend Fine Arts/Leisure" section of the Friday edition of *The New York Times***, there is always an extensive listing of the coming weekend's free and inexpensive city activities. The column titled "Spare Times" lists everything from museum shows to walking tours, street fairs, free films, neighborhood festivals, fun runs, and bicycle tours as well as lots of stuff to do with kids. The pages also carry informative articles and full-length and capsule reviews of art gallery and museum exhibitions. It's a very handy guide to turn to, especially on those Fridays when you're whining in your apartment about not having anything to do this weekend.

An invaluable resource to New York's museums is the magazine *Museums New York*, which is published monthly and can be purchased at museum shops and newsstands. In *Museums New York* you'll find a comprehensive guide to all the museums, listing opening and closing times, articles about current exhibitions and a list of most of the galleries throughout the city.

And, of course, *New York Magazine, The Village Voice, The New York Post, New York Press, The Daily News* and *The New Yorker* all carry exhaustive listings of most everything that is happening in the city.

WEBSITES:

www.allianceforarts.org

www.artistsnyc.com

www.broadway.com

www.broadwaystars.com

www.culturefinder.com

www.entertainment-link.com

www.internetbroadwaydatabase.com

www.moviefone.com

www.newyork.citysearch.com

www.newyorkmag.com

www.ny.com

www.nyc.gov

www.nytheatre.com

www.nytimes.com

www.papermag.com/guide

www.playbill.com

www.readio.com

www.showbusinessweekly.com

www.stagebill.com

www.tdf.org

www.theatermania.com

www.theatredb.com

www.theinsider.com/nyc

www.timeoutny.com

www.villagevoice.com

CONTACT ME

Do you have a favorite low-priced haunt that I haven't included here? Know another way to save money or get the best for less? If so, forward your ideas to me. I'll follow up on all suggestions and those I deem eligible will be included in the next edition of this book.

Write to:

craigwroe@anactorpreparesnyc.com

or

An Actor Prepares . . . To Live In New York City
c/o Limelight Editions
118 East 30th Street
New York, NY 10016

CRAIG WROE is an actor, writer and teacher who has lived in New York City since 1984. His acting credits include appearances on London's West End, off-Broadway, film, television and several leading regional theaters throughout the country. He teaches acting at the School for Film and Television.